THE PARTY GROUPS IN THE EUROPEAN PARLIAMENT

The Party Groups in the European Parliament

JOHN FITZMAURICE
B.Sc., M.Sc.

SAXON HOUSE | LEXINGTON BOOKS

Published by
SAXON HOUSE, D. C. Heath Ltd.
Westmead, Farnborough, Hants., England.

Jointly with
LEXINGTON BOOKS, D. C. Heath & Co.
Lexington, Mass. U.S.A.

ISBN 0 347 01063 6

Printed in England by Eyre & Spottiswoode Ltd at Grosvenor Press, Portsmouth.

Contents

Preface

This study has several aims, which are both documentary and analytical. The working of the European parliament will be closely investigated and particularly the role of the party groupings. This will represent a continuation of the documentation of the growth of party groupings at the European level begun by such authors as Van Oudenhouve*. Inevitably there will be considerable historical background, since the European parliament is an evolving and organic institution, with traditions reaching back to the assembly of the coal and steel community, and beyond into the parliamentary traditions of the member states of the European communities.

The main focus of the study will, however, be analytical. It will seek to show how, from the history and working of the European parliament, party groups have evolved and beyond that why the rate of that development should have been so relatively rapid. It is a premise of this study, which can be readily substantiated by reference to both national and local decision-making bodies in western democracies, that the existence of political parties and the dominance of the political process by the party system is an inevitable fact of modern political life. In so far as this premise is accepted, the development of a latent party system within the European parliament must be judged a positive and propitious step: the extent, though, that this premise may be extended to encompass the view that a well developed party system is indispensable to the proper functioning of a representative democracy, and the fact that such a system can be found in a given institution is a measure of the political power and maturity of that institution, make one less optimistic about the state of the European parliament. It is therefore essential, and one of the major aims of this study, to examine the cohesion, unity and political maturity of the European political groups and the extent to which they complement or coexist with the national political parties and to attempt some analysis of the factors inhibiting their development.

It must be remembered that the European parliament, perhaps more than any other international body, is called upon to play its role within the framework of a larger political structure of which it forms a part. The working and concerns of the European parliament can only be intelligently understood against the background of the decision-making process of the communities in which it seeks to intervene. Accordingly, the total political environment and the decision-making process is analysed.

The basic aim has been to collect from the existing literature on the parliament, from official records and documents and from contacts with people involved in the decision-making process, as wide a range of data as possible. The information obtained is used selectively to illustrate the theme and further the analysis and at the same time provide the reader with an abundant documentation on the subject. It is by no means claimed that it is complete; the study is limited to charting the main lines of the subject, avoiding an in-depth treatment of aspects which could be (and in some cases have been) the object of a book in their own right.

* The Political Parties in the European Parliament, Sijthoff, Leiden 1965.

Acknowledgements

Acknowledgements are particularly due to Dr G. Pridham of Bristol University and to Professor D. Coombes of Loughborough University of Technology, both of whom have unstintingly given valuable support, encouragement and many useful suggestions.

Acknowledgement is also due to those institutions and their staffs which have given financial and documentary assistance to the research for this book. In particular the European parliament which arranged several study visits to plenary sessions and to the secretariat, enabling me to gain valuable insight at first hand into the working of the parliament; to the commission of the European communities and in particular to Mr J. J. Schwed, Head of the division 'liaison with the European parliament'; to the German Bundestag and the Dutch Second Chamber, which provided much documentary material and the setting for interviews concerning the activity of national parliaments. Naturally thanks are due to those members of the European parliament and the national parliaments who provided a vast quantity of extremely valuable insight and information. Other bodies – universities, research institutes, political parties – have also given courteous and valuable assistance. Thanks are also due to many friends, in particular Mr J. Vos and Mr A. Duff who have been the source of many stimulating ideas, some of which have found their way into this book. Naturally, too, my gratitude goes to my family for their help and their willing acceptance of the temperament of the author.

Finally, the judgements and opinions expressed in this book are the sole responsibility of the author and do not necessarily in any way reflect those of any of the community institutions.

J.F.

Abbreviations

EEC/CEE	European Economic Community
ECSC	European Coal and Steel Community
EP	European Parliament
Euratom/CEEA	European Atomic Energy Community
Treaty of Rome	Treaty establishing the EEC
Treaty of Paris	Treaty establishing the ECSC
CA	Consultative Assembly of the ECSC

National abbreviations   B (Belgium); D (Germany); DK (Denmark); IRL (Ireland); I (Italy); F (France); NL (Netherlands); L (Luxemburg); UK (Britain).

Political Parties

CD	Christian Democrats
DC	Democrazia Cristiana (Italian Christian Democrats)
SVP	Südtiroler Volkspartei (South Tirol German Minority Party)
PLI	Partito Liberale Italiano
PRI	Partito Republicano Italiano
PSI	Partito Socialista Italiano
PSDI	Partito Social-Democratico Italiano
MSI-DN	Movimento Sociale Italiano-Destra Nazionale (Neo-fascist movement)
CDU/CSU	Christlich-Demokratische Union
SPD	Sozialdemokratische Partei Deutschlands
FDP	Freie-Demokratische Partei Deutschlands
PLP	Parti de Liberté et du Progrès (Belgian Liberals-Francophone)
PVV	Partij voor Vrijheid en Vooruitgang
PSB/BSP	Parti Socialiste Belge/Belgische Socialistische Partij
PSC/CVP	Parti Social Chrétien/Christlike Volkspartij (Belgian)
PD	Parti Démocratique (Luxemburg)
PSD	Parti Social Démocratique (Luxemburg)
POSL	Parti Ouvrier Socialiste Luxembourgeois
UNR	Union pour la Nouvelle République (Gaullist)
UDR	Union des Démocrates pour la République (Gaullist)

UDE	Union des Démocrates Européens (Gaullist European Group)
EDU	European Progressive Democrats
SFIO	Section Française de l'International Ouvrier (Socialist Party)
UDCA	Union Démocratique des Commerçants et des Artisans (Poujadists)
UDCP	Union Centriste des Démocrates de Progrès
RIAS	Républicains Indépendants d'Action Sociale
KVP	Katholieke Volkspartij
AR	Anti-Revolutionaire Partij
CHU	Christelijk Historische Unie
PvdA	Partij van de Arbeid
VVD	Volkspartij voor Vrijheid en Democratie
PCF	Parti Communiste Français
PCI	Partito Communista Italiano

Organisations and Bodies

COPA	Confédération d'Organisations Professionales Agricoles
ASSILEC	Community Milk-producers Association
ESC/CES	Economic and Social Committee

All quotations from foreign language works and speeches are given in an English translation by the author.

PART I

Background and Organisation

1 The Decision-making Process in the Communities

The treaties establishing the European communities, dealing as they do with the total integration of six separate national economies into a single market governed by common rules and policies, can only lay down a general programme and a timetable for its accomplishment. The broad objectives enshrined in the treaties require detailed and concrete elaboration, a process which must of necessity take some considerable period. It is, therefore, impossible to specify in advance the specific measures which will meet the future difficulties resulting from changes in the economic situation and which will succeed in welding the six national economies, each with its own peculiarities, into a single economic unit. The treaties are therefore limited to statements of principle — broad objectives, the methods which may or may not be used in their accomplishment; the establishment of interdependent institutions empowered to carry out the 'action programme' specified in the treaties.

In view of the special nature of the communities, an institutional structure somewhat different from that in the member states has been adopted. Executive power is shared between two independent bodies one of which is subject to direct parliamentary control and supervision. Legislative power as a separate element, in the sense developed by Montesqieu, is absent. The power to enact community law resides in the two executive bodies acting in co-operation, subject to the consultation of the European parliament. Only the judicial power is separate in the classic sense, acting as a check on the legality of acts of the executive and legislative power, as in the general model of liberal democracy. The commission, a nine-member collegiate body, is independent of the member states which have in common accord appointed it, and responsible only to the European parliament. Article 155 of the Treaty of Rome summarises the task of the commission. It must act as the guardian of the treaty; in this role it will be required to enforce those provisions of the treaty which require no implementing legislation as well as the body of community legislation adopted to date. In addition, the commission is the motor of integration; it must provide the tactical scheme for the implementation of the programme laid down by the treaty. It must translate the declarations of intent, the prescribed methods of the treaty, into draft legislative acts. In this manner, the commission prepares the acts of the council. The council has the power to enact community legislation, but only (with some exceptions) on the proposal of the commission. The council of ministers consists of the ministers of the six Member States responsible for the matters on the agenda. Legislation will thus be the result of an inter-play between the independent 'European' body and the body representative of national opinion. The European parliament, which represents the currents of political opinion, must be consulted on major legislative initiatives and can force the resignation of the commission by a vote of censure. The powers of the parliament, insubstantial though they may be, do ensure a minimum element of accountability and openness in community decision-making. The Court of Justice exists to uphold the rule of law in the community and to ensure judicial remedies to those subject to the new domain of community law.

Thus the treaty establishes objectives and a timetable for their accomplishment by the institutions which it has created for that task. The institutions do not, however, have a *carte blanche* and must act (Article 4): 'within the limits of the powers conferred by this treaty'. Hence the commission must ensure that any draft proposals meet the requirements of the treaty both as to form and substance. Usually the treaty will prescribe a particular legislative form, but may permit discretion. For example, harmonisation of legislation liable to create distortions harmful to the functioning of the Common Market under Articles 100 and 101 may only take the form of a directive; agricultural market organisations may be established by regulation, directive or decision; competition rules under Article 87 may be established by either regulation or directive. Furthermore, the commission must meet the conditions and requirements of substance laid down by the treaty provision on the basis of which it proposes to act. These conditions may take the form of safeguards of the rights of member states, limitations on the nature of the market organisations which may be set up (Article 40), objective economic conditions which must be met before the commission may act, such as the requirement of Article 101 that the disparate legislation must create a 'distortion' before harmonisation can be justified.

Whenever, as a result of the injunction of a 'programme article' of the treaty, public debate, complaints or requests from interested parties or member states, or as a result of its own research, the commission concludes that it can and should act, internal procedures are set in motion which will culminate in a draft legislative text. Let us take the case of a price and subsidy regulation for an agricultural product. The first stage is a general directive from the commission to the services responsible, giving it a policy guideline. In our case this will be the direction general for

4

agriculture and within that direction general, Direction B (Produits vegetaux), Direction C (Meat and Poultry) or Direction D (Special Crops, Fisheries and Forestry) according to product and may well involve Direction E (Economie et Structure Agricole). Small informal groups will ensure co-ordination between these directions and major points will be resolved by the cabinet or by the commissioner himself. Other directions general may be involved, as will be the Service Juridique and the Office Statistique in technical capacities. Small, ad hoc representative groups ensure co-ordination between the services involved.

At this stage extensive consultations take place, both with national experts, who act more as technical advisers than national representatives at this point, and with interest groups. In the agriculture sector these groups are well organised and articulate at the community level, both through consultative committees for each product and through community-wide organisations, such as COPA and ASSILEC for dairy producers. Consultation is most valuable since potential governmental and pressure group opposition can be eliminated at this early stage, which can greatly improve the chance of the adoption of the draft by the council, especially since the community decision-making process ensures maximum leverage to blocking by minor or sectional problems.

Out of the consultations and internal discussions a preliminary draft is forged. As such a matter is of considerable political importance it cannot be dealt with by the written procedure, which involves sending the draft to all the members of the commission and calling for observations before a time limit, in the absence of which the proposal is adopted. This procedure is mostly reserved for formal and procedural matters. In this case a discussion in the full commission is required. This is preceded by discussion in the meeting of the Chefs de Cabinet. This meeting gives the draft detailed examination and seeks to reach a provisional agreement. Some heads of cabinet may reserve the position of their commissioner and, in any case, any agreement reached here can still be debated in full commission. Final adoption is the prerogative of the commission acting, if necessary, by a majority vote.

The formal draft text of the commission is now transmitted to the European parliament for information and to the council as a proposal of the commission. At any time during subsequent proceedings the commission may, in accordance with Article 149(2), amend its own proposal, which enables it to act as a conciliator between interests and frequently arrive at a compromise acceptable to the council. Article 43 requires that the council consult the parliament and may (Article 198) consult the economic and social committee. The economic and social committee is required to establish a specialised section for agriculture, which prepares a report on the proposals which is approved by the full committee, thus becoming the Opinion of the Committee.

The main work of examining proposals is undertaken by the twelve specialised committees of the European parliament. Article 26 of the Rules of Procedure of the parliament stipulates that the parliament deliberates on the report of the competent committee, a rule only dispensed with in cases of urgency. The parliament or, when out of session, its president, assigns a proposal to the appropriate committee and, where relevant, to up to two other committees in an advisory capacity. In this case the agriculture and the economics committees would be responsible for examining the proposal. The committee appoints a rapporteur who drafts a report as the basis for discussion. The committee is a microcosm of the political composition of the parliament and hence, although no formal party *caucus* meetings are held to discuss committee business, the views of the party groups rapidly emerge from the debate, but frequently national, regional and interest group attitudes are equally important. The commissioner and competent officials attend the committee to explain and defend their proposal and the rapporteur of any other committee which has been consulted may attend and take part in the debate. After several sessions a consensus will emerge and the report will be adopted in the form prescribed by the rules of procedure: an 'exposé des motifs' (a general commentary) and a draft resolution, containing a general comment in summary form and specific amendments, requesting the commission to amend its proposal in accordance with Article 149(2). This report is debated in the plenary session of the parliament. Here it is introduced by the rapporteur and the spokesmen of the party groups present their groups' points of view, and amendments can be presented and discussed. Here too the commission is represented and will seek to ensure that any critical amendments are rejected and that the parliament approves its proposal without reservation. At the completion of the debate, the resolution, as amended, is put to the vote and becomes the opinion of the parliament, which is transmitted to the council and to the commission.

The commission has pledged itself to make known its attitude to every amendment proposed by the parliament and since July 1971 has decided to adopt a revised proposal each time that an amendment proposed by the parliament is accepted, in accordance with Article 149(2), in order to give a greater legal value to the amendments proposed by the parliament. However, the commission, in the statements on the matter by M. Rey, has made it clear that it is an independent body, with discretion as to whether to accept an amendment or to reject it, and not the 'automatic advocate' of the parliament.

In the council, the opinions of the parliament and the economic and social committee are transmitted to the national delegations and form part of the dossier of the specialised group of the council responsible for the matter. There are a few standing groups, such as the agriculture and the economic affairs groups, but the tendency is to establish flexible ad hoc groups for each question. The groups consist of expert civil servants from the member states, and follow the same rules of rotation of the chairmanship of the group as the council itself. The members of the group will be those officials from the home ministry who deal with the subject, acting on instructions from their ministry. The task of the group is to undertake a detailed examination of the proposal at a technical level and to examine the opinions of the parliament and the economic and social committee, in order to discover the areas of agreement and disagreement and to reach as wide an area of purely technical agreement as possible. The group draws up a report for the committee of permanent representatives (COREPER), embodying its conclusions as to the technical validity of the draft, as to the areas of agreement and disagreement and indicating the divergence, if any, between the commission proposal, the opinion of the assembly or economic and social council and the recommendations of the group.

At the next stage more overtly political factors come into play, and the COREPER proceedings will be closely watched by the national ministries. It is at this stage, when the proposals are widely known in political circles and among the interest groups, that action by interest groups and deputies in the national parliaments may compel the co-ordinating committees for European affairs which exist in most of the six member governments to issue firm instructions to defend a certain national viewpoint. Such action can prolong COREPER proceedings for several years and entail reference back to the group for further consideration, and can lead to the burial of the proposal. The commission, which is represented in the groups, the COREPER as well as in the council itself, may seek to rescue its proposal by tabling a compromise designed to win acceptance from all member states. When the COREPER does reach agreement on a draft acceptable to all member states, the text goes to the council as a 'Point A' on the agenda, where it will normally be adopted without debate, as a pure formality. In view of the power of the council to amend a commission proposal, if it does so unanimously (Article 149(1)) the resulting draft may differ considerably from the original proposal of the commission and may not be acceptable to it, let alone to the parliament. Where only agreement to differ can be reached, or where the subject is of such political importance that, as a matter of principle, the issue must be decided by the ministers themselves, the case goes to the council as a

'Point B' on the agenda, for full debate. The representatives in COREPER are by and large professional diplomats and this is reflected in its procedure, which approximates more closely to a classic inter-governmental conference than to a decision-making organ of a 'quasi state'. COREPER attempts to prolong discussion in the search for unanimity-making compromise, in the effort to reduce 'Point Bs' to the minimum. In reality these are limited to questions of overriding political significance, to issues where a publicly known divergence of opinion exists between member states or too urgent for the ordinary procedure. Although this system does some violence to the spirit, if not the letter, of the treaty, it is justified by the impermanent nature of the council, which could not in any case, in some mere fifty brief meetings per year, arbitrate every issue.

At the level of the council itself the procedure is broadly similar, even if more general and more political. Here again the goal is consensus and here again the commission plays an essential role as a conciliator, bringing forward a compromise to break a deadlock and commend itself to all the member states, whilst at the same time defending the essence of its own position. At this level the formality and cumbersomeness of the pre-liminary procedure is abandoned in favour of an informal and flexible approach, to the extent that within the space of a single night's marathon session four or more compromise packages may be introduced from commission or ministers, trenchantly debated and rejected in whole or in part. The discussion seeks to reach unanimity around a compromise offering some benefit to each member state. Unanimity may be a positive requirement of the treaty, but even where a qualified majority would suffice (that is to say 12 out of 17 votes in favour of a commission proposal, where France, Germany and Italy each cast four votes; Belgium and the Netherlands each cast two votes and Luxemburg one vote) such a possibility is well in the background. The tendency towards unanimity, already established, was given impetus by the Luxemburg agreement of 1966 which ended the constitutional crisis. The result of this agreement has been that, whilst the *de jure* position has remained unaltered, in fact unanimity has been sought, even if the treaty does not require it, whenever the 'vital interests' of a member state are invoked. This position, which is a matter of principle for France, has not been infrequently invoked as a matter of convenience by other states and has seen its meaning extended to cover apparently minor matters, hence virtually excluding the operation of the majority principle, which nonetheless remains in the treaty. Our example of agricultural prices would almost certainly, Article 43 notwithstanding, require unanimity.

When a text has been agreed by the council, it is sent to the 'Groupe des Juristes-Lingues' who must draw up an agreed version in each of the four official languages of the community (Dutch, French, German and Italian). This task is important because any version will be equally valid in any later juridicial proceedings. After formal approval in council, the text is published in the *Journal Officiel,* if it is a directive or a regulation, or is notified to the party concerned if it is a decision. The text shall, in accordance with Article 190, refer to any proposals or opinions obtained pursuant to the treaty and shall be reasoned; failure to meet this requirement can lead to the annulment of the act by the Court of Justice (see Case 24 − 62 German Federal Republic *v.* Commission). The Act will come into force upon notification in the case of a decision, or in the case of a regulation or directive upon the appointed day, or twenty days after publication.

The manner of execution and application of a text will depend on its form and content. In the words of Article 189 of the treaty: A decision is binding in every respect for the addressees named therein. Regulations shall have general application. They shall be binding in every respect and directly applicable in every member state. Directives 'shall bind any member state to which they are addressed, as to the result to be achieved, while leaving to domestic agencies the competence as to form and means'. Many regulations are in outline form only, requiring amplification to be effective, delegating to the commission, in accordance with Article 155, the power to make subsidiary regulations or directives, which will have the same scope as indicated in Article 189. This procedure is much used in the field of agriculture, where numerous detailed rules are needed on an almost daily basis, and also in the field of trade legislation. Here the council has instituted a check on the commission in the parent regulation: the 'Comité de Gestion' in agriculture or the 'Comité de Legislation' in other fields. These 'Comités' must give an opinion on draft regulations. Where they give a negative opinion by the same weighted majority vote as in the council itself, the regulation must be approved by the council or lapse.

The regulation has the same effect as domestic law and is applicable without any further procedure and must be enforced by each member state by the normal law enforcement procedures. In some cases the enforcement is alone, or parallel to the states, the responsibility of the commission. This is the case for the regulations made under Articles 85 and 86 against monopoly abuse, rules against discriminatory subsidies, coal and steel price rules. In these cases, the commission is empowered to undertake its own investigations and impose penalties on any enterprises which are in breach of the community law. Failure to comply with a decision may similarly entail penalties. Application of directives is the duty of the member states concerned, by means of such domestic measures as they deem appropriate and subject to such general criteria as are laid down in the directive. Where for any reason a state does not enforce or apply community law, and is therefore in breach of its treaty obligations (Article 5), the commission, as the guardian of the treaty, may commence the procedure of Article 169, which can lead to a judgement from the court that the state is in default and order the state to comply with the ruling. Such a ruling is usually successful in ensuring compliance with the community law.

At the stage of execution and application of community law a control and supervision can be exerted. The European parliament follows carefully the action of the commission and may intervene in a number of different ways. In Resolution no. 2 of 22 April 1970 and subsequent correspondence, the council has pledged itself to inform the appropriate committee of the parliament of the reasons which led it to depart greatly from the opinion of the assembly in adopting acts with financial implications and to take similar measures in respect of other acts to the extent that the council considers appropriate. This procedure is initiated by the committee under the procedure for oral questions and the council should respect a time limit of thirty days, where possible. The committees of the parliament may conduct any investigations, study missions or hearings, at which interested parties may be heard and may request the presence of the responsible member of the commission to explain a policy. Committees and political groups may table oral questions with or without debate, which require either the council or the commission to prepare a reply. In this way information as to the execution of policy may be obtained and changes sought. The individual member of the parliament may also table written and oral questions for the same purpose. In the national parliaments deputies may bring pressure to bear on their own governments through special committees on European affairs and through the usual channels, with a view to the governments taking certain action in their own execution or application of community law, or taking up the matter at community level. Individuals may attempt to influence policy through national deputies or members of the European parliament or utilise the petition to the European parliament (see Article 45 of the Rules of Procedure). Interest groups may act at the national level or through their community-wide federations — trade unions, industrial enterprises, COPA (farmers), etc. These representative bodies have direct access to the commission through their offices in Brussels and through numerous advisory committees on which they are represented.

It is axiomatic that, under the rule of law, each new source of law calls forth a corresponding legal remedy. Legal remedies in the community operate on two interrelated levels. Subject to certain conditions, the treaty provides for the right of direct judicial challenge of a contested act before the Court of Justice of the communities. Articles 173 and 175 give to member states the widest possible right to contest any act of the community creating legal obligations. An *in re ipsa* interest is imputed to the states; that is to say, they may attack an act even though they have no narrowly construed 'interest' in the act. Equally, they may compel community bodies to act where continued inaction is a breach of the treaty. The position of private parties (natural and legal persons, that is individuals and firms) is somewhat different. Legal remedies are only accorded to them to permit them to defend their 'interests' and not to protect the general good. For this reason they may not contest a directive, since this binds only member states. As far as decisions are concerned, a private party may contest a decision addressed to him. Other decisions may only be contested in so far as the decision 'is of direct and specific concern' to the party (Article 173). The court has interpreted this provision limitatively, so as to exclude most actions (see Cases 64 − 69 and 106/107 − 63). A regulation, as a matter of public rather than private interest, may not be contested unless it is in reality a decision in the disguise of a regulation.

The treaty lays down the grounds on which an act may be contested: that the act complained of is *ultra vires*; that the enacting body has violated the treaty or any subordinate legislation; that the enacting body has violated an important procedural rule; that the enacting body has misused its powers. As has already been noted, the institutions of the community must act strictly within the powers conferred by the treaty; hence where there is no treaty provision or valid act to justify the act complained of it will be *ultra vires*. Where the body enacting the provision has violated the treaty or some parent regulation, either by misinterpretation or because conditions imposed, either of an objective, economic or legal character, have not been met, the act is void. The court has made it clear that not all violation of procedural rules will lead to annulment. The key rule is the obligation to motivate an act. Misuse of power is the French administrative law notion of 'détournement de pouvoir', which is hard to render in English terms. It entails the use of powers which are in themselves valid for a purpose other than, or at variance with, that for which they were intended. The complainant must act within two months of the norm contested entering force. If the complaint is justified, the court annuls the act, or in the case of a regulation only that part which the court may consider necessary. Article 215 permits the court to award damages where a party has been harmed by illegal or negligent action by the community.

Regulations, decisions and those treaty provisions which are self-executing — that is, require no implementing legislation — may form the basis of domestic legal proceedings, either through the enforcement procedure of the member states or in a civil action. Here, too, community law may therefore be challenged. Where there is complete clarity or a previous ruling of the Court of Justice exists, domestic courts may interpret and apply community law, thereby passing judgement as to its validity. In the interests of integration and the uniform interpretation of community law, Article 177 of the treaty provides a mechanism by which domestic courts faced with a problem of validity or interpretation of community law may seek a preliminary ruling from the Court of Justice, which it may then apply to the specific case at issue. This procedure is obligatory on national courts against whose decision there is no appeal. In that way national and community courts share the task of ensuring the rule of law within the community.

Thus our review of the decision-making process of the community is complete. We have seen the meticulous process of consultation and checks and balances at every stage: checks which can be so formidable as to inhibit excessive action, but which must absolve from any charge of autocracy, or authoritarianism.

2 Historical Background: the Common Assembly

What comes out of this examination of the decision-making process of the communities is the fundamental weakness of the European parliament. Power in the communities lies firmly in 'bureaucratic' and inter-governmental bodies of the traditional type. However, it is sometimes salutary to remember that, set against the previous development of European history, the mere existence of a body such as the European parliament is remarkable and that the excessive hopes for the 'federalist vision' exemplified by Altiero Spinelli and others were born of a period of instability in the wake of the Second World War, which led into the blind alley that the nation state either was dead or would wither away in total discredit. We can now see that such standards apply too harsh a measuring to the existing institutions. Such warnings, notwithstanding, it remains true that the parliament is weak, too weak, which in turn creates problems in regard to the mobilisation of political forces and public opinion on a European level. The lack of political institutions (as distinct from an administrative apparatus) on the community level has caused political forces to ignore Europe, to be uncertain how and through what channels to involve themselves, or to reject integration as a bureaucratic tool of governments and industry, unrelated and even inimical to the concerns of the peoples of the member states.

In specific terms, the parliament's weakness would seem to lie in its unrepresentative character, its lack of control over the appointment of the commission, its lack of significant budgetary or legislative powers and, above all, the apparent failure to mature to the established parliamentary role, tending to remain a pressure group for further integration. It is the Coal and Steel Community which is the model for the institutional system of the communities; here, at least in theory, there was an executive – the high authority – endowed with an autonomous power of decision and responsible to the assembly and a special council of ministers, which had to consent to certain of the more important acts of the high authority: the council therefore resembled a senate or second chamber in a federal system and might well be compared with the German Bundesrat. This structure gives, at least in theory, the same picture, if in a somewhat attenuated form, as is found in a parliamentary system at the national level. In the later (and more important) communities the same apparent structure has been adopted, without any rethinking, but in deference to the susceptibilities of the governments the balance of power within the structure has been utterly changed. The council is the body with a power of decision. The role of the integrated 'executive' — the commission — is limited to the right to make proposals to the council and to administer policies already adopted upon delegation from the council. This is a totally different situation from that prevailing in the Coal and Steel Community. The council has become the legislature and, through its reticence in delegation and the fact that the commission lacks powers of decision and action, has in reality become the executive of the communities. The traditional dialogue between parliament and the executive has been replaced by the dialogue between the commission and the council. The position of the European parliament in the decision-making process of the community has not been logically considered. The formal power to pass a motion of censure on the commission (Article 144, Treaty of Rome) and thereby force its collective resignation, though in itself a most revolutionary power for an international assembly to possess, has been almost totally ineffective in realistic political terms. There has been no threat that the weapon would be resorted to since the days of the Socialist Group's attack on the coal policy of the High Authority during the debate on the Fourth General Report (1956). The assembly is without power to influence the appointment of the commission, which is in the hands of the member governments who in practice merely agree on the national representation in the new commission and the president, leaving the actual appointments to each member state in isolation as far as its own nationals are concerned. Under the present circumstances the parliament would not succeed in ensuring that a more 'political' commission were appointed if it were to employ the weapon of the censure motion. This problem is reinforced by the fact that in practice the commission and parliament have tended to have a virtual identity of views in opposition to those of the council, which has resisted the supranationalist intentions of both the commission and the parliament. This has meant that parliamentary control over the commission in a more generalised sense has had little meaning. Furthermore, there is no clear delineation of responsibility. The real power of decision belongs, formally, to the Council, which is not and cannot be responsible to the European parliament. The final shape of a policy will depend on the complex interaction between the commission, the author of the initial proposal and the council, which must decide thereon. The parliament cannot hold the commission responsible for the end product, only for the initial proposal — but everyone knows that this is only a draft. Inevitably political responsibility is defused.

The parliament was not endowed with legislative powers, nor with any real power over the community budget. In the Coal and Steel Community there was no obligation to consult the parliament on any proposed measures, though this was frequently accepted voluntarily by the high authority. The budgetary process of the community did not require the intervention of the parliament, nor did the fixing of the levy of up to one per cent of turnover in Coal and Steel products which was one of the main elements of the income of the community. Under the Rome treaties, the concept of consultation was introduced. In respect of certain policy measures (agricultural prices, the social fund transport policy, etc.) the council was obliged to consult the parliament. It is generally agreed that this consultation must occur in such a way as to enable the parliament to deliberate and issue an opinion in time to influence the commission and the council, although even this minimum requirement has not always been met.

It is clear from Case 5/57, Netherlands *v.* High Authority, that failure to consult the European parliament is viewed by the Court of Justice as a major violation of procedural form and would therefore lead to the annulment of the legislation in question. This is, however, the limit of the legal obligation imposed on the council. There is no requirement that the opinion of the parliament be accepted or even considered by the council. Schutzer, in an article in the *Common Market Law Review* (1967)[1] considers that the council is in fact obliged to assist the parliament in carrying out its role under the treaties and that therefore it must furnish information necessary for the parliament to work efficiently. This is underlined in the *Illerhaus Report,* Document 114/1963-4. The parliament has also sought to discover the reason why its opinion has been disregarded by the council and was informed (see written question 55/67) that in certain cases this information will be supplied on request. There have been developments from this modest start to closer relations with the council. The parliament may of course seek to ensure that the commission amends its proposal under the Article 149(2) procedure, by invoking the responsibility of the commission to the parliament. Even if the commission does agree, and this is as we have seen by no means inevitable, there is no guarantee of a favourable reaction from the council. As Schutzer puts it in the article already quoted: 'Since the Parliament possesses no right of "avis conforme" (concurring opinion), its co-legislative authority depends solely on the control it exerts over the Commission'. This realisation has led the parliament, not without some reservations, to seek closer relations with the council. As part of the Luxemburg Treaty (22 April 1970) package, the council adopted certain resolutions which indicated a willingness to participate in the budgetary procedure on the basis of a dialogue with the parliament and to ensure that the commission provides the parliament with more information as to the financial implications of its proposals:

> The Council pledges itself to maintain the closest cooperation with the Assembly during the examination of acts with financial implications and to explain where necessary, the reasons leading it to reject the opinion of the Assembly.

In the case of other measures the obligation of the council is less far-reaching; as a result of a prolonged correspondence between the council and parliament a procedure was adopted whereby the Council:

> . . . pledged itself to explain its reasons for rejecting the opinion of the Assembly on important acts.

In less important matters the council: 'Would judge the appropriateness of giving an answer and would define its content'. The request must be made by the competent committees of the parliament in accordance with the procedure for oral questions without debate. This procedure, limited as it is, represents an interesting attempt by the parliament and the council to set up new channels of influence within the community decision-making structure and may lead the parliament to seek to influence community legislation as much through the council as through the commission.

In essence the budgetary procedure of the Rome treaty represented a mere refinement of the usual consultative procedure. The commission drew up a draft from the initial estimates of the other institutions, which was then adopted, with possible amendments, by the council, which then sent the project to the parliament which was given one month to examine the project. If no amendments were voted, the budget was considered adopted. If there were amendments, the council was required to re-adopt the budget by a qualified majority vote (see Articles 199 and 203 of the Rome treaty). This procedure gave the assembly both an extremely limited time to consider the budget and very little influence, in that its decision was in no way final and its amendments could be removed by a mere qualified majority – the same vote by which the original draft was adopted. The Luxemburg treaty of 1970, which amended Article 203 of the Rome treaty, represents a marginal improvement in the budgetary powers of the parliament which was rendered inevitable by the decision to create a system of 'ressources propres' for the communities. This would deprive the national parliaments of control over significant revenues which would henceforth belong directly to the community and be appropriated to community uses by community institutions. Under the procedure for the 'normal' period (after 1975) established in the Luxemburg treaty, the parliament will be able to propose amendments to the whole budget as in the past, but the consequences of amendment will vary according to which parts of the budget are amended. As before, the institutions draw up estimates which the commission assembles into a draft and transmits the draft to the council before 1 September each year. The council adopts the project by a qualified majority and transmits it to the parliament before 5 October. The parliament then has an increased period to consider the project — forty-five days. Amendments may then be adopted by an absolute majority. If within fifteen days the council has not rejected the amendments of the parliament, the budget is adopted. If the council rejects the amendments by a qualified majority, the parliament must reconsider the project. For those expenses other than those which '... découlent obligatoirement du Traité, ou les actes pris en vertu du Traité', the parliament has the final word — by a 3/5 majority — within the limits of a complex formula based on the evolution of the Gross National Product of the member states. This is of course an extremely limited power because the major part of the expenses of the community is involved with the common agricultural policy and certain other policies which are fixed in advance or which are unpredictable, such as those of the social fund. In fact, the parliament has only the final decision over some 4 per cent of the budget.[2]

In some ways as serious as the 'constitutional' weakness of the parliament, and less easy to document, is the failure to become a mature political institution, the arena for the clash of opinions over the future development of the communities. Instead, the parliament has tended to remain a pressure group for integration, rather than reflecting the full diversity of political tendencies within the community. There has been a preference for broad, generalised resolutions, capable of any interpretation and at times lacking in political bite — in order to present as far as possible a united front in pressing further integration on the council. This situation, noticeable as it is at present, should not be exaggerated, especially in view of the relatively short traditions of the parliament — it must be remembered that it took the British parliament many centuries to become a mature and powerful political institution. The problem is in part the result of the specific weaknesses — in terms of powers of control and supervision — which we have already examined; it is, however, more fundamental than that. The composition of the parliament has created its own problems. In the early stages both France and Italy designated their delegations to the European parliament by a system of absolute majorities, which excluded the Communists and the parties of the extreme right such as Poujade's UDCA. In Germany, the KPD was excluded from the ESCS common assembly before the party was declared unconstitutional by the Bundesverfassungsgericht in 1956. Only the Netherlands and Belgium have faithfully chosen their delegations by proportional representation since 1951. Since 1968 the entry of the PCI has to an extent alleviated the unrepresentative character of the parliament. However, the French Communist party is still excluded, with some 23 per cent of the vote in France. The representation of political parties is not the only problem to arise in this connection. The treaty requires that, until the parliament is elected by direct universal suffrage (Article 138(1) and (3), Treaty of Rome), the members of the parliament should also be members of their own parliaments. This raises the problem of making an effective job of both the national and the European mandate, especially when neglect of the national mandate can have repercussions on electoral success at home: for example, a Dutch member, Hr Van Rijn, seems to have been relegated to an unfavourable position on his party list in 1963 due to excessive concentration on European parliamentary work. There is a tendency for the delegations to 'choose themselves', being composed of only committed supranationalists. On this point David Coombes[3] comments:

> The majority of the members of the Parliament have been selected largely because of their willingness to serve and because of an existing interest in or commitment to the European movement.

In addition there is the problem of the national political parties not concerning themselves with the community to any large degree, preferring to concentrate their effort on the national level, as has traditionally been the case. It was of course a vital part of the 'engrenage' thesis of integration, which in large measure lay behind the 'communities method' that increasing economic integration would lead to the taking of even more decisions at the community level and that this development would lead public opinion, the press and media, interest groups and political parties to respond by redirecting their focus from the national level to the new community decision-making centres. This has of course happened, but not to a sufficiently dramatic extent to cause the political parties to direct their main activity, or even a significant part of their activity, to the European parliament. The reasons why this preference for the national focus continues to exist and to impede the development of powerful community level political bodies and the formation of political groups whose main focus and effort is concentrated at the European level are an important aspect of this study.

Having set the European parliament in the context of the decision-making process of the communities and attempted some realistic analysis of the influence of the parliament within that framework and pinpointed some of its weaknesses, we are in a position to turn to the party groupings themselves and to examine their origins, basis and development from the days of the common assembly (1952). Much of the inspiration for the development of specifically trans-national or supranational party groups came in the early, formative stages of the common assembly, when the European idealism underlying such a development burned most brightly. It is therefore indispensable to examine in some detail the process by which the groups came into being and how and why they developed as they did. Above all, it is imperative to reach an understanding of the significance of this new departure, which was and is unique among international assemblies — a significance which was well understood by the participants and ardently desired by them.

The treaty setting up the Coal and Steel Community was signed on 18 April 1951, and came into force on 25 July 1952. The treaty provided for an assembly of seventy-eight members; eighteen members to come from each of France, Germany and Italy, ten from Belgium and the Netherlands and four from Luxemburg. The assembly was to: '...exercise the supervisory powers which are granted to it by this Treaty' — ECSC treaty, Article 20. The assembly held its inaugural session to elect its officers and to draw up its rules of procedure on 10 September 1952. Early on the tendency to form groupings along political lines became evident. In view of the exclusion of the Communists, Nenni Socialists and the extreme right wing groups such as the French UDCA and the Sozialistische Reichspartei (SRP) from Germany it was natural for three embryonic groups to emerge representing three broad tendencies of political life in the six member states of the new community: Socialist (Social Democrat), Christian Democrat and Liberal. Each of these broad tendencies was clearly recognisable in the national political arena and could readily be transferred to the European level, with only limited problems of co-operation across the national frontiers. In this the assembly was following normal parliamentary usage:[4]

> If any legitimate doubt as to the statute of this Assembly should arise, it is in traditional parliamentary practise that the solution should be sought, not in unjustified comparisons with Assemblies, Commissions or other Organs of an international character.

The early debates on the rules of procedure, as well as the form in which these were finally adopted, give ample evidence of the conscious effort being made to facilitate – nay, encourage – the formation of formal party groups of a trans-national character within the assembly. The office of president was at once politicised by the contest between the Christian Democrat Brentano and the Socialist Spaak, who only stood on condition that the Socialists supported him *en bloc.* He was thus elected by 38 votes to 30. The bureau was to consist of a number of members unequal to the number of member states; it is clear that the purpose of this measure was understood from the speech of Monsieur Blaise.[5] The bureau was to reflect the political composition of the assembly (3 Christian Democrats; 2 Socialists; 1 Liberal) rather than the national composition. The Rules of Procedure (RP) gave official recognition of the role of the groups in Article 33 bis, which was based on the *Struye Report.* The objective was to give *de jure* recognition to a situation that already existed in practice. In order to encourage the formation of groups the procedure was made as simple as possible:[6]

1   The delegates may form political groups according to persuasion.
2   Groups shall be formed by handing a declaration of formation to the president, which declaration shall include the name of the group, the signature of its members and the composition of its executive. This declaration shall be made public.
3   No person shall be a member of more than one group.
4   The number of members necessary to form a group is nine.

The rules do not impose on the members any obligation to join a group. Neither do they explain what political conditions of allegiance are required for a deputy to be accepted as a member of a given group, nor is any statement of policy required from the group. The president is not given any power to reject any declaration of formation which may be handed in to him. The sole obligation placed on the member is that he may not join more than one group. The sole limitation placed on group formation is that of size. Minimum size is fixed at nine – a block on the formation of many small splinter groups. By sheer mathematics the maximum number of groups which could be formed in the 78-member assembly was eight. The rules do, of course, require that groups be formed on the basis of political persuasion, which would, it seems, exclude (and this was intended) the formation of purely national groups. In addition to official recognition groups were soon given financial aid from the funds of the assembly. The principle was easily accepted with only one dissentient – Monsieur Korthals. The bureau drew up a proposal for the distribution of funds, which entailed a bloc grant of 500,000 BF to each group and an additional 10,000 BF per member to be paid to each group. There was some opposition to this proposal, on the principle that community funds should not be paid to the groups and also on the grounds that there should be no discrimination with regard to size (Mollet). The proposal was nonetheless adopted by assembly. Thus the groups were given a material and legal framework within which they could develop as best they might. Of course, implicit in this system was the right of any member of the assembly to remain unaffiliated to any group if he so chose. In the early years two members availed themselves of this freedom. Monsieur Korthals, the Dutch Liberal, refused to join the Liberal group in the assembly, since he considered the group too 'illiberal'.[7] The other member who did not join any group was Monsieur Debré, who evidently did not share the European enthusiasm of the majority of the other delegates, and so it was logical enough for him to remain an independent member of the assembly. In theory, such members did not suffer any loss of influence, but obviously, in a climate of opinion which looked upon the groups as the formative influence in the assembly, the reality was that such members were rapidly deprived of any influence over the work of the assembly.

The major work of the assembly was, in common with the European tradition, to be carried out in the seven standing committees of the assembly. Article 35 of the Rules of Procedure stipulated that, in the composition of the committees: '. . . due regard be had to an equitable representation of the participating states and the various political tendencies'. However, no procedure is laid down for the nomination of the candidates for the committee. In the first instance this function belonged to the national delegations; hence the requirement of equitable political representation was merely a limitation on total freedom of action, an adjusting factor. From 1955 on the presidents of the political groups were invited by the president to submit their nominations for the committees and these were usually endorsed without debate, thus giving predominance to the political factor. The observance of the rule of national representation was the responsibility of the bureau. Certain special committees were formed, such as the working group and the comité de redaction (this committee had to draw up a draft report on the annual report of the high authority). On these bodies there was at first no clear predominance of political representation. In respect of the working group, appointment of groups and the committees was to be on an equal basis. In the discussion of this proposal by President Pella, some opposition had been voiced to retaining any national basis for representation. Monsieur Kreyssig (Socialist) rejected national representation as outmoded. In practice, the committees did not avail themselves of their rights and the working group came to be appointed exclusively by the political groups.

The comité de redaction was composed in the first instance of the chairmen of the committees of the assembly which had examined the annual report and the president of the assembly. In the second year of its existence, the bureau proposed to broaden the composition of this committee to include five representatives of the groups who were eventually appointed without regard for nationality.

The bureau, which had initially been constituted with a representative from each member state, nonetheless attained roughly fair representation of the three groups. On the death in office of Monsieur de Gasperi, president of the assembly in 1954, the question had to be faced of how to replace a member of the bureau; it was desired to reduce the nationality element in the bureau and hence a rule was framed to meet the situation. The official would be replaced by a member of the same political group and not of the same nationality (RP 6). As the bureau came to discuss more political and less purely organisational issues, the convention grew up that the presidents of the groups were invited to attend meetings of the bureau whenever political items were on the agenda. Thus, here too, political representation became dominant and the political groups were directly consulted on matters which aroused major political controversy, through the presence of their presidents in the bureau for such discussions.

The rules of procedure (RP 11 and 12) provide for a committee of presidents which was to draw up the agenda of the plenary sessions of the assembly. In order to bring to bear the necessary knowledge of the work of the standing committee on which the agenda had to be based, the committee was composed of the president and vice-presidents of the assembly and the chairmen of the standing committees. As early as the March 1953 session Monsieur Mollet (Socialist) was arguing in favour of the participation of the political groups in this body. Gradually the custom of inviting the groups to attend was developed; there was a good precedent for this, in that rules already allowed the high authority and the council of ministers to be invited to send representatives to the committee. With the revision of the rules in May 1954 the opportunity was taken to provide for the invitation of the representatives of the groups. This 'invitation' allowed the representatives to take part in the meetings, but stopped short of full voting rights.

In the organisation of committee work the political groups came to play an increasing role. The appointments of presidents and vice-presidents of the committees were made along party, and not national, lines. A member of a committee who was unable to attend would appoint a 'suppleant', replacement from his own group irrespective of nationality. In the all-important question of the appointment of rapporteurs, party considerations became uppermost. The rapporteur had the responsibility of leading the discussion in committee and drafting a report which would gain the acceptance of his committee and then, once adopted, of presenting the draft report, with its draft resolution, to the plenary assembly and replying to the debate and giving his views on the proposed amendments. In short, his role is rather similar to that of a British minister, steering a bill through the House of Commons. Such appointments came to be made on the basis of prior agreement between the party groups.

On 20 and 23 June declarations of formation were handed to the president in respect of three groups which were to continue throughout the life of the common assembly and beyond into the European parliament when the latter was formed in 1958. These were, in order of size:

Christian-Democrat	38 Members	President:	Sassen (Netherlands Katholiek Partij)
Socialist	23 Members	President:	Mollet (France SF10)
Liberal & apparentes	11 Members	President:	Delbos (France Radical)

Six members did not join any group: four French Républicains-sociaux (Gaullists) and two Liberals. This figure was, as already mentioned, reduced to two from 1956 onwards.

Each group was required by the rules of procedure to have an executive and was, as we have seen endowed with some financial resources out of the community funds, otherwise organisational and material questions are left to the groups themselves. The Christian Democrats appointed an executive with a president and eight vice-presidents; the Socialist executive consisted of a president, vice-president, secretary-treasurer and two members; the Liberal executive was limited to a president, a vice-president and a secretary. The Christian Democrats' internal organisation was based on a set of rules. The general administration devolved on to the bureau aided by the secretariat, but only within the framework of the general policy laid down by the group as a whole. In addition, working groups were established to follow important matters. A key role was played by the secretary general who, although an official of the group, enjoyed considerable political influence. He maintained close contact with the president and among the members. He was empowered to undertake studies, negotiate with the high authority and make political recommendations to the group. The Socialist secretary general was more limited in his role; however, an efficient secretariat maintained liaison between the members and gave some coherence to the work of the group. The main detailed work of drawing up policy proposals lay with two working groups. Legal questions and economic and social affairs, with its three sub-committees — on coal policy, cartels and transport. Political directives were then adopted at full group meetings, which were called both in and out of the plenary sessions of the assembly. The Liberals were less ideologically cohesive and were in any case the smallest group — a fact which was reflected in the less substantial character of their organisation. There were no working groups and the full group met rather infrequently. This was to some extent compensated for by the activism of the secretary general, Monsieur Drèze, who was influential both in Belgian and international Liberal circles.

The increasing organisation of the groups and the tendency to politicisation of the proceedings of the assembly led to group collective viewpoints being presented. The normal parliamentary procedure was applied: the president controlled the debate and gave members the right to speak. This right was originally given to individuals in the order in which they had given in their names to the president before the debate began. Even before the formal recognition of the groups, collective viewpoints came to be expressed. So it was that in the debate on the financing of the groups in March 1953, Messieurs Mollet, Sassen and Delbos presented the views of the Socialists, Christian Democrats and Liberals respectively. Increasingly from then on debates came to be characterised by group statements followed by a few shorter interventions by individuals, who either disagreed with their group standpoint or who wished to raise some point of detail. Although there was no legal justification for the convention, it more and more came to be the case that the group spokesmen were permitted to take the floor immediately the rapporteur had completed his presentation of the report, thus giving them certain dominance over proceedings and completing the impression of politicisation of the assembly, which has been a constant feature of the developments we have examined.

Within less than two years of existence, the political groups had obtained a dominant position within the organisational structure of the assembly. The groups had been recognised by the rules of procedure and had gained financial support from the budget of the assembly. The office of the president of the assembly had become the subject of a political contest; the political, rather than the national 'proportz', principle had been accepted as the basis for membership in the bureau and in the standing committees and any special committees which might be set up. The groups had gained the right of attendance at the important committee of presidents and hence some influence over the agenda of the plenary session. The posts of rapporteurs and chairmen and vice-chairmen of committees were allotted on party lines, bringing group influence into play in the vital committees, which did the main detailed work of the assembly. The practice of holding group meetings before plenary sessions and appointing group spokesmen gave a party accent to the proceedings in the plenary sessions unique among international bodies.

The groups had become dominant and party was the main organisational principle in the assembly. Rules and structures can only act as a framework from which meaningful action can grow; they are not a substitute for organic development. Indeed, one would not expect the political solidarity and cohesion so evident on the national plane to develop with the same speed as had the formal structure which we have just examined, for even the formal structures of this kind had only developed over centuries in the member states. What concerns us here is the extent to which the groups developed a corporate identity and cohesion and distinctive policies and styles which differentiated one from another and to what extent such differentiation had brought about political controversy in the work of the assembly, having at the same time regard to the difficult position of the assembly in the sense that it was not a 'legislature' in the accepted sense and did not therefore easily split into a majority whose task was to support the executive and a minority opposition group which was an alternative government majority.

Up to now, we have confined ourselves to the manner in which the groups became organisationally dominant. In fact, at the same time parallel developments had occurred in the development of the political consciousness of the groups. At first political activity was evident, but conflict and differentiation among the groups was not apparent, except on smaller issues, which might be attributed as much to personality questions as to serious political differences. The election of the president of the assembly saw the first political division. Monsieur Spaak stood with the clear support of the whole Socialist group against the German Christian Democrat, Herr Brentano. Spaak had made the support of the Socialist group as a whole a condition of accepting nomination as a candidate. He was elected by 38 votes to 30 for his opponent. This indicates that Spaak did enjoy the solid support of his group, but that the same could not be said for Herr Brentano who would, without doubt, have been elected if he had obtained the solid support of the Christian Democrat group, as this group had at that time almost an absolute majority in the assembly (38 members out of 78). In the debate on the first draft budget the question of political groups was raised. The rapporteur considered the formation of groups essential to the assembly in performing its task of controlling the high authority. In the same session, Monsieur Mollet and Monsieur Sassen supported this view.[8] Also in the March session there occurred a difference of opinion between Monsieur Mollet (Socialist) and Monsieur Sassen (Christian Democrat) on the question of the groups. Monsieur Mollet wanted there to be no discrimination in the funds made available to the groups, irrespective of size. In the plenary debate on the *Vermeylen Report* on financing the groups, statements were made on behalf of all three of the as yet unrecognised groups: Messieurs Mollet, Sassen and Delbos (Liberal).

From this it is clear that the early sessions had of necessity concentrated upon questions of organisation, which had in spite of some group intervention not led to the groups' gaining any distinct identity. However, a recognisable pattern soon asserted itself. The assembly began to seek to extend its limited role. The assembly was endowed with one real power: to pass, by a two-thirds majority, a vote of censure against the high authority, which would then be compelled to resign. Upon this power the assembly sought to build. On the resignation of the first president of the high authority in early 1955, the three political groups presented a joint resolution, which required that the six governments should consult the assembly before the new president was appointed. Secondly, the new president was required to make a policy statement to the assembly, immediately on taking office. The first part of the Resolution met with no response whereupon Monsieur Pella, president of the assembly, undertook a tour of the six capitals and urged the appointment of a political figure rather than a technocrat. In this the assembly was satisfied with the appointment of Monsieur René Mayer. Monsieur Mayer presented to the assembly a Declaration of Policy (21 June 1955) in the manner of an incoming prime minister. This statement gave rise to a debate in which the group spokesmen held a prominent place. This system of executive statements as a preface to statements by group spokesmen in reply, followed by a general debate, was to become traditional in the assembly. The other model was the committee report, introduced by the rapporteur, upon which the high authority and the group spokesmen commented, leading to the adoption of a resolution. The key feature in the system is the dialogue between the groups and the executive, much in the manner of a national parliament.

Another feature of this early period was the catalytic effect of the Socialist group. At all times it was this group which took the lead in asserting the powers of the assembly, in imposing control on the high authority, in increasing the role of the groups within the assembly and, above all, in provoking political controversy. Referring to critical comments on the working of the community by Monsieur Mollet, Van

Oudenhouve states: 'The Socialists' enterprise had a contagious effect on the other groups, who were soon to adopt the same course'. It was then the increasingly cohesive attitude of the Socialists and their critical stand in relation to the policies of the high authority which provoked a response from the groups. However, it should not be imagined that 'party politics' were at this stage well developed. Indeed, individual viewpoints were still the norm and some national positions obtruded. In particular, the German SPD and the French SFIO adopted national standpoints. At this time, for reasons of internal politics, the SPD was most critical of the ECSC formula and rejected the formation of a political community on the same model; hence, they were sharply differentiated not only from the assembly as a whole, but also from their fellow Socialists.

At this stage the groups concentrated on concrete issues of policy, avoiding more generalised, ideological statements. This was necessary since every group standpoint represented a complicated and, at times, delicate compromise between the positions and special interests of the component national parties. Nonetheless, distinct lines of battle could be discerned through the standpoints adopted. In the debate on the *Second Annual Report* of the high authority (May 1954), all three groups appointed spokesmen and their statements indicated characteristic concerns, which were to find an echo throughout the life of the assembly. For the Socialists, Monsieur Carcassone[9] advocated an equalisation of wage levels in the community, standardisation of social policy and community-wide collective agreements. For the Christian Democrats, Monsieur Sassen showed himself unenthusiastic about wage equalisation policy, but demanded a statement from the high authority on cartel policy.[10] Characteristically, Monsieur Laffargue for the Liberals warned against excessive planning and dirigisme which would blunt the dynamism of private enterprise. Here we can see the traditional concerns of the three main streams of political life in the member states gaining an echo on the community level. Here we see the Socialist concern with wages and conditions of work and social services and evidence of a dirigiste approach to the problem. We see the Christian Democratic concern with effective competition and control of monopoly power to ensure the efficacy of the market system. The Liberals we see in their classic role as the defenders of private enterprise. Such concerns were again evident in the replies to Monsieur Mayer's declaration on 22 June 1955. In the debate on Euratom of March 1956 the Socialists were ranged against the Christian Democrats and the Liberals. Their spokesman, Monsieur Dehousse, underlined the Socialist commitment to general controlled disarmament and demanded that all fissile material should be the property of the community. On the other hand, Sassen (CD) emphasised that private property and initiative were axiomatic in the thinking of his group.

Such differences were to lead to direct confrontation and bitter controversy which would cast the Socialists in the role of an opposition and so force the Christian Democrats and Liberals to support the high authority in the manner of a government majority in a national parliament. The first such clash concerned the levy on coal and steel turnover. The ECSC is unique among international organisations (until the institution by the Treaty of Luxemburg, 1970, of 'ressources propres' for all three communities) in possessing an independent source of revenue and indeed, a supranational taxing power. This community tax (Article 50, Treaty of Paris) is in the form of a levy on coal and steel turnover, to be fixed by the high authority at a rate not to exceed 1 per cent. The rate of levy is fixed by the high authority on its own authority – it is not required to consult either the council of ministers or the assembly. Since the high authority is responsible to the assembly it would be expected that the high authority would consult the assembly on such a vital political issue. In May 1955 the high authority reduced the rate of levy from 0.90 per cent to 0.70 per cent and that without prior consultation of the assembly. As might be expected, this decision provoked an adverse reaction in the assembly. All were agreed on the lack of consultation. However, the Socialists went beyond a mere procedural criticism, which indicated a distinctly Socialist approach to problems of public finance and expenditure. A reduction in the levy meant a reduction in funds available for expenditure on investment grants and social policy; this situation was deplored by the Socialists. On the other hand, the Liberals and Christian Democrats were not critical of the principle of a reduction in the rate of the levy – merely in the manner in which the reduction had in the case at issue been imposed. Two contradictory resolutions were before the assembly. The Socialists therefore demanded a roll-call vote. This vote exposed the differences of opinion which existed; the Socialists voted *en bloc* for their own resolution and solidly against the draft resolution submitted by the Liberal group, as indeed did the Liberals, *mutatis mutandis.* The Christian Democrats voted solidly against the Socialist resolution, but split into three factions on the Liberal resolution: one for, one against and one group abstained. This division was not along national lines: all the national parties were themselves split on this issue.

Even more violent political controversy erupted in the debate on the *Fourth Annual Report* of the high authority. Monsieur Nederhorst indicated that the Socialist group had come close to tabling a motion of censure against the policy of the high authority.[11] A month later, after the conclusion of the debate on the *Report,* Herr Kreyssig launched a violent attack on the high authority on behalf of the Socialist group. It was alleged that the high authority was indifferent to the needs of social policy, had no coherent coal policy and had undermined the supranational character of the community. Such an attack forced the other two groups to defend the executive. In substance, if not in fact, the action of the Socialists had been an expression of no confidence in the high authority, which had been rejected by the other groups, who thus appeared to support the executive. The November debate on coal policy enabled the Socialists to return to the attack. Here the Socialists complained that the high authority was failing to exploit the powers conferred on it by the treaty. Here again the other groups were forced to defend the high authority.

It is clear that the Socialists were following a distinct political line which brought them into conflict with the liberal assumptions on which the policy of the high authority was based and with their defenders in the assembly. The Socialist group was translating to the European plane their traditional concern for public expenditure and state intervention in economic affairs and their instinctive distrust of private capitalism. This led them into a direct confrontation with the other groups in the assembly. The Socialist group appeared more and more as an opposition group. As Van Oudenhouve states: 'By this separatist tendency, the Socialist Group revealed themselves unequivocally as a supranational opposition to the executive'. It is evident that the attitude of the Socialists was responsible in great measure for the politicisation of the assembly, provoking as it did a response from the other groups, who were forced to define their position in respect of the high authority. The assembly divided into two blocs — those who supported the line pursued by the high authority and those who attacked it — in short, 'government' and 'opposition' blocs were forming. In other words,[12] the members of the assembly's major task consisted in choosing between liberalism and dirigisme at the community level. The treaty contains elements of both liberalism and dirigisme and, hence, can support either point of view; in consequence, the Socialist group were able to emphasise the dirigiste aspect of the treaty and the Liberals were equally able to reject this element in favour of a liberal approach, whereas the Christian Democrats could attempt to synthesise the two elements. It was the catalytic effect of the Socilists' action which was responsible for this state of affairs:

> Statements by the Socialist Group forced the other parties to come into the open ... The increasing attacks by the Socialists drove the Christian-Democrats in particular to take up the defence of the executive, which cast them *de facto* in the role of a government party.

Referring to the position of the Liberals in this respect E. Haas[13] states

> When the position of the Christian-Democrats meets the essence of the free enterprise and autonomy wishes of the Liberals, they act as a member of a government coalition. But when the Christian-Democrats are in two minds about High Authority policy, as they often are, the aspirations of the bulk of the Liberals come closer to meeting the role of a tacit opposition group blackmailing the Government into action by the threat of joining the opposition formally.

Thus we have a system in which the Christian Democrats, with, for the most part, Liberal support, act as a government party against the vociferous opposition of the Socialists. Political positions were, it should be remembered, not generalised, carthesian statements, but rather concrete responses to the particular issues, rooted in the traditional perspective of each group. These positions did not amount to a political programme on the European level. No group was prepared to draft such a programme. Indeed, very serious obstacles would have stood in the way of such enterprise: the economic character of the treaty did not lend itself to generalised political positions, nor had there been time for such positions to mature and, above all, the heterogeneity of the groups' composition militated against such an approach. Only a piecemeal, ad hoc approach could maintain the fragile unity of the groups. Efforts to distil the doctrine of the three groups by the working group chaired by Monsieur Fohrman failed and the *Report* of Monsieur Gozard to the Council of Europe[14] in which he surveyed the doctrine of the groups was rejected by the groups themselves. Our only guide to the policies of the groups can be their own statements made in successive debates on the major issues of community policy. The cumulative effect of such statements would be to give an indication of the position of a particular group on the main issues.

The main issues which should be examined are: wider problems of integration; coal policy; social policy; competition, manpower and investment policy. From the earliest days of its existence, the assembly was confronted with the question of further European integration. On 11 September 1952, Dr Adenauer, President of the Council of Ministers, asked the assembly to draw up a draft treaty for a European political community. For this task the assembly was augmented by an additional nine members drawn from the larger states, (Germany, France and Italy). This augmented body received the name of the Ad hoc Assembly. The drafting work was undertaken by a 26-member constitutional committee.

In this committee the Christian Democrats were overrepresented, with fourteen members, and the Socialists had a mere five members, fewer than the Liberals. The draft was adopted by the seemingly impressive vote of 50 for, 0 against and 5 abstentions. Of course some 32 members were absent from the vote. Calculations show that the 'true' result, apportioning the absentees for and against and counting abstentions as opponents, would be closer to 67 for the draft and 20 against. At all events, the two blocs showed splits in the party groups. The 'Nos' consisted of the German SPD, which rejected the whole concept of a political community on the grounds that such a body would impede German reunification; the French Socialist Party, which wished for greater co-operation on the basis of the fifteen members of the Council of Europe and rejected a political community which excluded Great Britain, with its strong Labour Party. The French Gaullists rejected the federalist emphasis in the project. Two Liberals opposed the project: Monsieur Maroger (France) feared German hegemony in the new community and Monsieur Schaus (Luxemburg) feared that the smaller states would be dominated by the larger powers. The supporters of the project consisted of the entire Christian Democrat group and the Liberals, minus two. The Socialist parties split along national lines, with the other Socialist parties (from Italy and the Benelux Countries) supporting the project. In fact this project was of little real importance due to the failure of the European defence community. By the time of the 'relance européenne' at the Messina Conference in 1955 there had been considerable change in the attitude of the SPD. As early as December 1954 the assembly had been able to pass a resolution based on the *Teitgen Report,* by a large majority, which included the Socialists. In the numerous discussions on the matter in the wake of the Messina Conference (June 1955), and during the drafting of the Treaties of Rome, the assembly was able to speak with an almost unanimous voice, with the Socialists having no difficulty in supporting the principles involved without internal dissention.

In concrete consideration of how the general principle of more integration should be implemented, there was by no means the same harmony. As in the past, the Socialist group had definite and specifically Socialist viewpoints on the exact form that the future community should take. For them, a Common Market would have to be not a mere 'free market' but an 'integrated market', in which there would be integrated, economic, commercial and fiscal policies, the aim of which would be to foster economic growth and social progress on a community-wide basis. The Christian Democrats, too, emphasised the need to go beyond a mere customs union. For them the touchstone of the enterprise would be a dynamic release of economic forces within the new economic union, but with proper safeguards by way of government regulation and social policy. The Liberal group welcomed integration but were less clear about its practical implementation. Indeed, in respect of the 'relance', it might be said that the Socialists had now overtaken the Liberals in European zeal. On Euratom, the projected Atomic Energy Community, which likewise emerged from the Messina Conference, there was general ageement in principle among the groups. All were agreed on the notion of a common market in nuclear material and personnel. However, the Socialist group had distinct views on the form which the community should take. For them it was essential that the community should ensure the use of nuclear energy for peaceful purposes alone, which would require strict controls at all stages. In addition, they demanded community ownership of fissile materials, a definitely Socialist position. The Christian Democrats and Liberals, although in favour of disarmament, were not prepared categorically to forswear the military use of atomic energy. On the question of ownership of fissile materials, these groups were totally opposed to public ownership of fissile material and wished to reserve for private enterprise the prime role in this field. Indeed, only by passing over both these issues was the assembly able to adopt a resolution on the subject. Naturally, the resultant resolution, adopted with only one dissentient (Debré), was virtually meaningless.

One of the major problems with which the community had to wrestle was the coal crisis. Within a short time of the signature of the Treaty of Paris the shortage of coal, which had formed the economic background against which the treaty had been negotiated, gave way to a prolonged and deep crisis due to the fall in demand for coal and the uncompetitive nature of European coal production. At a stroke, all the complicated provisions of the treaty for dealing with a dearth of coal were redundant and those which enabled the high authority to react to overproduction were shown to be woefully inadequate and dependent on conflicting national interests. After this crisis, it became evident that the supranational power of the community had strict limitations. Not unnaturally this crisis was the subject of deep concern in the assembly. The situation was extremely complicated, in that there was at first, in 1956, a rise in demand for coal, which could not be met, which led to importation of American coal, which ultimately provoked near collapse in the European coal industry. Hence there was a first phase in which the high authority had to ensure that enterprises did not exploit the shortage, followed by a period of total overproduction and run down. The issue was not raised until April 1956, when Monsieur Mollet gave a written statement to the high authority attacking their 'Memorandum on Coal Policy'. In the May-June sessions of 1956 a major aspect of the Socialists' attack on the high authority policy in general concerned coal policy. The Socialists maintained that strict control by the high authority was necessary and were critical of the failure of the high authority to employ the powers given to it by the treaty. Indeed, the preferred solution would have been supranational control and operation of the coal industry; for them the free market was untenable in the coal industry. The Christian Democrats did not adopt a genuine group standpoint, but in general refrained from criticism of the high authority and proposed a solution to the problem in the framework of an energy policy seen as a whole. The Liberals advanced arguments for 'making the market work', enabling the coal industry to operate efficiently within the private enterprise framework.

As we have already seen, the Socialists placed great emphasis on the development of a community social policy. This was not limited to debates on social policy, but permeated their approach to every question. In this they were frequently critical of the high authority, which they considered to have neglected this sphere of policy, in favour of a market-orientated approach. The stuff from which a community social policy might be fashioned is sparse indeed; there is no separate chapter of the treaty dedicated to social policy — rather a few disparate references to social objectives: wage levels, free movement of skilled workers, aid to employment of redundant workers under certain tightly controlled conditions. Usually such indications are limited to what is needed to ensure fair competition and the liberal market system. The high authority has merely a certain responsibility for making studies, initiating action or guiding the activity of member states. In fact responsibility rests almost entirely with the member states and community powers and instruments are almost non-existent. The assembly always displayed a disproportionate interest in this field of policy. The other two groups were not as forthright as the Socialists in presenting a distinct point of view. The Socialists always sought an extensive interpretation of the limited treaty provisions that did exist and criticised the high authority for inaction. In particular, the Socialists sought an upward harmonisation of wages and living conditions throughout the whole community. This was based on the notion of 'égalisation dans le progrès' found in Article 3 of the treaty. This view was first apparent in the May 1954 debate of the subject and was re-emphasised by Monsieur Nederhorst in the May 1957 session,[15] who was dissatisfied with progress achieved in this area. The Christian Democrats were reserved in their response to the position of the Socialists and did not see the need for harmonisation on any large scale, believing that this would in any case result from economic integration. On the question of the free movement of skilled workers, the Socialists were again, in May 1955, to strike a political note; for them, the implementation agreement, based on Article 69 of the ECSC treaty, was grossly inadequate, giving too great authority to the national governments and affecting too limited a category of workers. The most serious social problem that faced the community was that of re-adaptation of workers of enterprises forced to go out of production as a result of technological changes. Despite the fact that the real powers of the high authority were extremely limited in this field, the Socialists were active in demanding a more vigorous policy on the part of the high authority. At the May 1955 session, the attack was opened by Monsieur Sassen of the Christian Democrats, but was followed by Monsieur Nederhorst for the Socialists. Whilst Monsieur Sassen limited himself to questioning whether the reduction in the levy rate would not prove detrimental to the re-adaptation fund and demanding greater resolution from the high authority, Monsieur Nederhorst made a more categorical statement along the same lines. At the May 1956 session the issue was again raised. The Socialists took a more sombre view of the situation and this culminated in the Kreyssig 'Declaration' of June 1956, which violently attacked the inaction of the high authority in social policy. The Christian Democrats were unable to do more than to emphasise the importance of the matter — internal disagreement prevented a more substantial statement from the group. The discussion of the *Wigny Report* on the first four years of the community in February 1957, led to a new attack by Monsieur Nederhorst for the Socialists. He criticised the lack of results to date and argued for the creation of new sources of employment in the same areas rather than the shifting of workers to other areas. In the May debate Messieurs Nederhorst and Lapie criticised the new reduction in the rate of levy and argued in favour of extensive use of the re-adaptation policy to close marginal mines during periods when demand for labour was high in other sectors. The Christian Democrats were not able to make any meaningful contribution to the debate and the Liberals did not intervene.

Articles 65 and 66 of the ECSC, in particular, give the high authority precise powers over cartels and mergers. Indeed this is only logical, since free competition is the touchstone of the treaty. The first concrete case raised before the assembly was that of the Ruhr Coal Sales Cartel (CEORG) which was split into three separate sales organisations by the high authority. The Socialists were not satisfied with cartel policy in general; to them there was too little permanent public control and the high authority had failed to attack radically the existing cartel structure. These attitudes were reiterated in the May-June 1956 debates and particularly in the debate on the *Kreyssig Report* on the desirability of a treaty revision. Here the Socialists proposed a public law control body on which workers would be represented. The Christian Democrats were without clear guiding principles and adopted an empirical 'wait and see' approach to the problem, limiting themselves to demands that the high authority should act on the basis of clear principles (which were not formulated by the group) rather than on a case by case basis, as had been the case up to that time. The Liberals were not in favour of any radical approach to the problem and preferred to support the high authority, rather limiting their concern to the safeguarding of competition in general terms. On the problem of mergers, which the treaty does not seek to forbid but merely to place under the scrutiny of the high authority, the Socialists again took the lead in formulating a coherent position. The question did not come into the open until the special debate on the problem in May 1957.[16] Here the Socialists indicated that they had no prejudice against mergers as such, but *were* critical of the high authority, which in their view had not developed a clear policy and had been too weak in opposing abuses of market power, since many of the mergers which had been approved had brought no benefit to the consumer. The Christian Democrats formulated no precise view and argued in favour of a standing policy towards concentrations. The Liberals were silent. At the February 1958 session, the Liberals took the view that, economically, mergers were inevitable and beneficial, but should be controlled to avoid degeneration into political influence. This line approximated to that which the Socialists adopted at this time. The Christian Democrats took the view that the problem was indissoluble from that of cartels and should in any case find its solution within the framework of the General Common Market.

The treaty takes considerable interest in the problem of investment policy. The high authority is required to publish at intervals statements of general objectives in regard to investment policy and capacity expansion. In addition, the community has been given rather more direct means of guiding investment policy. Article 54 of the treaty permits the high authority to require notification of investment projects and to issue an 'avis motivé' on them. Out of its funds the high authority may make loans or issue guarantees to enterprises to assist investment which would raise production, lower costs or increase sales. From levy income the high authority created a guarantee fund and hence was able itself to raise loans, such as from the USA, and hence granted, by 1958, loans totalling $173.1 million. Early on in January 1954 differing views were expressed in the assembly on the type of investment policy to be pursued. Speakers[17] emphasised the political significance of the debate and the need for a choice as between the dirigiste and liberal alternatives. In the May-June 1955 debates, Messieurs Deist and Nederhorst for the Socialists advocated a controlled investment policy, by which the high authority would direct investment into priority channels and ensure general co-ordination of investment policy. The Liberals categorically rejected control by the high authority. There was no Christian Democratic standpoint: individual speakers were split as to whether co-ordination was needed or whether investment was the sole concern of enterprises. Here the matter rested until November 1956. Again the Socialists were the most positive, demanding that some force be given to the 'avis motivé, or else control would pass to the national governments. The Liberals called for more publicity of priorities and the Christian Democrats limited themselves to a rejection of dirigisme.

Looking at the different policy areas one can agree with Van Oudenhouve:

> ... wage and labour conditions, and, although to a lesser extent re-adaptation too produced one or two brief manifestations of party politics, the problem of free movement of labour never once generated any political tension ... Steadfastness characterises the Socialists, who, as their numerous contributions show, aimed at influencing decisively the trend of investments by broader based financing and the publication of relevant details, all this under the impulse of a vigorously acting High Authority.

We can reasonably conclude that only the Socialists had by the dissolution of the assembly gone any way towards the formulation of concrete, clear-cut ideological positions at the European level and that this alone had been the catalyst to the politicisation of the assembly.

Notes

1 'Legal aspects of the work of the European Parliament'.
2 As indicated in chapter 14 (esp. pp. 207-8) the budgetary procedure is under current review.
3 *Politics and Bureaucracy in the European Communities*.
4 *Further Report* (Document 919).
5 C.A. Proceedings, no. 1, 11th September 1952.
6 Article 33 bis.
7 T. Westerterp, 'Europese Fractievorming' *Internationale Spectator*, July 1958.
8 C.A. Proceedings, no. 2, 11th March 1953, pp. 12, 14.
9 C.A. Proceedings, no. 6, 14th May 1954, pp. 118-19.
10 C.A. Proceedings, no. 6, 14th May 1954, pp. 125-8.

11 C.A. Proceedings, no. 13, 9th May 1956, pp. 419-23.
12 M. Teitgen, rapporteur for the political affairs committee.
13 *The Uniting of Europe.*
14 Council of Europe, Document 705.
15 C.A. Proceedings, no. 24, 26th June 1957, pp. 661-2.
16 Debate on the *Fayat Report.*
17 Herr Deist, C.A. Proceedings, no. 5, 14-16 January 1954, pp. 97-8.

3 The European Parliament: Organisation and Powers

3.1 The rules of procedure

The European parliament came into being in early 1958 as a result of the Treaties of Rome establishing the European Economic Community and the European Atomic Energy Community and the Convention relative to certain Institutions common to the European Communities. This last makes it clear that one single assembly is to be established for the three communities. Indeed, this was not the original intention and was only conceded at the last minute after energetic pressure from the common assembly and the consultative assembly of the Council of Europe.[1]

The problems of organisation and structure which had confronted the common assembly were absent, in so far as the practice and experience of that assembly over six years could readily and with only minor changes be adopted in the new situation. Indeed, the institutional structure of the two new communities was in most respects similar to that of the Coal and Steel Community, except that the equilibrium between the institutions was altered in favour of the Council of Ministers which, in the new communities, was the main body endowed with decision-making powers, to the detriment of the supranational body (the commission) which was of course placed under the control of the assembly. In addition, the policy fields involved were of a different order; true the Euratom Community was as much a sectorial body as the Coal and Steel Community, but the EEC had jurisdiction over the whole economy of the member states and potentially over social and fiscal policies.

Naturally this change would greatly widen the horizons of the Assembly, but did not present any immediate practical difficulty. As far as the parliament itself was concerned its role was expanded. In the terms of Article 137 of the EEC Treaty, the assembly 'exercises the powers of deliberation and control conferred upon it by the Treaty'. Specifically the number of members was raised from 78 to 148 – divided as follows:[2] France, Germany and Italy each 36, Belgium and the Netherlands each 14 and Luxemburg 6 – and, more important, Article 138(3) places an absolute obligation on the assembly and the council of ministers to adopt a convention providing for the election of the assembly by direct, universal suffrage. Under the Rome treaties, the assembly may pass a motion of censure against the commission at any time, not merely during the debate on the *Annual Report* (Article 144, EEC). The assembly has a right to discuss the budget and propose amendments which must be discussed by the council, but may be rejected by a qualified majority. Since the Treaty of Luxemburg in 1970, the position of the assembly on the budget has improved: the assembly may fix its own budget without outside control and may, as before, propose amendments to the whole budget, which must be considered by the council. From 1975, the assembly will have the final word over that section of the budget which does not depend on acts adopted in accordance with a treaty stipulation. There is argument as to the meaning of this provision, but it would seem to exclude the assembly from control over some 95 per cent of the total budget. A statement in the Treaty of Luxemburg that the 'Assembly adopts the budget' has been taken by the assembly to confer upon it the right to reject the budget in toto, as from 1975. That is to say, if amendments proposed by the assembly were to be rejected by the council, the way would be open for the assembly to reject the whole budget; the object of this exercise would be 'to provoke new and more acceptable budgetary proposals'.[3]

In addition, it had become clear from the common assembly that a true parliamentary tradition was developing which would not be satisfied with the limited *a posteriori* control formally accorded to it, as is stated by S. Buerstedde:[4]

> From the start the Consultative Assembly saw its role not merely as the exercise of an *a posteriori* control of the High Authority. It sought rather to intervene fully in the decision making process of the ECSC.

This fact was recognised by the new treaties. The assembly was to be consulted before the more important legislative acts were adopted.

We can see that the new assembly, combining the parliamentary powers for all three communities was greatly fortified both in scope and power. In so far as mere statistics can give some indication of a level of activity, it is instructive to compare the volume of work of the common assembly and the European parliament. Over the whole life of the common assembly from 1952 to 1958, 110 reports were adopted, whereas for example in the year 1970 the European parliament adopted 242 Reports — twice the total output of the common assembly.

The present rules of procedure of the parliament, which differ little from those adopted in 1958, are based on the common assembly rules.

The changes which were made were those necessitated by the treaties themselves: the larger membership of the parliament; the consultation procedure; the budgetary procedure especially since the Treaty of Luxemburg in 1970; the requirements of the Treaty of Fusion (1965). Other changes were made to legalise custom, such as the participation of the group presidents in the committee of presidents.

The president of the parliament, elected at the annual March session, is responsible for the external representation of the parliament (Article 53), for the general direction of the work of the parliament, for the control of the sessions: he opens and closes the sitting, maintains order and calls members to speak. He is replaced when necessary by one of the vice-presidents, elected at the same time as himself.

The bureau is composed of the president and eight vice-presidents. The main task of the bureau is administrative and internal. With the co-operation of the secretary general, the bureau organises the secretariat and draws up the organigramn of the institution (Article 49, RP). On the basis of a report by the secretary general, the bureau draws up the draft budget for the parliament itself, which is then considered by the finance and budgetary committee. The bureau must also make a report at the start of the annual session, on the basis of which the appointment of members is validated. It must also receive the nominations for committee posts and is charged by Article 37 of the rules to ensure an equitable national and political balance in committee membership.

A new body was created to integrate the political groups more closely and formally into the fabric of the parliament. This was the enlarged bureau. This organ consists of the bureau and the group presidents who are now full members of this body, rather than, as before, having a rather shadowy right to participate in the work of the bureau upon invitation. In practice, the bureau itself tends to meet less and less frequently, being transformed into the enlarged bureau, even for those questions where, formally at least, the bureau alone would be competent to act. The enlarged bureau controls the agenda of the assembly. It draws up the agenda of the plenary sessions, but in doing so is assisted by the committee of presidents. This body is composed of the enlarged bureau and the presidents of the standing committees, whose task it is to furnish information on the state of committee work which must form the basis of the agenda. In the same way, Articles 46 and 47 stipulate that an oral question for debate, tabled by any member, a committee or political group must be considered by the enlarged bureau, which may transform it into a written question or place it on the agenda of the parliament. However, if the question is put by a political group it must be placed on the agenda. If there is a vacancy in the bureau, the political group to which the former holder had belonged proposes a candidate for the office, which must then be ratified by the enlarged bureau.

At the base of the work of the parliament are the committees. The parliament has the right to appoint standing and ad hoc committees, but the normal procedure has been to appoint only standing committees. There are at present twelve:

1	Political committee	29 Members
2	Economic and Monetary committee	29 Members
3	Budgets committee	29 Members
4	Agriculture committee	29 Members
5	Social affairs committee	29 Members
6	Public health and environment committee	29 Members
7	Legal affairs committee	29 Members
8	Transport and regional policy committee	29 Members
9	Cultural affairs committee	27 Members
10	Energy research and Technology committee	29 Members
11	Development and Cooperation committee	35 Members
12	External Economic Relations committee	35 Members

Each of these committees has a bureau — president and two vice-presidents. The quorum for a valid vote is fixed at one-third of the nominal membership, unless at least one-sixth of the membership raises an objection, in which case half the members must be present before a vote can be valid.

Article 22 of the rules of procedure provides that a request for an opinion received either from the commission or the council is referred to the appropriate committee, which must be done either by the parliament itself or, out of session, by the president. In accordance with Article 30, the competent committee may be assisted by up to two other committees who have an interest in some aspect of the question. Article 26 makes it clear that as a general rule the parliament deliberates only on the report of the competent committee, which gives the committees a key role in the procedure of the parliament. Only where the matter is declared urgent can the report be dispensed with or given orally. Such treatment can only be requested by the president of the parliament, the commission or the council of ministers, or ten members of the parliament. It is granted as a right if at least one-third of the members so request in writing. A procedure which can also save time, at least in respect of proposals of limited interest or of an extremely technical nature, is that of consideration without debate. This procedure is used at the request of the competent committee, provided the commission does not object.

The committees may constitute sub-committees and send a small group of members on a study mission in order to elucidate specific questions. For each question a rapporteur is appointed and he must draw up the report, which must contain a draft resolution (Articles 42 and 44) an 'exposé des motifs' and the opinions of any other committees which have also been consulted; on the invitation of the president of the committee the commission and the council may take part and the committee may by special decision invite any other person to attend. Any member of the parliament may attend, but not take any part in the proceedings, unless he is invited to do so; however, a member of the committee may be replaced by any other member, who may then take full part. This is a means of allowing interested non-members of the committee to take part. Any other committee consulted may send its president, rapporteur and up to five members to explain their opinion.

In plenary session, the rapporteur opens the debate and may subsequently be heard at any time. In addition, the commission and the council may be heard at their request — a right conferred not by the rules of procedure but by the treaty itself. The rapporteurs and presidents of any other committees concerned may also be heard at any time. The rules (Article 31) give priority to the spokesmen of the political groups, but (Article 28) the president may propose a time limit on speeches, after consulting the groups and committee presidents. The rules themselves limit interventions on procedural matters or to propose or oppose amendments. Any member may propose amendments, but these may be referred to the competent committee and must be so referred if the committee requests it. If there are amendments proposed to the budget these must automatically be considered by the competent committee.

3.2 Nomination of members

Initially, the rules (Article 36) required 17 members to form a group and the same groups as had existed in the common assembly were reformed. In the first session (March 1958) there were 67 Christian Democrats to 38 Socialists, 35 Liberals, and two unaffiliated members. This reflected the same relationship between the strengths of the groups as had been the case in the common assembly. As far as national origins were concerned, the Germans (19) and Italians (25) dominated the Christian Democrat group and the German SPD, the Socialist group. In the Liberal group the small conglomeration of French 'moderate' parties accounted for 20 of the 35 members. In the Christian Democrat groups there were eight national parties, in the Socialist group seven, but in the Liberal group sixteen, of which three were Italian and eight French. By the next year the Fifth Republic had been established in France and the parliamentary elections of 1958 brought to the 'Assemblée nationale' some 200 UNR members and that led to eight being appointed to the European parliament. In this way the Liberal group rose to 41, the second largest. The UNR members were given the status of 'apparentes' in the Liberal group, a form of association with more administrative than political significance. The increasing friction between the France of General de Gaulle and the other five community member states found its echo in the European parliament. The UNR members did not share the supranational approach to European problems which in general characterised the Liberal group. In particular the press conference of January 1963, at which General de Gaulle excluded Britain from the communities, caused great controversy and bitterness as between the UNR members and almost the entire remainder of the parliament. It was at this point that the UNR members sought a change in the rules of procedure to enable them to form a group on their own. With the reduction of the number required to form a group to 14, they were able to form the 'union démocratique européenne' (UDE) in January 1965.

The method by which members of the parliament are designated has always been within the province of the national parliaments, the treaty limiting itself to stipulating that the members must already be members of their national parliament. The rules of procedure (Articles 3 and 4) state only that the parliament verifies the credentials of its members and gives no right to examine the national procedures used, as the treaty leaves this open to the choice of the member states. It only states how a mandate can be lost: ending of the mandate conferred by their national parliament; death; resignation from the European parliament; loss of the national mandate, in which case the member may remain in office until his successor has been designated by the national parliament, up to a maximum period of six months. It is clear that control of the nomination procedure lies entirely in the hands of the national parliaments; therefore any bias in the composition of the delegations cannot be challenged. Indeed, one of the objects of this freedom was to enable certain countries, particularly France, Germany and Italy, to exclude any Communist or other extreme left representation. It was always a matter of criticism that the European parliament was unrepresentative and to the extent that the Italian extreme right *was* represented in the form of MSI and PDIUM (Monarchists) deputies, biased against the left. As Coombes puts it:

The majority of the members of the Parliament have been selected largely because of their willingness to serve and because of an existing interest in, or loyalty towards, the European movement.[5]

In respect of the Italian delegation this situation took on the proportions of a scandal in the period after the 1963 election. Up to twelve of the members were at one time either dead or else no longer members of the Italian parliament; some had quite simply been defeated in the 1963 election. It was the internal debate over the designation of Communist deputies which caused the delay in renewing the delegation. Socialists wished to see a completely representative system, in which the composition of the two chambers would be faithfully reflected in the European parliament delegation. The continuation of the centre-left government in Italy after the 1968 election made the adoption of this formula in place of the absolute majority system inevitable. The Italian Communists thus appeared at the European parliament in 1969. The other member states, except France, do not have this problem. The Netherlands and Belgium both send members chosen on a proportional basis from both the first and second chambers in the Dutch case and from both the senate and chamber of representatives in the Belgian case, but in both countries the Communist parties and, for that matter, extreme right wing parties have been too weak at the national level to claim representation in the small (14 member) delegations. Luxemburg has only one house in her parliament and too small a delegation (and Communist party) for there to be any difficulty on this point. Germany sends only deputies from the Bundestag, since the Bundesrat is in reality more a 'conference of the Länder' than a parliamentary body in the normal sense of the term. Only in the case of the first Bundestag could the problem of Communist representation have arisen. Here the KPD could scarcely have qualified for even one seat in the small, 18-member German delegation to the common assembly. From 1956 until the 1969 election the KPD was outlawed by a decision of the Bundesverfassungsgericht in accordance with Article 21 of the German basic law. In the 1969 election the party and its allies failed to gain any seats in the Bundestag.

Only in France does this problem continue to present any real difficulty.[6] As in Italy, the French parliament (the national assembly sends 24 of the French members and the senate 12) has always designated members by the majority method. This means that the majority of the assembly could in theory appropriate all the seats in the delegation and exclude the opposition. This has not been done, but this method has enabled the majority to limit the places allotted to the opposition parties to certain parties to the exclusion of others. Under the Fourth Republic the Communist party and the UDCA of Poujade (which elected some 56

45

members to the 1956 assembly) were both excluded. In the Fifth Republic the electoral system of 'scrutin majoritaire à deux tours' has tended to limit Communist representation in the assembly to well below what would be expected on the basis of their constant 20 per cent share of the poll. Indeed, at the 1958 elections only ten PCF members were elected — too few to form a group under the 'Règlement' of the assembly and hence ineligible for the European parliament delegation without any policy of deliberate exclusion being necessary. This, it should be noted, did not occur due to any marked reduction in voting strength, which would have as before entitled the PCF to some eight members in the European parliament. At the 1962 election the communist party elected 41 members and hence could form a group, but remained excluded from the European parliament, although on the grounds of numbers they might have two or three members (as did the smaller centrist group). In the 1967 election 73 PCF members were elected and the UNR and their allies only just retained the 244 seats required for an absolute majority. The parliamentary situation was thus more open and the question of PCF representation was openly discussed and would have been supported by the 'Fédération de la Gauche', but the majority system excluded this. Since the 1968 elections, with only 33 PCF members, the question has at least on the grounds of numbers been of less importance. As far as the future is concerned any conclusions must be speculative. It must be expected that there will be more pressure in the future for the represent-ation of the PCF in the French delegation. The special circumstances of the 1968 election make it almost inevitable that the number of PCF deputies will increase at the next election. In addition, the fact that, for this election, for the first time since 1936, the Socialist and Communist parties will fight the election not only with an electoral alliance but with a common programme (adopted 28 June 1973) presented to the electorate as a government programme, makes it inevitable that there would be PCF members in the European parliament *if* this coalition were to gain a majority at the election: in particular, in view of the somewhat changed attitude to the communities which the PCF has shown in accepting the common programme. In this joint programme, the Communist party has accepted a much more positive view of the European communities than hitherto. The party accepts the 'reality' of the communities and, following the recent Soviet Party position, takes it as an objective feature of the political landscape. Furthermore, the PCF has moved to a position closer to that of the Italian party: the Communists not only exist, but to break them up would have serious consequences for France; hence the goal should be action from within to democratise the communities to turn them into 'a Community of the workers'.

All of this brings us to the question of the origin of the European mandate and the independence of the member. As we have seen, the members of the European parliament are for the present indirectly elected, that is to say elected by the national parliaments. Article 138 of the EEC treaty speaks of 'delegates which are chosen from the national Parliaments'. It should not be inferred that this means that the members are delegates *of* the national parliaments, but merely that election from the national parliaments represents a convenient manner of selecting the members of the European parliament at this early stage of integration. Indeed, Article 137 gives a different construction. It is this article which gives a general description of the assembly and its role, stating: 'The Assembly, composed of Representatives of the peoples of the Member States of the Community . . .' It is therefore clear that the members of the European parliament are not mandated delegates of their national parliaments. They have a dual mandate due to election as national members and election as members of their delegation to the European parliament, which is then validated by the European parliament itself. If a member is the representative of the people of his state and not of his national parliament then he must act in accordance with the mandate he has received from the people, which is usually a party mandate, since only through his party membership can the political affiliations of a member be clearly seen. Hence, if a member changes his party affiliation in the course of a legislature, should he resign from the European parliament? He is under no legal obligation to do so, but the considerations discussed above constitute a pressure to do so. Indeed, the German member, Elbrächter, resigned his seat in 1958, when he left the 'Deutsche Partei', because he considered his mandate to be 'party dependent'.[7]

If a member is the representative of the people of the state from which he comes, and if his mandate is at least to some extent party dependent, then it follows that he is not a representative of the parliament which has sent him, nor is he a national delegate bound to defend his own state and the policies of his government. Indeed, he might be a vociferous opponent of that government and, as such, retains the right to criticise its European policy which, with the expansion of the activity of the communities, gives a wide scope. The transference of *purely* domestic political controversy is not considered correct. In line with their 'intergovernmental' view of the communities and their antipathy towards a supranational viewpoint it has led the French UNR members to take a somewhat more restrictive view of what constitutes the proper freedom for a member of the European parliament. At the time of the 1965-66 community crisis caused by the French withdrawal from community institutions, the UDE group attacked French opposition members of the European parliament because they had used their position as members of the European parliament to attack the policy of President de Gaulle while outside France. The UDE appeared to consider that the parliament was not competent to pass any judgement on the policy of a member state and that the fact that French members should do so was an abuse of their position. The UDE reminded these members that, owing to the majority rule for the election of members to the European parliament, they owed their seats to the generosity of the majority and that if they persisted in using that position to attack French policy such 'generosity' might not be repeated. One might say that the implied threat of expulsion or non-renewal of mandate was not a serious one; it is nonetheless indicative of an attitude of mind that it could have been made at all.[8]

3.3 The consultative procedure described

Since the European parliament has no legislative powers in the ordinary sense of the word:

> Since Parliament possesses no right of 'avis conforme', its co-legislative authority depends solely on the control it exerts over the Commission's proposals,[9]

it is forced to seek to influence the commission which is politically responsible to it and the council, which is in no legal sense placed under the control of the parliament. The parliament must seek to impress its views on the council through the consultative procedure. On this point Buerstedde[10] states:

> In this (the extension of control to the Council), the point of departure was the view that the Council and Commission were a double executive in which the weakest part, the central community organ, alone was subject to community parliamentary control.

Or, as an alternative conception:[11]

> The Council is considered as the very strongly developed federal part of a bi-cameral legislature, whose second and hitherto weakly developed part, the European Parliament, which as a result should not control the Council, but rather achieve a gradual strengthening of its position in this as yet unbalanced double legislature.

These extracts serve to illustrate the problem; however one looks at it, the European parliament has only a consultative role, which is further weakened by the dual nature of the executive and particularly by the special nature and composition of the council of ministers. One can indeed agree with William Pickles when he states: 'If it had only to deal with a single executive, the Parliament would only have needed some representative and popular backing to begin to exercise some degree of control.'[12] The parliament has been largely concerned to ensure that it has fully asserted its right to be consulted on the important political questions facing the communities and to ensure that the commission and council should in fact be influenced by its opinions.

It is in the consultation process that the parliament can be seen at its best advantage. This is because it has, as we have seen, no legislative powers and the general debate, so much a feature of the House of Commons, is rare almost to the point of being non-existent. The budgetary debate has as yet not assumed the importance that would be its due in a national parliament and in any case follows the same outline procedure as the consultation process. We shall therefore study this process in some detail.

The concept of consultation is not found in the Treaty of Paris, where the power to enact legislative norms is in the hands of the high authority, a body responsible to the assembly. Hence it is only in the Rome treaties that this procedure is found. The Treaty establishing the EEC provides that the parliament must be consulted in eighteen cases where the community is endowed with a normative power.[13] The Euratom treaty also provides for consultation where major legislative powers are given to the community (security norms, inspection procedure, the role of the common research centres).

In these cases the situation is quite clear. Consultation of the parliament is an obligatory procedure required before the act in question can come into force. The Court of Justice has ruled[14] that consultation is an obligatory procedural rule to the extent that non-consultation would justify annulment of the act in question under Article 33 of the ECSC treaty or under Article 173 of the EEC treaty. The court has defined with some precision what is required, stating in the case cited: 'The organ consulted must possess all the information necessary to enable it to undertake a study of all the points of importance and to examine every possible solution.' This ruling makes it clear that an over-hurried consultation, without giving the parliament the supporting data or explanations, would not (in theory, at any rate) satisfy the treaty requirement. The court does not consider that the 'right to be consulted' means that the parliament can in effect veto a proposed text by the expedient of failing to issue its opinion. All that is entailed is that the parliament must have the opportunity to pronounce: if it does not do so within a reasonable period the council may proceed without an opinion from the parliament. Naturally, there can be room for dispute as to what constitutes a 'reasonable' period and that period would in any case vary from case to case, depending upon the importance and complexity of the matter. The parliament has complained of undue pressure and, indeed, of consultation being reduced to a mere formality by the time limit set. One can cite the example of the association agreement with Greece; the parliament was not consulted until after formal signature of the agreement, with the result that any changes proposed would have only an academic interest as at that stage renegotiation of any or all of the agreement would be to all practical purposes impossible. Almost at random one can take another example: at the first sitting of the June 1972 session, Mr Vredeling raised the matter of a report by the external economic relations committee on a commission proposal concerning development aid. The committee had been under pressure from the council to present the report in June, but it came about that no early council decision could be expected, making it possible to postpone consideration of the report which could in the meanwhile be subject to greater discussion in committee. In spite of these difficulties, in most cases a satisfactory solution can be found to meet the needs of both the parliament and the council. The parliament has, however, suggested that the council should make greater use of the right granted to it under Article 139 of the EEC treaty, to call the parliament into special session, which could be used where the urgency of the matter justified such action, rather than the application of pressure to issue an opinion in a hurried and insubstantial manner.

The treaty makes it clear that the parliament must be consulted on certain matters and the Court of Justice has reinforced this provision. However, in practice, difficulties have arisen in the application of this rule. The development of the community has led to a more sophisticated range of instruments being used than those enumerated in Article 189 CEE or Article 14 CECA. Much of the legislative work of the communities depends on prior 'Programmes' or 'Memoranda'. These basic documents serve to establish objectives and a timetable, which are then given a legal form. In addition, there has been a growing tendency to use 'mixed' procedures: decisions of the governments of the member states meeting in the council; protocols; agreements, and so on. These may vitally concern the communities and may indeed be substitutes for a community act. These procedures have considerable political importance and can have the effect of reducing the community legal process proper to mere formalism, reiterating agreements already reached in political terms. Such procedures

of course exclude the delicate balance of institutional influence established by the treaty: there need be no proposal of the commission (though
the commission has usually been involved and may have instigated the
procedure), there need be no consultation of the parliament and the
control of the Court of Justice is excluded. The parliament has been less
concerned with form than with substance; it has sought to be consulted
wherever major political choices have been involved, whatever the actual
formal text may be. It has sought to ensure that its limited consultative
power is not even further diluted through complex, and at times
confusing, 'packages' reached in the council after the commission has
substantially amended its proposal from the form in which it was put
before the parliament. The parliament is not opposed to the commission
playing the role of conciliator or mediator in the council, but has merely
sought to avoid any reduction in its own role or confusion as to the
political responsibility for the final decision. The parliament has clearly
defined its position:

> The Commission ought to invite the Council to reconsult the
> Parliament whenever its initial proposal is modified to the extent
> that it differs substantially from its original form.[15]

This general statement of principle was subsequently explained; the
parliament was not prepared to see its own role attenuated, even if an
assertion of its rights would make the legislative procedure even more
complex and heavy than is already the case: 'The Parliament must be
properly consulted . . . even if, to this end, several consultations on the
same text are needed.'[15] In the same report, the parliament showed its
concern to be consulted on all matters where major political choices were
involved; it was clearly here rather than on technical questions that the
parliament could and should make its voice heard: 'The Parliament must
be consulted on the whole package of texts which go to define a policy
option for the Community . . .' This is clearly a plea for consultation both
on proposals which have been subject to amendment by the commission
under Article 149(2) CEE in the course of proceedings and on those
proposals, which, though of major importance, do not require a consultation under the terms of the treaties. Here two examples come to mind:
harmonisation of indirect taxation under Article 99 CEE and measures
ensuring the free movement of labour under Articles 49 and 51 CEE. The
emphasis here is, as we should expect, on matters of political consequence.
One might discern in the above statement a demand to be consulted on
proposals which do not fall under the definitions of Articles 189 CEE, 14
CECA or 161 CEEA; however such a demand is made explicit.

> The Parliament shall be consulted on drafts which, even if they
> do not fall under the terms of article 189 of the EEC Treaty
> and of article 161 of the Euratom Treaty, do fix the political
> content of Community policies.[17]

Here the parliament is addressing itself to the problem of that whole range of terms – memorandum, programme, declaration, request to the commission, etc. – which have no legal status, but which amount to declarations of intent on the part of the council, to be completed by legally binding acts at a later date. The parliament considers that, unless it is involved at this preliminary stage, it will lose all influence, since subsequent action will be mere execution of earlier decisions.

A related question, and one with yet other important repercussions, is that of which institution should consult the parliament, the council or the commission. This question was considered in a Report[18] which considered the legal and political aspects of the problem. At present the council consults the parliament as the parliament had itself requested in 1958. From the legal point of view much tends to the view that the council should consult the parliament. The usual formula, 'Le Conseil, sur proposition de la Commission et après consultation de l'Assemblée... leads to the conclusion, from a mere grammatical angle, that it is the council which consults the parliament. There is no text which expressly provides for a consultation by the commission. In the event that an act should be annulled because of procedural violation, it would be the council which would be legally responsible to take the necessary measures to rectify the situation, making it logical that the council should consult the parliament. Several reports of the parliament have endorsed this view, for example: 'The originality of the Treaty is that in a large number of cases the Assembly must be consulted. By whom? By the council.'[19] Or: 'Normally, the Assembly is consulted by the Council.'[20] In 1958 the commission consulted the parliament on the question of protection against ionising radiation (14 October 1958). The competent committee of the parliament refused to consider itself formally involved. Indeed, its president informed the committee of presidents (23 October 1958): 'l'avis est donné à l'institution habilitée de prendre la decision'. However, the provison of Article 149(2), which permits the commission to amend its proposal right up to the point where the council takes a decision, would make it more logical that the commission should consult the parliament before presenting its proposal to the council. In fact, the legal arguments are not conclusive and a legitimate doubt may exist, even if it seems likely that on balance the council should consult the parliament. Article 22 of the rules of procedure of the parliament leaves both possibilities open. The Rey Commission declared itself to be ready to raise the question with the council and considered that the problem might be solved by agreement between the two institutions as provided for in Article 162.

The parliament felt that on political grounds it would prefer the commission to consult it. The parliament is better placed to control the commission and hence to ensure that it is consulted on all major matters and to ensure that it would be consulted upon amendments to the original proposal. Furthermore, if the commission consulted the parliament at an earlier stage it could incorporate into its proposal amendments from the parliament and these would have legal value under Article 149(1) denied to amendments of the parliament addressed to the council under the present procedure. As noted, the Rey Commission accepted this position, but declared that the commission, whilst under the political control of the parliament, in general terms, was not its automatic advocate and would maintain its freedom of action whatever procedure was adopted. The parliament on the basis of these arguments decided that the commission should raise the matter of a change of procedure with the council. As yet no formal change has occurred, but there is more flexibility in arrangements than has been the case in the past, to the extent that the commission does now consult the parliament on texts which will not lead to adoption of a legally binding act.

When in session, questions are referred to committee by the parliament itself, otherwise by the president. One committee is responsible for preparing a report, but up to two additional committees may be asked to give an opinion or may themselves request the right to do so. This procedure is flexible and avoids major difficulty about which committees should be responsible for a report. For example, in the case of the *Report on the Euratom Research Programme* for 1972[21] the Committee for Research, Energy and Atomic Problems was responsible with opinions from the Legal Committee and the Finance and Budgetary Committee. A committee will, over time, build up a position and develop certain concerns, which give a continuity to whatever it undertakes and which will be evident even in the opinions it gives to other committees; for this reason it is important in some cases to refer a particular question to a particular committee and hence there may be some behind-the-scenes dispute on this issue.

The committee is a microcosm of the parliament itself. The rules of procedure require that the bureau should observe national and political balance in proposing the committee appointments. In actual fact the question of national balance is considered somewhat less important and may be treated with a certain flexibility. In the 1972-73 session the composition of the committees was based on a more or less fixed formula. On the large 29-member committees there are generally 11 Christian Democrats, 8 Socialists, 5 Liberals, 4 UDE and 1 non-inscrit Italian (PCI). There is some deviation from this formula in that, on the agriculture committee, the Socialists have 9 members, as they do on the legal committee. On three of the large committees, the Christian Democrats only had 11 members. On the finance and budgetary committee the adjustment was necessary to find a place for Hr Engwirda, a Dutch member (D'66) who belongs to no group. In the smaller committees the usual formula was 6 or 7 Christian Democrats, 4 Socialists, 2 Liberals, 2 UDE and 1 PCI. Again, some adjustment was needed to place Thiry (FDF-RW) on the Turkish association committee. It could not be said that there was any detectable formula on national lines. On all but the two smallest committees, every member state was represented. Germany, France and Italy usually have 7, 8 or, at the most, 9 members on the larger committees, but on two committees Italian representation is as low as 3. Belgium and the Netherlands would have at the most four members each and Benelux representation was constant at about seven. In total the position of each group is: [22]

CD	119	Belgium	25 or 1.8 per member
Socialist	84	Germany	78 or 2.2 per member
Liberal	47	France	78 or 2.2 per member
UDE	40	Italy	60 or 1.7 per member
PCI	12	Luxemburg	15 or 2.5 per member
		Netherlands	30 or 2.1 per member
	302		

As far as individual committee service is concerned, sheer statistics would require that each member should sit on 2.05 committees. In fact the norm is two committees (91 members). There is a tendency for the number of members sitting on three committees to increase (33 members in 1972-73 as against 24 in 1971-72). Eighteen members sit on one committee only and the president is allotted no committees. There is no marked tendency for office holders (in the bureau or presidents of committees or groups) to limit their committee posts; in fact, to a certain extent the reverse is the case. Most of the members of the bureaux of the groups sit on two committees and four committee chairmen sit on three committees. In spite of this fact, one should be wary of correlating activism with committee service, since some of those generally recognised as the most active members — such as Vredeling, Richarts, Kriedemann and Hougardy — do not belong to three committees. Of those who do belong to three committees, 13 are Christian Democrats, 9 Socialists, 6 Liberals and 5 UDE. This seems a fair balance worthy of little comment. Of those who belong to only one committee, six are Italian PCI or other unaffiliated members and the remainder are largely Liberals and UDE, of French or Belgian nationality. Attendance in committee meetings is variable and is naturally dependent on commitments in the national parliaments and upon the importance of the matter to be discussed, but average attendance in the larger committees is 15: it may fall as low as 11 or so and will not rise above 20. It is quite usual for at least one of the members present to be replacing another member. This may be because the real member of the committee cannot be present or to enable the replacement to participate in a discussion which interests him. To take an example at random, at the meeting of 30 March 1971 the committee for external economic relations adopted the *Report* of Monsieur De Winter.[23] At this meeting Monsieur Dewulf (Belgian Christian Democrat) replaced Hr Westerterp (NL) and Hr Meister replaced Hr Starke. In such cases, a member will be replaced by a member from his own group, but often from another country.

There is some tendency for members to 'self-select' themselves on to the committees in accordance with their particular interests. It would be too strong to say that the committees are mere extensions of the lobby, but there is certainly a tendency for committees to become the bailiwick of certain interests and points of view and for a certain solidarity to develop along those lines. The agriculture committee, for example, has always had a large number of members from the French and Belgian Liberal parties and from the 'marginal' agricultural areas of the community, as well as members with a direct connection with agriculture or agricultural pressure groups, such as Signor Vetrone (COPA), Dupont (ASSILEC – the EMC Milk Producers' Organisation) and Vredeling (Dutch Agricultural Co-operative). In the transport committee, eight of the seventeen members have or have had a direct connection with transport industries and three others (Cele, Bertrand and Meister) have shown interest in the subject to a specialised extent.

The key figure in committee work is the rapporteur. In theory his task is merely to represent loyally the views of the committee; however, the reality is different. The rapporteur is in a strong procedural position both within the committee itself, where he leads the discussion, and in the plenary session, where he opens the debate, pronounces on amendments and may, as we have seen, speak at any subsequent stage in the debate. Beyond that, he will lead the debate within his own group and hence can shape its postion on the question. Procedural advantages apart, he has a notable political advantage: he can seek to orientate the committee from the start and it is he who must shape the compromise necessary to obtain the adoption of his report. Under these conditions, it is not surprising that the designation of rapporteurs should sometimes on occasion conflict. In theory, he is the free choice of the committee by vote, but in fact the matter is settled by agreement among the groups. As between the groups, a fair distribution is worked out, often in accordance with particular interests of the various groups. Due to the personal expertise of particular individuals and the dominance of the Christian Democratic group in terms of size, certain important questions may seem to go invariably to a given group. However, an effort is made to ensure that overall no imbalance results. One major report given to one group may be compensated for by several lesser reports. National balance is less sought; there would no doubt be some corrective action taken if in a given committee all the rapporteurs appointed in a short space of time were of the same nationality, but no conscious 'proportz' is attempted: [24]

Country	Rapporteurs	Percentage	Percentage by size of delegation
D	33	29.2	23.1
F	30	26.6	23.1
I	5	4.4	23.1
B	16	14.2	12.8
NL	25	22.1	12.8
L	4	3.5	5.1

Compare the distribution of rapporteurs by political groups:

Group	N	Percentage	Percentage by size of group
CD	55	48.7	47
Socialists	40	35.4	29
Liberal	16	14.1	20
Non-inscrit	2	1.8	4

Certain members have gained a reputation in certain fields and can therefore count on nomination as rapporteur for most reports falling within that given field. When he was in the parliament the Belgian Socialist, Monsieur Dehousse, was rapporteur for all the reports on the problem of direct elections. Monsieur Jozeau-Marigné has become the expert on procedural questions and parliamentary law and has thus drafted many reports on these questions. Hr Aigner has been rapporteur for the budget of the parliament both in 1971-72 and for 1972-73. Hr Vredeling, Richarts and Brouwer have become the main rapporteurs for the Agriculture Committee. Mademoiselle Lulling, the Luxemburg Socialist, has concentrated on social policy and women's rights and has drafted many reports in these fields. Monsieur Spénale has specialised in the budgetary powers of the parliament.

The task of the rapporteur is a delicate one; he must carry the committee with him and, given the practice of seeking as near unanimity as possible, his room for manoeuvre is limited. At the same time he must not find himself forced to write a report that goes against his own political principles. He must limit conflict and seek compromise, but not to the point of meaninglessness. The approach adopted will depend on several factors: personality and interest of the rapporteur; the political import-ance of the subject; the technicality of the subject. In some cases, although this is now rarer, the committee will hold an exchange of views on the matter, often in the presence of the commission, without any formal text having been drawn up. This discussion assists the rapporteur in discovering the 'sense of the committee'. The rapporteur may be given some considerable assistance by his own group and its secretariat if the matter is of sufficient importance. Here one can mention the report which the German Christian Democrat, Müller, will present on behalf of the political committee at the forthcoming Summit Conference of the Ten. The Christian Democratic group has already held extensive discussions on this question which will give the rapporteur a useful orientation. In such circumstances one would expect the rapporteur to specify very precisely to the committee staff the nature of his report. In other less vital cases the rapporteur may do no more than read and correct a draft made for him by the staff. Some reports of a complicated and technical nature, such as tax harmonisation, matters related to the agricultural levies and restitutions, are, and let us state this frankly, in reality the work of committee staff. The rapporteur must always remember that he is the agent of the committee and not of his political group, and that he is not free to limit himself to his own opinions. Hr Nederhorst gave an admirable summary of the task of the rapporteur:

As the rapporteur of a committee in which different political views are represented, I sought in the first place not to write a report which would gain me the plaudits of socialist colleagues, but which would have provoked strong opposition from other political views. Without violating my own principles, I felt myself obliged to make a report which could be accepted by members of the committee other than my own political allies.[25]

The rapporteur will draft a report and then continue to redraft it until unanimity is obtained or until only minor and not very significant areas of conflict remain or a small but irreconcilable opposition has become manifest. Such a small opposition will not lead to complications in the plenary session, nor will it be such as to reduce the weight of the resolution vis-à-vis the council of ministers. This system leads to extended discussion on minor points and frequent redrafts of the text. It may mean that the final resolution is double its original length in order to balance all views. Members do sit in groups, but there is no formal concertation between the groups on a given committee, except that the Socialist group does have committees composed of the Socialist members of each of the standing committees which can meet in caucus if necessary and the working groups of that group do sometimes examine a problem which will come up in committee. Members tend therefore to speak in their own names only. Opposition is rarely carried to the length of voting against the report. A member may move an amendment, and then reserve his position for his group meeting in the hope that he bring his group to espouse his point of view in the plenary session, or he may reserve his position quite simply for the plenary session itself. In the common assembly, where, as we have seen, there was at times violent controversy as between the Socialists and the other groups, of 110 reports and 30 complementary reports only ten were not unanimous. The same tendencies have been at work in the European parliament. As Lyon states[26] 'They were long and balanced resolutions, in which the outline of a precise political standpoint was drowned in vague, generalised considerations.' Since 1963 two events have made for less harmony; the first, the formation of the UDE. This group has found no difficulty in working with the other groups in committee on economic and social questions, but has frequently been hostile on the positions taken up by the other groups on institutional matters, which has been reciprocated in violent opposition to the policies of President de Gaulle. At times compromise has not been possible and the UDE members have abstained on certain reports and even voted against them. The second event was the entry of the Italian Communists in 1969. This group diverged from the other members of the parliament not only on questions of supranationalism, but also on basic economic and social matters. One might have expected more conflict than has in fact been the case. The Communist members have been of a high quality and have taken their work in the European parliament seriously. They have accepted the parliamentary game and have attempted to use the parliament as a platform for their views and as a means to engage in a dialogue on Europe. In the committees they were given no posts of responsibility nor any rapporteurships (until 1974), but have intervened in the discussions in a moderate and reasoned way and have in general adopted a constructive and conciliatory attitude. They have proposed amendments in order to state their position, but also in a positive spirit, and indeed their amendments have occasionally been accepted. Usually they avoid political responsibility for a report by absence from the vote or by abstaining, but PCI members have at times directly voted against a report and also have voted in favour of the draft. One can cite numerous examples of these positions:

Report of Mr Aigner on the draft budget of Parliament for 1971/72.[27]

Signor Fabrinni voted against the report.

Report of Mr Van der Gun on problems posed by the elaboration of an incomes and wages policy.[28]

Madame Carettoni-Romagnoli abstained.

Report by Mr Oele on the future tasks of the Joint Research Centre.[29]

Signor Leonardi abstained.

Report by Mr Van Amelsvoort on the draft directive on the fixing of a common rate of stamp duty.

Signor Fabrinni voted against the report.

Report of the Finance and Budgets Committee on that part of the IVth General Report falling within its competence.

Here Signor Fabrinni voted for the report.

In the committee meetings it is usual for the commission to be represented. According to the rules of procedure, the commission and the council do not have an automatic right of participation, but must be invited by the president. In the case of the commission invitation and acceptance is almost automatic. The parliamentary committees wish the commissioner in person to attend as frequently as possible and there has at times been friction on this issue. At its meeting of 30 June 1971, the commission decided that in the event the commissioner responsible was unable to attend the committee he should be replaced by only his head of cabinet or his deputy, a director-general or director and, in exceptional cases, by head of division. The council is not represented in the committees by a minister (except in the political committee where a report is given in accordance with the Davignon procedure) and rarely by an official from the secretariat of legal service. Here one must not be too dogmatic because new procedures are being developed in the budgetary field which have led to greater contact and co-operation between the council and the parliament and under these procedures too the president of the council has appeared before the Finance and Budgetary Committee. The right to invite outside experts or organisations by a special decision of the committee has not been greatly used. There have been some hearings on the American model, but this device has been used infrequently. When the Social Affairs and Public Health Committee was drawing up its Report[30] it held a meeting (14 October 1972) with certain employers' and trade union organisations: 'Union des Industries de la Communauté européenne'; 'Conféderation européenne des Syndicats libres dans la Communauté'; 'Organisation européenne de la Conféderation mondiale de Travail and Secretariat permanéent CGT-GCIL'. The legal committee heard the representatives of the professions concerned (meeting on 22 January 1971) when drawing up its Report.[31] It should, of course, be remembered in this connection that the social partners, agricultural and professional bodies have their own representative body, established by the treaty, the Economic and Social Committee, which, like the parliament, must be consulted under certain conditions. Furthermore, in view of the weakness of the parliament these bodies have preferred to build up a complex of community level committees and a lobby system based on the commission:[32] 'Having no real grip on the power of the Community the European Parliament is rarely lobbied.'

The report of the committee, when it emerges from the processes which we have been considering, will consist of the 'exposé de motifs', a general consideration of the question — an analysis of the background to the proposal and its content; it will also contain a draft resolution, which if adopted will become the opinion of the parliament. This draft resolution will contain a general statement on the proposal and may comment on specific points in the proposal and may request the commission to adopt certain amendments to its text in accordance with the procedure of Article 149(2) of the EEC treaty. The report must also contain the opinions of any other committees and may contain a statement of any minority position within the committee. In addition it will contain procedural information, such as the majority by which the report was adopted.

Before passing on to consider the procedure in plenary session, some attention should be given to the role of the secretariat of the parliament in committee work. One of the five 'Directions générales'[33] of the secretariat is entirely concerned with assisting the committees of the parliament. The more important committees have a secretary and secretariat of their own. This goes for the Agriculture Committee, the Social Affairs and Public Health Committee and the Energy, Research and Technology Committee and the Budgets Committee. Other committees are served by a general secretariat. In the 1972-73 budget of the parliament[34] it was suggested that the economic committee and the transport committee should be given their own secretariats. The task of this 'Direction Générale' is to assist the rapporteurs and presidents of the committees of the parliament. They do the detailed work in the preparation of the meetings, such as dealing with problems of the agenda, but, more important, they do the research and detailed work on the draft reports and make the necessary contacts with the commission and other bodies. The extremely competent work carried out by the committees and the excellence of certain reports depends in large measure upon the secretariat of the committee. It should also be remembered that the secretariats of the political groups attend the committee meetings and are in a position to furnish assistance to those members of the committee from their group and to the rapporteur, if he comes from their group. They also act as the watchdog for the group and can ensure that any matters arising are brought to the attention of the group as a whole.

As we have seen, the enlarged bureau draws up the agenda for each session on the basis of information supplied by the committee of presidents. Certain questions may be treated without debate at the request of the competent committee and with the agreement of the commission. Otherwise each matter is debated. Unless the urgent procedure is proposed no report which has not been distributed at least twenty-four hours in advance may be discussed (RP 13). In the debate the rapporteur starts the proceedings by introducing his report. Priority is given to the group spokesmen, who may (and this is usually the case) be limited to a maximum period, say half an hour for each group. Groups may appoint two spokesmen, either to reflect the different tendencies within the group or to divide the subject matter between two specialists. It is only for the most important questions that each group will appoint a spokesman; for example, in the February session 1972, out of eleven matters discussed, only on three of them (including the 'Programme d'activité 1972' and the 'Situation économique de la Communauté') did all the groups participate.[35] Debates are frequently fairly technical and non-controversial; to take a typical session, in December 1971 there were only two highly political debates: on the question of mine safety and on generalised preferences for developing countries — in both cases the political note was struck by the Socialists. The draft report has filtered through both committees and the meetings of the groups, but even so it can happen that opposition can be carried into the plenary session both from committee and group. A member of the committee may state his opposition in the committee without engaging his group: for example, in the debate on the report by Mademoiselle Lulling[36] Monsieur Liogier opposed point 5(3) of the draft resolution, which would have allowed bodies seeking the assistance of the fund to communicate directly with the commission, but did not engage his group. Such matters are often then discussed in the group and, if the group does not accept the view of the member, he may revive the issue in the plenary session. Hr Gerlach (German Socialist) opposed the creation of 280 new posts in the 1972-73 budget of the parliament in the Finance and Budgetary Committee and then in the Socialist group, where he felt obliged to go against the group line and vote against the report and table amendments in the plenary session.[37]

As has been seen, the individual speakers follow the group spokesmen and may be allotted a shorter period; it is at this point that the commission and the council may intervene in the debate. The responsible commissioner will make known his position on the report in general and on any amendments demanded by the parliament. The council does not take as active a part as the commission. In fact, until recently, the presence of a minister was a rarity and still tends to be the exception. Lately the council has participated in the budgetary debates and has reported to the parliament on the progress of political co-operation under the Davignon procedure; in addition, ministers have also appeared in less important debates and seem to be seeking a more active contact with the parliament.

Amendments may be put forward by any member, but it may be demanded that they be referred to the competent committees; indeed, if that committee so requests the amendment must be so referred. It is usual for the rapporteur to comment on amendments and sometimes spokesmen from the groups do so.

Finally, the draft resolution is put to the vote. Only if the result is in doubt after a vote by raising the hand, or by sitting and standing, or at the request of ten members, can a roll call vote be taken; such votes are rare. If adopted the report is transmitted to the commission and the council.

The vote is taken on the draft resolution, not on the proposal of the commission itself.[38] Hr Westerterp (in 1970) put forward the view that the parliament should vote on the text of the commission and that the amendments which the competent committee might wish to table would take their place with other individual amendments. This procedure would make the commission a direct participant in the debate trying to defend its text rather than an observer in an exchange between the rapporteur and committee majority on the one hand and the rest of the parliament on the other. This procedure would make the commission more ready to defend the amendments of the parliament before the council. Monsieur Jozeau-Marigné considered that the present procedure did not disadvantage the commission which would make up its mind on amendments on their merits irrespective of the procedure followed in the parliament. He considered that the new procedure would undesirably undermine the role of the committees and hence reported that no change was desirable.

Another problem follows: what happens if the draft resolution of the committee is rejected by the parliament? The main problem examined by the report[39] is the interpretation of a negative vote. The report is concerned to avoid a situation in which the parliament would be politically weakened by pronouncing in a contradictory manner, leaving it open to the other institutions to interpret the will of the parliament. There should be no possible doubt as to the intentions of the parliament. If the draft of the committee is adopted *in toto* there is no possible doubt, but if amendments proposed by the committee are rejected, without an amendment to restore the text proposed by the commission being carried, there could be doubt as to the intention of the parliament. Where the committee accepts the proposal of the commission without amendment and its resolution is rejected, the result is quite clear: the parliament has issued a negative opinion on the proposal of the commission. If, however, the committee had modified the initial text, then it would be difficult to be certain as to the interpretation of a rejection. Would it represent an acceptance or rejection of the proposal on which the parliament had been consulted? In the cases where doubt could exist, it must be eliminated or else the parliament will be weakened. Two possibilities can be considered: either the parliament must give an opinion in the form of a resolution (argument taken from Article 22 of the rules of procedure); in this case, the competent committee must redraft its resolution until an acceptable form is found, taking account of the discussion in plenary session; this procedure could be followed whether the imprecision arose from a direct rejection of the resolution or from contradictory amendment. The other view holds that reference to the committee should only occur where amendment had made the text unclear. A vote rejecting the resolution terminates the procedure and signifies a negative opinion. This view holds that the parliament is entitled to give its opinion in the form of a negative vote, just as well as in the form of a resolution. Further, it holds that continued 'navette' between the committee and plenary session weakens the parliament and in any case considers it improper that the committee should, in effect, be required to interpret the will of the parliament. It is therefore proposed that this negative vote should simply be notified to the institutions concerned.

Notes

1   H. Furler, 'Parlamente über die Nationen' *Die Politische Meinung,* April 1957.

2   Further changed by the Treaty of Accession to 198, Britain can send 36 members and Denmark and Ireland 10 each.

3   *Spénale Report* Document No. 226/70 1971.

4   *Der Minister Rat im Konstitutionellen System der Europäischen Gemeinschaften,* p. 175 (De Tempel, Bruges 1964).

5   *Politics and Bureaucracy in the European Communities* PEP, Allen & Unwin, 1970.

6   W. Feld, 'The French and Italian Communists and the Common Market' JCMC, vol. VI, no. 3, 1968.

7   E.P. Proceedings, no. 4, 21 October 1958, p. 7.

8   E. Bubba, 'A propos de la designation des membres du Parlement européen par les Parlements nationaux' *Revue du Marché Commun* no. 89.

9   Schmutzer, 'Some legal aspects of the work of the European Parliament' *Common Market Law Review* 1967-68, no. 5, pp. 89-92.

10   op. cit., p. 223.

11   op. cit., p. 224.

12   'Political power in the Community' in Cosgrove and Twitchett (eds), *The New International Actors,* Macmillan, London 1970.

13   The most important cases are:
Measures abolishing discriminations based on nationality;
Measures establishing the agricultural policy (Article 43);
The right of establishment and performance of services (Article 54);
Measures in the transport field (Article 75);
Competition rules (Article 87);
Harmonisation of legislation (Article 100);
Measures concerning the European social fund (Articles 126 and 127);
Conditions of service of Community civil servants (Article 212);
Association agreements (Articles 220 and 230);

Application of Article 235 to extend the powers of the community (Article 235);

Amendment of the treaty.

14   *Affaires* 6 and 2/54.

15   Resolution of 20 October 1966, para. 6.

16   'Rapport de Monsieur Jozeau-Marigné sur les problèmes de la consultation du Parlement européen', *Document* 110/68.

17   'Rapport de Monsieur Jozeau-Marigné . . . ', op. cit.

18   Drawn up for the bureau by Monsieur Jozeau-Marigné.

19   'Rapport de Monsieur Jozeau-Marigné . . .', op. cit.

20   *Rapport von Karenbergh,* Sur le Règlement.

21   Monsieur Glesener's *Report* (Document 57/72).

22   Source: Parlement européen: Bulletin 12 June 1972; Liste des membres.

23   *Report on the Declaration and Resolution* adopted on 29 July 1970 by CECLA (Document 27/71).

24   Kanteyn, *L'Assemblée Commune de la CECA,* (Aspects européens, 1961).

25   Débats no. 37 of 19 February 1958.

26   *L'Assemblée Commune de la CECA,* Paris 1957, p. 31.

27   Document 57/71.

28   Document 50/72.

29   Document 17/71.

30   On the document, First Orientations for a Community Social Action Programme. Rapporteur: Mr. Vredeling.

31   On a draft directive on the right of establishment and the free provision of services in the field of finance, economic advice and accountancy. Rapporteur M. Armengaud (Document 30/71).

32   See D. Sidianski, 'Pressure Groups and the EEC'.

33   Direction Générale B: Commissions et Délégations parlementaires under Hr Van den Esde.

34   'Rapport de Monsieur Aigner sur le projet d'état previsionnel des recettes et des dépenses du Parlement européen pour l'exercice 1972-1973', *Document* 57/72.

35   *Compte rendu in extenso des débats.*

36   *Rapport de Mademoiselle Lulling sur la proposition de règlement d'application de la décision no. 71/66/CEE du Conseil du 1er Février 1971 concernant la reforme du Fonds social européen,* Document 32/71.

37   Amendment no. 4 from Mr Gerlach to the Report of Mr Aigner on the draft budget of the European Parliament for financial year, 1972/73.

38   See *Rapport de Monsieur Jozeau-Marigné sur une proposition de*

résolution presentée par Monsieur Westerterp tendent à modifier les articles 22 et 26 du Parlement européen.

39 *Avis à l'intention du Bureau sur la procédure de vote du Parlement et les aspects juridiques du rejet du rapport d'une commission parlementaire,* Redacteur: Monsieur Jozeau-Marigné.

PART II

The Political Groups

4 The Christian Democratic Group

4.1 Membership and organisation

The Christian Democratic group dates from the Common Assembly days, when, together with the Socialists and Liberals, it was one of the original supranational groups. The group has always been the largest in the parliament, but has never attained an absolute majority. At present the group has members somewhat in excess of one-third of the total membership. Enlargement has not led to much gain in membership, as neither Denmark nor the UK has Christian Democratic parties and because, when the Labour party boycott ends, the Socialist group will become the largest group. The membership of the group divides up as follows:

Christian Democratic Group

Member state	Bureau	Total	Affiliated parties[1]
Belgium	1	6	2 PSC/CVP
Germany	3	16	1 CDU/CSU (joint Bundestag Group)
France	2	2	1 UDCP (senate group)
Ireland	1	3	1 Fine Gail
Italy	3	16	2 DC & SVP (South Tirol German minority)
Luxemburg	2	3	1 PCS
Netherlands	2	6	3 KVP (Catholic), CHU, AR (Protestant)
Total	14	51	11

The group has the most formal admission criteria of any of the groups, in that membership is open only to members of those parties which are listed in the Rules of Procedure of the group. The group as a whole could expel a member, but this would be considered an extremely drastic measure and has never yet happened. As the figures show, the group is less compact than the Socialist group, in that it comes from nine national parties (or ten if one considers, as increasingly one must, the Flemish and Francophone wings of the Belgian Party to be totally separate). However, one of these ten, the Sudtiroler Volkspartei, is very small and of only regional significance. Three parties come from the Netherlands, the result of the split of the movement into Catholic and Protestant branches; however, at an international level these three parties have long worked closely together, forming the Dutch 'Team' in the first Christian Democrat international body, Nouvelles Equipes Internationales. The group is dominated by the large German and Italian parties (34 of the 52 members); since the virtual demise of the MRP, the whole 'Centre' in French politics has been in a state of flux and there has been no clear 'Christian' current; except for the two senators from UCDP the 'Centristes' have tended to prefer the Liberal Group.

As we have seen, the nomination of the members of the European Parliament is in the hands of the national parliaments, which adopt a wide variety of procedures, but these usually in practice mean that the national parties accorded representation propose members to fill their 'quota'. Impressionistically one can say that competition for the seats available is most severe in the smaller countries — Belgium and the Netherlands — as well as in Germany, at least to a certain extent.

There is considerable ideological differentiation within the group, which occurs in two ways: differences between the approach of the various national parties and through attempts to balance the tendencies found within the national parties in the delegation. The Dutch KVP is a more progressive party than the other Dutch parties in the group, largely because it is within the Dutch Catholic church, rather than in the Protestant churches. There the new thinking has been going on, which has led to the formation of certain splinter or 'ginger' groups on the left wing of the KVP, such as the Radical party. The ARP and the CHU, Protestant and more Conservative, work closely together and at times a merger has been contemplated. The Italian party has for historical and domestic political reasons taken a more 'statist' position, whereas the German CDU/CSU has tended to take a more free-market approach, based on the Social Market Economy system of Dr Erhard.

It is difficult to document efforts at internal balance in naming the national party quotas, but care is taken to ensure representation of all significant tendencies.[2] Four of the Belgian Christian Democrats come from Flanders and two from Brussels and Wallonie, which represents the balance of electoral strength of the party in each area. The Belgian party has always included representatives of agricultural interests and on the other hand trade union orientated members, such as Monsieur Califice. The German members are drawn both from the CDU and from the CSU (13 CDU and 5 CSU). The members of the German CDU/CSU cover a wide range of economic interests: Agriculture (3), Industry (5), Academics and lawyers, both Protestants and Catholics, regional interests (e.g. Hr Klinker from Schleswig-Holstein) and the affairs of the refugees and expellees from the DDR (Hr Jahn and Hr Riedel, the latter being a member of the Bureau of the Exile CDU). Liberal views are mixed with doctrinaire anti-planning members. Analysis of the Italian Christian Democratic party[3] indicates that the party is a loose coalition of tendencies ranging from the neutralist and syndicalist groups centred round Gronchi Dossetti and the review Forze Soziale to the atlanticist, laissez-faire tendency which opposed the 'opening to the left' in 1963, grouped around Mario Scelba. One can point to representatives of these tendencies in the Italian delegation: in their time Rubinacci and Sabbatini from the CISL (Christian Trade Union) and, on the other hand, the long service of Scelba in the European Parliament. Regional interests have not been ignored (Pintus from Sardinia), nor have agricultural interests (Vetrone, president of COPA, and two others).

The plenary group meeting is the sovereign decision-making body of the group. The bureau is an executive and preparatory body composed of a president and 13 members, there being no other officers. Membership of the bureau follows a mixed pattern. All member states have basic representation of at least one member in the bureau and then weight is attached to the strength of the national parties, giving Germany and Italy each three members and leaving France with only two. The requirement of a basic national representation means that the Benelux countries, with only 16 members of the group, are over-represented in the bureau with 5 members (cf. three for Italy which also has 16 members), partially corrected by limiting the Belgian representation to one. The group is assisted by a number of working groups, set up on a more or less permanent basis; at present there are two (e.g. Agriculture, Promotion of Capital Ownership among the Workers).

The role of the secretariat (which is common to the EUCD and to the group in the Consultative Assembly and in the Council of Europe) should not be underestimated. In a supranational body the permanent officials can do much to reconcile divergent views and national styles as well as provide the vital element of continuity in the work of the group. The group has a secretary general (at present Signor Ferragni, an Italian) and two assistant secretary generals, at present French and German. For the year 1972, the budget of the parliament provided for 29 officials to assist the political groups, of which 14 were Category A, 3 were Category B and 12 were Category C. This was raised to a total of 41 (23 in Category A) in the supplementary budget to take account of enlargement. For 1973, 63 posts are provided for the groups (29 in Category A, 4 in A3, 10 in A4, 2 in A5 and 7 in A6, plus 6 in A7). Nine posts are in Category B and 25 in Category C. The Christian Democratic group had, up to 1973, some 7

Category A officials raised to 10 by the addition of one in A5/4 and two in A7/6.[4]

The secretary general is a political personality himself, often with previous experience of working in other community institutions and may himself have national political aspirations. He is active and influential. He is present at meetings of the group and takes part in the discussions; he will prepare the way for the compromises needed to reach a common point of view. He is also present at meetings of those organs of the parliament in which the groups are represented (the Bureau 'élargi' and the 'Comité des Présidents') and negotiates on behalf of the groups with the other groups and with the commission and does much on a day-to-day basis to ensure liaison with the national parties. His right to present proposals to the bureau and to the group as a whole gives him an important mediating role. The group secretariat is also represented in the committee meetings and thus follows the detailed work of these bodies, so as to be able to undertake research to assist the group members on the committee or a Christian Democrat Rapporteur. Beyond this involvement in the day-to-day work, the secretariat has to think out and research longer term policies and strategy and prepare the conferences of the UEDC and the parties of the Six.

In view of the 'dual mandate' of the members of the group; in view of the weakness of the European Parliament and in view of the fact that effective decision-making power in the community is in the hands of the council, whose members are individually responsible to their own national parliaments, it is natural and most necessary that the group should seek outside links and contacts. Organic links arise from the dual mandate-membership of the home parliament and national party group, which create opportunities and obligations. Members may 'echo' issues at home by making reports on their activity in the European Parliament to their national parliaments and parties and by participating in debates on European policy in their home parliament. We shall return to the use made of these links, but what interests us here is the link created by the group and by the national Christian Democratic parties.

Before the Second World War links were rudimentary compared with the socialists. The Christian parties in Germany and Italy were swamped by Fascism. The newly formed CDU, the MRP and the Italian party, together with the surviving Swiss Catholic party, revived co-operation after 1945, leading to the foundation in 1947 of the Nouvelles Equipes Internationales (NEI). This organisation included national 'teams' from all western European countries and Czechoslovakia. The team could either be a party, as in the case of the CDU, an association of parties (the Dutch KVP, ARP and CHU) or a group of personalities or organisations (e.g., the

British team). This hybrid structure led Neunreither to characterise it as 'halfway between the European Movement and the organised party'.[5] This body soon became western European in character and policy, but with some outside contacts with the exile parties in eastern Europe (who were members), with (from 1964) the Nationalist party of Malta and, on the basis of a biannual conference, with the South American sister parties in OCDA. The aims and role, as well as organisation, of NEI were vague, being to promote contact between parties and personalities sharing the acceptance of Christian Democratic principles. This led to the formation in 1961 of the World Union of Christian Democrats (UMDC). This body holds a congress and has an executive of 12 members.

Such links — either in NEI or UMDC — were inadequate to the needs of the much more closely connected Christian Democrat parties of the Community, engaged as they were in the common pursuit of European integration. Hence the European Union of Christian Democrats was formed in 1964, with its secretariat in Paris. This body sought to create links based largely on the Community and has, unlike NEI, been organised as a confederation of parties only. The sporadic, *ad hoc* conferences and meetings of presidents and secretary generals of Christian Democrat parties of the Six held since 1958 were brought under UEDC and the Christian Democrat members of the commission were invited to attend. In April 1970 a conference of presidents of Christian Democratic parties of the Six was formally constituted as a permanent body, to meet at least three times a year, or when called into session by the president of the EUCD and the president of the group in the European Parliament jointly.[6] This Permanent Conference tends to devote itself to discussion of one concrete problem, rather than the adoption of general policy statements. For example, the meetings of April 1970 and May 1971 considered direct election and the enlargement of the powers of the parliament.

The group is the decision-making body. In 1970, it held 46 meetings, more than one per day of session. Meeetings are usually held on the first day of the session and two or three times during the week of session as the agenda demands. Meetings are also held outside the sessions; for example in 1972, Journées d'études were held at Rennes (23-25 May) and at Stuttgart (25-27 September). The individual member must give one week out of two to his European work; the group meets at least monthly, even out of the sessions; and the bureau meets for at least one half day per month.[7] All the matters on the agenda of the parliament are discussed in the group meeting and sometimes, also, matters currently before the committees, especially where the rapporteur for the question is a member of the group. For example, the Christian Democratic group devoted a long and careful discussion to the *Report on the Preparation of the Summit Conference* (presented in July 1972) for which Hr Müller was rapporteur, well before the political committee had completed its deliberations on the *Report*. In this way the rapporteur would become aware of the views of his own group and the attitudes of the Christian Democratic members of the committee could be co-ordinated. As we shall see, several points of view developed on this issue. A member of the Competent Committee (the rapporteur, if the rapporteur is a Christian Democrat) will be alerted to present an exposé to the group on each matter. On this basis the group will seek to arrive at a common standpoint, and to decide whether the matter warrants the appointment of a group spokesman who will be responsible for presenting in the plenary session the essence of that common view (not his own view). The task of the group is to 'filter' or 'arrange' national and ideological positions to reach a compromise. Compromise is necessary both with the commission and with other groups because the parliament, having so little real power, is forced to attempt to persuade rather than impose its view. This requires the parliament to show a united front and to work, as far as possible, in harmony with the commission, which alone can give some legal significance to the views of the parliament by embodying them in an amendment to its own proposal. The Christian Democratic group is aware of the need for compromise and hence avoids extreme positions, seeking to rally the whole group and, hopefully, most of the parliament to a common standpoint.

Formally the group is autonomous, independent of the national parties and free to take such decisions as it thinks fit. If it is to be effective and coherent it must adopt objectives broadly acceptable to the national parties and work closely with them to attain these objectives, through the organisational structure which links them together. Above all, the group must avoid positions which are unrealistic to the national parties and must not succumb to that schizophrenia described by Spinelli[8] in the case of a German deputy who demands a more advanced Community position of the German Minister of Agriculture in his capacity as President of the Council of Ministers and yet upbraids him in the Bundestag for not defending German national interests more stoutly.

There are many examples of co-operation designed to meet this. During the discussion of the proposals for Economic and Monetary Union, a meeting was organised between the group and experts of the national parties. Monsieur Werner (Luxemburg Prime Minister and a Christian Democrat) attended a meeting of the group to explain his report to the council, which formed the basis for Economic and Monetary Union. During his term as President of the Council, Signor Ferrari Agradi (Italian Treasury Minister, Christian Democrat) addressed the group on the monetary crisis. The Christian Democrat members of the commission are always invited to group meetings and frequently attend. Christian Democrats who are not members of the group participate in the Journées d'études (longer, several day sessions devoted to a particular subject or subjects). In 1972, for example, at the Stuttgart Journées (25-27 September) a report on the reform of the international monetary system was presented by Signor Colombo and one on the common commercial policy by Hr Narjes. At Luxemburg (5-7 May 1971), devoted to the institutional development of the Communities, the definition of a Christian Democratic policy for Europe and the role of EUCD, the reports were all given by non-members of the group: Hr Heubl, a Bavarian Minister, Monsieur Werner and Signor Rumor (President of EUCD).

A good example of how this complex involvement works out in respect of particular policies is the important case of the Summit Conference in Paris and the institutional questions associated with it. These points were considered at the Rennes Journées d'études (23-25 May 1972). The meeting heard a report from Hr Müller, Rapporteur of the Political Committee for the Resolution on the Summit Conference. On this basis, the group drew up its position in advance of the vote in parliament in the hope ultimately of influencing the Summit Conference of Heads of State and Government of the Enlarged Community. Also considered was a report drawn up by Hr Lücker.[9] This report is the fruit of the deliberations of a working party in which, through UEDC, the national parties were represented as well as the group, assisted by the secretariat which, as it is common to the group and UEDC, is able to act as a bridge between the two, keeping in touch with the leaders of national parties and of the group. The report is to be debated by the national parties and adopted by them and will in due course form part of a general programme. In this way, the report will be binding at both European and national levels and both the national parties and the group will be pursuing the same objective by different, but parallel, means. This is most important in the institutional field where profound changes would need unanimity in the council and unrelenting pressure on national ministers to be realised and then would need ratification by the national parliaments; hence pressure at both levels must be exerted and both levels must be in step. What is sought is that all parties and the group should speak with one voice and act concertedly towards a common goal, each attacking the obstacles from a variety of angles.

4.2 Policy

Having examined the organisational structure and decision-making processes of the group, we shall turn to the policies of the group. Although one can say that Christian Democracy is a recognisable political 'tendency', it is difficult to make any meaningful generalisation about the philosophy of the group. It can be said that the Christian Democratic outlook takes man, the individual, as its focus. It accepts that man is a social being and lives in a community to which he is responsible and which is responsible to him. It is concerned with man in this social setting and emphasises a hierarchical system of responsibility extending from the individual, to the family unit, to the local community, to professional organisations and associations, through the state to the European and world communities, each accepting a share of responsibility appropriate to that level and not usurping the rightful responsibilities of other links in the chain. In this way the often cruel effects of blind market forces or the rule of the stronger on the individual must be mitigated by constructive use of instruments of social policy. What this means in individual policy areas is rather imprecise and open to dispute. On these issues the group is divided and on some objective measures is not greatly more cohesive than the Liberal group, but appears to be so. Adapting the analysis of Heidenheimer,[10] which applied to the CDU (after all, the dominant party in the group), one can say that the cement which holds the group together is support for integration.

There is no doubt of the overall objective to be pursued:

> For us the final goal has always been to create a political community of a sui generis, federal type, hence we are opposed to all measures which would tend to maintain the Council as an intergovernmental body, compensating conflicting interests and governing in an almost absolutist manner.[11]

For the group modern problems can no longer be solved in the national context alone, but must be faced at the European level and solutions found at that level, which will require the close involvement of political forces and the development of a European ideology by the group. This leads the group to emphasise and seek to extend the political character of the community; thus Lücker refers to the tasks of the Paris Summit in these terms:

> The Summit Conference must fix the necessary political directives to bridge the gap which exists between the political

development and the economic and monetary development.

The logic of this position is to seek to extend the powers of action of the community to new fields not expressly laid down in the treaties, but made possible by the level of integration already achieved:

> We demand that the Summit take decisions on the policies to accompany economic and monetary union which are not expressly laid down in the Treaties.[12]

In spite of a well justified reputation of being in the vanguard on institutional questions, the group is less clear and less clearly united on the strategy by which these aims are to achieved. The group president, Hr Lücker, inclines to a long run approach, emphasising 'ideal' solutions. For example, he proposes a text which begins:[13] 'A European Government is established.'

The group as a whole, well represented by Hr Müller, rapporteur for the political committee on the Summit Conference, holds a more pragmatic view. This shows that divergences do not necessarily follow national party lines — both Lücker and Müller are Germans, but one, Lücker, is CSU, and both have their allies and opponents throughout other national parties. However, the Müller tendency is overwhelmingly in the majority in the Group and corresponds to the line of the CDU/CSU Bundestag Group.[14] This view seeks to make important changes in the decision-making procedures of the community without amending the treaties in the short run, following the method proposed by the *Vedel Report,* seeking in short to achieve 'a dramatic change in institutional habits'.[15] In general terms the treaty is seen as the centre, if you will, of three concentric circles, the second being economic and monetary union, which is held to belong to the community sphere. On the periphery of this second circle lie the new policies made necessary by the existing level of integration and by economic and monetary union: social policy, regional policy, industrial policy. The third circle, linked only tenuously with the others, represents political co-operation — foreign and defence policy.[16] The relative urgency of action in each sphere is disputed, some placing more emphasis on the democratisation of the community as against extension of competences (the Dutch), but the grand design and the gradualist approach is well accepted.

One member of the group, Signor Scelba, a former Italian Prime Minister, has adopted an even more cautious, almost Gaullist, view. For him, the essential fact which cannot be bypassed is that all progress depends on the political will of the nation states which form the community, particularly the larger states, such as France and Great Britain. No policy should be adopted which would alienate those member states, which implies making haste slowly. For Signor Scelba the Summit Conference might make important progress on this basis, without violent confrontation and without major changes in the treaties.

As far as specific (and immediate) changes in the respective roles of the institutions are concerned, the group has clear and definite ideas. The group considers that the present intergovernmental character of the council is strictly temporary, but in a spirit of realism accepts the Luxemburg Agreement (1966) on majority voting with reservations. The group accepts that it is reasonable for a member state to seek to defend its 'vital interests' and that, in such cases, at the present stage of integration, it should not be overridden but a compromise acceptable to all should be sought. However, the part of the treaty thus 'put on ice' should be strictly limited. The content of the phrase 'vital interests' must be clearly defined in advance and limited in extent to prevent its abuse as at present. The group is concerned at the cumbrous and long procedures, particularly the delays encountered in the Council of Ministers, which it would wish to see remedied by much greater delegation of matters now decided by the council to the commission, as Article 155 permits. Whatever progress may be made in the short run by co-operation between institutions, in the long run a revision of the treaty is inevitable in order to bring about the necessary changes in the institutional equilibrium of the communities:

> A revision of the treaties is essential in order to improve the governability of the communities... and to ensure that the increased political importance of the Community in the world is echoed in appropriate institutions.[17]

It is clear that the position of the European Parliament is central to this issue and that the main burden of any such changes must be to improve its position to ensure the democratic legitimacy of the community. The group is categorical about the need to carry out these changes within the shortest possible time. It follows the conclusions of the *Vedel Report*, holding that the question of the powers of the parliament is paramount and can no longer be evaded by reference to the ancient dispute over direct election:

> We consider that the increase in the powers of the Parliament cannot be put off until it is directly elected. Of course we demand direct elections, but the failure of the Council to act in fulfilment of its obligations to adopt a single electoral law for the whole Community,

cannot serve as a pretext to avoid giving the Parliament real legislative powers.[18]

The group supports the measures proposed by the *Furler Report* and considers that the programme for reform outlined in the *Vedel Report* might be the way. Whatever the legal forms eventually chosen, the essential is that the parliament should be given the right to participate directly in the decision-making process of the communities. Hr Lücker summed up the view of the group in these terms:

A real right of participation by the Parliament in decisions on acts with legal effect and in particular those with financial consequences; greater budgetary powers; right of approval of appointment of Commissioners.

We should set out consideration of the policy of the group on economic and social issues against the statement by Van Oudenhouve[19] that: 'They usually reach agreement on the purely political level, but are liable to suffer internal stresses as soon as economic or social issues arise.' As we have seen, there are within the group varied tendencies: the Italian 'statists', trade unionists and doctrinaire economic liberals. It is probably true that, as Heidenheimer found for the German CDU/CSU, support for integration and a certain European policy is the cement holding together those of disparate views. In the early Bundestags the CDU only voted unanimously on one out of five occasions, largely on foreign affairs; party discipline was lax on internal affairs, but was heavily imposed on foreign policy issues, thus keeping the party from falling apart on these domestic issues. In the European group, economic and social issues can be minimised, left on one side or glossed over by compromise. This does not mean that the group has no policy on such questions, but merely that positions sometimes lack precision and incisiveness, that lengthy debate may be needed and that a wide range of views is tolerated. The group believes, as we have seen, that man should be at the centre of policy, not its object; he must not be sacrificed to the free play of market forces, whose excesses must be corrected by judicious use of social policy. The group is pragmatic and lacks ideological prejudice. It is not opposed to state intervention, but merely seeks to limit it to its proper role; that is, to those areas where others cannot assume responsibility. For example, Hr Löhr stated:[20]

I think that this Parliament should state clearly that the attainment of parity for our women in the socio-economic field is in the first instance a matter for the social partners.

Here, as often, the responsibility of employers and trade unions is preferred to state intervention, which is considered unnecessary and intrusive. Within this pragmatism, there are, as we have seen, nuances: the 'statism' of the Italian party, based on the Italian experience, where a large part of the economy is controlled through ramified state holdings (e.g. ENI and IRI). In Germany, by contrast, again based on the national experience of the social market economy system of Dr Erhard, the emphasis is on the free play of market forces; indeed the CDU government long opposed the efforts of the EEC commission (as it happened, under a CDU president, Dr Hallstein) to introduce a modest system of planning at the European level and certain CDU members (in their time Burgbacher, Dichgans) reflect this anti-planning view.

The key economic problem conditioning all others is inflation:

> But in place of the ill of mass unemployment, we now face the other ill of creeping inflation.[21]

This problem is seen as a danger to the whole edifice of integration:

> I am not prepared to give over the fate of European unification to some new economic tendency or other. I am convinced that the issue of assuring a relative stability of our price level is a life and death question for Europe.[22]

The causes of inflation discerned by the group lie in excess demand caused by excessive wage rises beyond the increase in productivity and by excessive state expenditure — two preoccupations of the group:

> ... excess of demand over available real resources can be made responsible: too strong investment without increasing productivity; too high government expenditure; too high surplus on the balance of payments or all these at once.[23]

The solution to the problem cannot be found without extensive action at the community level; indeed this holds good for all economic problems. At the same time the group's concern for the free market is evident, as is its fear that dirigisme will become permanent if once admitted. Referring to the need for a co-ordinated economic policy Artzinger stated: 'Centralisation, so one might think, would bring back unhappy memories at least in Europe'. In line with its general political approach, the group firmly demanded that the required co-ordination be given a new and effective institutional form:

> I am convinced that we cannot ensure the development and later convergence and uniformisation of our economic policies without an institutional development in the council.[24]

There is in the position of the group a certain unresolved contradiction: the general political line supports ongoing integration at the fastest possible pace, which requires that political authority should be created at the community level and exercised so as to influence the behaviour of other structures, also in the economic field. Since the economies of the member states are at present organised on national lines, industry, agriculture, labour, professional organisations, will not set the pace, but must be led, which requires a certain amount of dirigisme. This contradiction does not invalidate the position of the group, but it intrudes at times and will have to be resolved at some stage by a conscious choice.

Energy problems have always attracted considerable attention at community level, both because of the fact that two of the three communities are concerned directly with energy and because of the basic importance of energy, especially imported energy, to the whole economic life of the community. The Christian Democratic group has always followed these problems closely and Hr Springorum (German CDU) has become something of an expert in this area (he is from Bochum in the heart of the Ruhr and a former mine engineer and mine manager). The main fear of the group is that the favourable energy situation which Europe has enjoyed up to now may be in the process of long term shift:

> There are clear signs that the surpluses of the 1960s will become shortages, unless we pursue an energy policy which will remove this danger.[25]

He was not optimistic that the necessary measures would in fact be taken:

> Unfortunately our Group cannot avoid the feeling that neither the Council nor the member states conceive of the policy in sufficiently long-run terms as is necessary in the energy field in view of its inflexibility.[26]

The importance of the energy is such that the group abandons its usual preference for free-market arrangements and demands action by governments and by the commission to meet the situation:

The energy supply of the community is too important to be left to chance in the world market and all political and economic risk should be excluded. This energy policy requires long-term planning and we welcome the fact that the Commission intends to bring forward more concrete proposals in the field of energy policy, which will concern trade policy, supply and stocking policy.[27]

The group is concerned that Europe should be assured supplies of energy at reasonable prices and that this aim should be pursued as part of economic integration. State intervention — both by national governments and by the community as such — is not excluded where the situation requires it. Above all, a coherent energy policy for the community is sought in which indigenous sources can play an equitable part, taking account of the special characteristics of both the supply situation and of the demand for energy.

Like energy and transport policy, agriculture was placed in a special category on account of its particular economic structure and the high level of state intervention. It was to be the object of a common agricultural policy, with special rules and structures. The treaty leaves the exact form of the policy uncertain, largely because the differences between structures and policies in the member states were such as to make concise agreement impossible. Because of the inherent difficulty of the matter, because of the drive by France to construct the common policy — a vital French economic interest — and because of the size and political importance of the rural sector (unlike the UK), agriculture has taken a disproportionate share of time energy and financial resources in the community since about 1961. Naturally, the European Parliament has been closely involved, the more so because agriculture is the one genuine 'supranational policy' of any large-scale political importance. Farmers early realised that the vital economic decisions affecting their sector were no longer taken at national level, but by the community.

The Christian Democrats have shown a great deal of interest in the argicultural policy, both because of its inherent interest and because of the large rural vote for Christian Democrat parties. In Germany, three Länder have a greatly above-average proportion of the work force employed in agriculture: Bavaria, Lower Saxony and the Rhineland-Palatinate; all of these show an above-average CDU/CSU vote. Six members of the European parliament come from the Bavarian CSU, including Hr Lücker, the group president. In Italy the whole of the south has over 30 per cent of the working population in agriculture; in all the regions of the south the DC vote is above the national average. In Abrozzia, Puglia, Molise and Basilicata, where the proportion employed in agriculture (1968) exceeds 45 per cent, the DC vote was over 50 per cent and in places reached 65 per cent, as against the national average of 39.3 per cent in 1968 and 38.1 per cent in 1972. It is among these agricultural deputies that the two Italian agricultural federations, the Confagricultura and the Coltivatori Diretti, have gained their great influence. There have been in the European parliament powerful spokesmen for the agricultural interest on the Christian Democrat benches: Monsieur Dupont (president of ASSILEC, the Belgian dairy farmers' organisation), Vetrone (president of COPA), Van der Ploeg (Dutch Catholic agricultural workers' syndicate), among others.

Despite this general concern and connection with agriculture, there have been differences, and at times wide divergences of opinion, within the group. The Italians have defended Italian agricultural interests against the generally 'northern European' orientation of the CAP, which has led to their making special demands in the fruit, wine and tobacco sectors and laying great emphasis on structural reform. They have often taken this line, together with other (if not all) Italian members, in a national bloc (e.g. debate on the *Lulling Report* on a policy for tobacco, July 1969). This has led to conflict with German interests, especially in the case of wine and tobacco. The Germans initially opposed the structural policy, as one of irrational subsidy and preferred to use price policy as a means to guarantee farm income. The Mansholt approach has now reluctantly in some cases been accepted by the German members on social grounds. On the other hand, the Belgian members have always been more favourable to the structural/social approach and have advocated aid to Italian farmers. The Dutch members of the group have on the whole been less connected with agriculture (at present only one of the seven members) and in any case are more likely to be connected with Agricultural workers and co-operatives than with small-scale inefficient farming. Holland has the lowest food prices in the community; Dutch members therefore en bloc oppose high prices in agriculture and the Christian Democrats and Liberals from Holland often vote with the Socialist group on this issue.

As a whole the group has accepted the Mansholt Plan, even if it has some difficulty in accepting some of the faster targets for the reduction of the work force proposed by the plan, but the principle involved is accepted. The group does accept the need for a modification of the price policy. Prices must be fair, but not excessive. The group accepts that price policy alone cannot raise agricultural incomes to parity with equivalent occupations nor assist the marginal Italian and French farmer, to which end a structural/social policy must be developed. The group is concerned that agriculture should not be viewed in isolation; general integration and economic and monetary union is vital to the success of the agricultural policy:

I have stated in this Parliament that the 100 per cent integration of agriculture in the Community framework must not be taken as an excuse not to undertake ongoing integration in other sectors; for if this were to be the case we should be confronted with a grave crisis in agriculture within a very short time.[28]

The group considered it positive that the council had broken the price freeze for agricultural products but was uncertain, indeed sceptical, as to the overall effect of the measures taken and their adequacy. Commenting on the price increases, Brouwer said:

The strange thing is that the actual effect on the income of the farmers will be slight in view of the inflationary tendencies of the last three years. There remains much uncertainty as to whether the percentages adopted will in fact raise the income of the farmer or whether much of it will get stuck in the distribution sector. The real question is: will the farmer have more money in his pocket? Here there is uncertainty.[29]

This would be settled, in the view of the speaker, if all new price proposals contained an element of adjustment to cost increases which was explicitly so called. The most positive part of the package for the group is the fact that structural reform and price policy have been connected up:

Our Group has always insisted that there was an unbreakable bond between price policy and structural policy. It is of course necessary to control all the instruments needed to solve the problems of European agriculture and horticulture. I consider it the most positive aspect of the Council Decisions that we now have a global instrument for the future of agriculture.[30]

For the group, there has always been a strong link between agricultural policy and social and regional policy. Regional policy is not only a matter of assuring internal and international competition, but also a question of social justice and solidarity. The group would wish to see greater activism in this policy sector and would encourage medium and small scale dispersed industries (this would seem to be a political as well as an economic aim). More active participation in the formulation of regional policy should be sought from regional bodies. A greater role should be found for private capital in regional development. The regions themselves should be more effectively organised to articulate their concerns at European level. In order that regional development follows some basic principles, in order to avoid unplanned, anarchic, competitive and even conflicting action, the diverse activities involved should be co-ordinated by the commission.

In spite of a recent and opportune reform both the legal powers and the financial resources at the disposal of the European social fund are considered inadequate to the requirements of the situation. The group shows a characteristic preference for dispersed responsibility, with only co-ordination, not direction or management, from the centre. The group welcomed the commissions's *Memorandum on Social Policy* (1972), but considered that many of the priorities could best be attained through 'concertation' of the employers and trade unions in each sector and, above all, at community level and in a community consciousness. As far as possible the social partners should bear the responsibility with community intervention only where they failed to reach agreement. Even where legislation was involved the social partners should be closely associated with its elaboration and execution.[31]

As the largest group, the Christian Democrats have played an important role in the parliament, particularly in their unwavering support for the most far-reaching integration from the start. In spite of the manifest difficulties of reaching a common position on social and economic questions the group has held together and attained a greater 'subjective cohesion' (whatever any 'objective measure' might say) than the Liberal group, by their support for integration, by emphasising those things which are common to all Christian Democrats and by a willingness to compromise on economic and social issues, even at the risk of having thereby to evade certain issues and of losing incisiveness on others.

Notes

1   Source: European Parliament, *Liste des Membres,* 12 June 1972.

2   Information supplied by Signor Ferragni, secretary general of the group, in conversation with the author.

3   See F. R. Willis, *Italy Chooses Europe,* New York 1971.

4   Source: Rapport de Monsieur Aigner sur le projet d'état prévisionnel des recettes et des dépenses du Parlement européen pour l'exercice 1973.

5   *Le rôle du Parlement européen dans la formation de décision des Communautés Européennes,* Colloque, Lyons, 1966.

6   See DC Europe, no. 19, 16 May 1970, Press Conference of Hr Lücker, 27 April 1970.

7   Information supplied to the author by Monsieur Califice, former

D

member of the group and now a minister in the Belgian government.

8   *The Eurocrats: Crisis & Compromise in the European Communities.*

9   Report drawn up by Hr Lücker on behalf of the mixed working party of the group and the UEDC, on the institutional future of the enlarged community.

10   Article, 'Foreign Policy and Party Discipline in the CDU' *Parliamentary Affairs*, vol. XIII, 1959-60, pp. 70-84.

11   Press conference held on 25 May 1972 at Rennes by Hr Lücker, president of the group, after the Journées d'études.

12   Lücker, loc. cit.

13   Rapport au nom du Groupe de travail mixte sur les principes d'une réorganisation institutionelle et constitutionelle de la Communauté élargie.

14   See: 'Aktionsprogramm der CDU/CSU für Europapolitik', in *Union in Deutschland*, no. 3/1972.

15   A phrase used by Monsieur Dewulf in conversation with the author.

16   For a development of the position of this outer circle see: CDU/CSU Action Programme, Section II (Aussenpolitik).

17   Lücker, loc. cit.

18   Lücker, loc. cit.

19   Lücker, loc. cit.

20   Debate held on 20 April 1972 on 'Equal Pay for Women'.

21   Artzinger, in the name of the group in the debate on the economic situation in the community, *Débats,* 21 April 1972.

22   Artzinger, loc. cit.

23   Artzinger, loc. cit.

24   Artzinger, loc. cit.

25   Springorum, Debate on Energy Policy in the Community, *Débats,* 21 April 1971.

26   Springorum, loc. cit.

27   Springorum, loc. cit.

28   Translated from Dutch by the author: Brouwer (NL-KVP) in the debate on the statement of Monsieur Cointat, president of the council on the decisions of the council of 25 March 1972, *Débats,* 22 April 1971.

29   Brouwer, loc. cit.

30   Brouwer, loc. cit.

31   See the intervention of Hr Vandewiele in the debate on the commission memorandum, *Débats,* 13 June 1972, pp. 40-3.

5 The Socialist Group

5.1 Membership and organisation

The Socialist group is the second largest group in the parliament and the sending of a delegation by the Labour party would make it the largest party. It is in fact the only group to have in it members from all nine member states (until Mr Taverne resigned). The present composition of the group is:

	Bureau	Total group	Affiliated parties
Belgium	1	4	PSB/BSP
Denmark	1	4	1 (Social Demokratiet)
Germany	2	17	1 (SPD)
France	1	7	2 (Socialistes & Radicals)
Italy	1	7	3 (Republicans, PSI & PSDI)
Luxemburg	1	2	2 (PSD, POSL)
Netherlands	1	6	1 (PvdA)
Total	8	47	

The largest element is the German SPD, which dominates the group; together the Italian and German Socialists account for some half the members of the group (24). This dominance has been reduced by enlargement. The group contains a small number of constituent parties (11) with a high average membership. If one excludes the recent split in the Luxemburg party there is only one Socialist party from each state. In addition, the Italian Republican party and the French 'Radicaux de Gauche' are affiliated to the group ('apparentes'). Therefore with these small exceptions all the members come from Social Democratic parties, and all with the exception of the French party, in government or recently in government and with very similar traditions and concerns. This gives the group a certain basic cohesion.

The rules of procedure of the group provide[1] that any member of a party affiliated to the office of Social Democratic parties of the European community may become members of the group at their request. Other members may apply, in which case the matter shall be decided by the group, upon a report from the bureau. Clearly the bureau would wish to establish whether in its view the member (or his party) has the necessary credentials, which would depend on the position of the party or individual in both national and European politics. Presumably the participation of the Italian Republican party in centre-left government since 1963 has facilitated its acceptance in the group; equally the fact that the French 'Radicaux de Gauche' form a single group with the Socialists in the national assembly has led to their membership of the group as 'apparentes'. The case of Dick Taverne was more difficult; he was sent to the parliament after his return to the Commons at the Lincoln by-election. He had defeated an official Labour candidate at the Lincoln by-election and was returned to the European parliament by the Conservative majority in the House of Commons. For a long period the Socialist group had hoped that the Labour party would change its attitude and until that hope had died Taverne was not admitted to the group, and then only as an 'apparente'. (He has since resigned from the European Parliament.)

The Danish Social Democratic members have constituted a national party bloc within the group. On matters of an institutional nature such as budgetary powers, political co-operation, European union, defence co-operation, the Danes have been unable to follow the advanced integrationalist thinking of the group. On several occasions a Danish Social Democrat has spoken in dissent from the group position, making it clear that in doing so he also spoke in the name of the other Danish Social Democrats. This was notable in the debate on the budgetary powers of the parliament. Here both in the debate on the interim report of M. Spénale and on his final report Finn Christensen indicated that the Danes did not support the concept of the 'last word' for the parliament; this in his view would represent an effective transfer of the sovereign powers of the Danish Folketing over and above what had been sanctioned by the Danish people at the Referendum. 'It would be absolutely inadmissible to give the Parliament the right of veto . . . I am opposed to any change in budgetary powers which would require the amendment of the Treaty.'[2] In spite of the relatively tight group discipline, which will be considered later, this distinctive attitude has not given rise to any special problems within the group. The particular political conditions in Denmark which have made such a stand necessary are well understood, if not approved by the group.

The rules make no clear reference to party discipline. Rule 7 lays down that any member who brings forward 'weighty political reasons' shall not be bound by a decision of the group. In addition, members are required (Rule 19) to take an active part in the work of the committees of the parliament. The rules provide for no sanctions against a member. It is, however, clearly understood that the group may in extreme cases expel a member; this has not occurred as yet, and could only occur if the member had consistently acted in a manner incompatible with continued membership, in a way going beyond the normal bounds of political dissent. In practice, more informal sanctions are available, such as criticism in the group meetings, warnings or censure.

The group meeting is the 'sovereign' body; all the other organs of the group being in a subordinate position. The group itself draws up its policy positions and appoints group spokesmen to present the views of the group to the parliament. The group, on a proposal from the bureau, appoints the Socialist members of committees and delegations of the parliament. In order to make a valid decision a quorum of at least half the members of the group must be present; decisions are taken by simple majority vote. The group meets both in and out of session. In 1970, the group held 28 meetings, approaching one per day of session. The usual procedure is for the group to meet on the first day of each session and often several times in the course of the session. Here all the questions to be debated in the plenary session are considered and it will be the responsibility of a member of the appropriate working party or committee to present a short report on the matter. That person would usually be a member of the competent standing committee of the parliament. Votes in the group are reduced to a minimum, the consensus approach being preferred. The group does not direct its members to vote — that is, there is no formal 'consigne de vote' — but, unlike the other groups, the Socialist group does from time to time adopt the reverse procedure of giving its members a free vote ('liberté de vote'). This was clearly explained by Monsieur Dehousse in a debate in 1967.[3] It is not infrequent that a member will speak and vote against the stand of his group. His only obligation is to declare his opposition (Rule 7) and to inform the chairman in advance of his intention to speak in the debate in his own name (Rule 5). For example, in the debate on the five directives for the reform of agriculture, applying the resolution of the council of 25 March 1971, held in November 1971, Hr Kriedemann voted against the draft resolution of the agriculture committee, notwithstanding the fact that it had the approval of the Socialist group and that Hr Vredeling, a member of the bureau of the group, had been one of the rapporteurs. In the debate on the 1973 budget of the parliament, Hr Gerlach voted against the report of the committee for finance and budgetary matters, in spite of the fact that the group voted in favour.

The bureau of the group is an administrative and preparatory organ. The bureau consists of seven members: chairman, three vice-chairmen and three members. The rules require a minimum membership of six. It is specified in Rule 10 that the chairman, vice-chairman and other officers must be elected in special ballots. It is also laid down that the outgoing bureau may make proposals for the election of its successor. The term of office of the bureau is one parliamentary year. At the present time the bureau is composed of two Germans and one member from each of the other member states. The president is a Frenchman and the three vice-presidents are from Germany, Italy and the Netherlands. There is thus some provision for national weighting in the bureau, though none is required by the rules of procedure. As indicated, the tasks of the bureau are mainly of an administrative and preparatory character, as well as providing continuity in the work of the group. This role is clearly defined in Article 12 of the rules: to deal with matters referred to it by the group for study or decision; to maintain contact with the Socialist groups in the parliaments of the member states, with the office of the Social Democratic parties of the European communities and with the Socialist International to present proposals to the group; to co-ordinate the work of the organs of the group; to supervise the work of the secretariat and to draft the budget of the group.

The group is assisted by two working groups: one for legal affairs and the second for economic and social affairs. At the annual session of the parliament the group appoints the members of these working parties. Non-members may be invited to attend the meetings of the working parties. Within its field of policy each working party is responsible for following the work of the standing committees of the parliament and preparing the position of the group, but may not take any policy decisions. In addition, these working parties act to co-ordinate the work of the Socialist members of the standing committees. The legal and political affairs working party was very active in discussing the Socialist position on the resolution of the political committee on the proposed meeting of heads of state and government (rapporteur, Hr Müller, Christian Democrat). The critical response of Hr Kriedemann to the statement on the programme of the commission made by Signor Malfatti in the February session was drawn up in this working party.

Articles 13 and 20 of the rules provide for the establishment of committees of the Socialist members of each of the standing committees of the parliament. These committees are chaired by the Socialist member of the bureau of the standing committee of the parliament. The chairmen of these committees are required to call meetings of their committees to prepare for the standing committee meetings where important matters are to be discussed. This preliminary meeting must take place if the standing committee is to appoint a Socialist rapporteur for any question. If the chairman of a committee so requests, the secretariat shall draw up a summary of the committee meetings and circulate to all members of the group a memorandum on any matter within the terms of reference of the committee. In general terms, these twelve committees have the task of co-ordinating the work of Socialist members of the standing committees and preparing, together with the working parties, the decisions of the group. It must be remembered that these committees consist of no more than ten members, all used to working together, and can thus adopt extremely informal procedures.

An important contributor to the work of the group is the secretariat. The Secretariat is provided for in the rules of procedure (Rule 16). The secretariat is responsible for assisting the Socialist members of the parliament in the performance of their duties in plenary sessions or in committees and in assisting the organs of the group. Further, the secretariat is to draw the group's attention to problems affecting the communities and preparing studies on them. In this way, the secretariat provides expert assistance and continuity to the work of the group. The group appoints a secretary general and one or two assistant secretaries. The secretary general is responsible for the supervision of the secretariat and for the distribution of work. The remaining staff are engaged by the secretary general, with the agreement of the chairman and the treasurer. The staff are appointed on a temporary basis and do not enjoy the security of tenure of the permanent staff of the parliament and commission, but in general follow the same career structure. In this way it is possible for the groups to achieve flexibility and make short term appointments of people with a political commitment, without going through the lengthy process of appointment normally required. The group was allocated ten A grade officials in the 1972 budget and this has been increased in the 1973 budget to 13, by the addition of one official at A 5/4 and of two officials at A 7/6. The secretariat follows the work of the parliament and is able to draft positions on the various issues which come up for debate, to act on the directions of the bureau and the group in drawing up documents for study. The secretariat is represented in the committee meetings and thus is well acquainted with the state of any question. The secretariat draws up, on request, reports of all meetings of group organs: bureau, working groups and committees, and thus contributes to the information of the members. In particular, the execution of decisions made by the bureau is carried out by the secretariat. The secretary general has some political influence, in that he is not only in close touch with events, but works closely with the chairman and bureau members in the day to day activity and is empowered by the rules (Rule 17) to make proposals to the group.

Certain reforms of both organisation and approach are now under active consideration by the group. The impending enlargement, which would greatly increase the size and diversity of the group, makes it more than ever imperative that more compact and incisive working methods should be adopted. In addition, the greatly increased workload of the parliament and the need to ensure political direction also tend in that direction. In the first place, the division into two working parties has made the terms of reference of each too unwieldy and widely drafted and has led to an imbalance, with the majority of the detailed work being required from the working party on economic and social affairs. The many topics have to be examined by both working parties. The facts that the working parties have such wide terms of reference, and can in any case do no more than prepare matter for discussion in the full group meeting, has led them to function less than satisfactorily and has led to there being too little interest and active participation in their work. It has been proposed, therefore, to increase the number of working parties to four, with a small active membership and the right of attendance being accorded to other interested members. It has not as yet been decided how the terms of reference of each working party would be drafted, but one can for example envisage a special working party being established for agriculture. It is also under consideration that the role of the bureau should be strengthened so as to place it in a better position to co-ordinate the political activities of the group than has been the case hitherto. It would be the task of the bureau to establish a medium term action programme, which would establish priorities for the group, its organs and the secretariat. This programme would lay down those political issues on which it was proposed to concentrate and on which the group would seek decisive action. This would naturally not prevent individual members from following up their own particular interests, but would ensure more overall direction in the work of the group. It would ensure that the group had a plan and no longer merely responded piecemeal to issues as they came up; the bureau, the working parties and committees would particularly carefully prepare the ground for debate within the group on these issues; the secretariat would be able to devote its energies to these questions and thus apply its (limited) resources more rationally. The amount of formal, routine work done by the group meetings in discussing minor matters could be reduced to make way for more far-reaching debate on priority matters. The bureau would meet at the start of each session to discuss the agenda and, on the basis of work done in the working parties and committees, could dispose of certain unimportant questions which aroused no controversy and on which no group opinion was required. This would mean that not every item would automatically be discussed in the group, which would then be able to devote more time to essentials. Such a reform would make the group more cohesive and effective and need in no essential way reduce democracy within the group.

Traditionally, the Socialists have been internationalist and it was the Socialist political forces who, in the nineteenth century, first gave political action an international dimension. It is therefore natural to discover that, in this field, the Socialist parties lead the way. They have expressed the conviction that the establishment of 'supranational' institutions at the European level requires a corresponding adjustment from the political forces:

> *Notes* that a democratic structure for a united Europe accompanied by fuller economic, social, monetary and political integration cannot be achieved without a supranational structure for the democratic and, in particular, the Social Democratic forces, and that closer cohesion of the concerted political action by the Social Democratic parties are therefore necessary.[4]

As in the case of the other groups, personal links exist through the dual mandate system. Members of the group are also members of national parliamentary groups. As we shall see in our more detailed examination of this question, this gives the individual member some opportunity to raise European issues and to seek support for European positions within his home group, but this opportunity should not be exaggerated, since there is some evidence that the active member in the European parliament may not be able to exert much influence in his home parliament. It is unlikely that he would be an office-holder in the national group and lack of time will severely limit his activity on the domestic level. There are certain exceptions, particularly among the Dutch members, who manage to combine and co-ordinate activity at both levels. Here Hr Vredeling (Socialist) is a good example. He spends some 80 per cent of his time on European affairs generally, both in the European and Dutch parliament; he regards the two levels of activity as indissoluble. He thus devotes little time to purely Dutch problems.[5] The Dutch are unusual in the respect and tolerance accorded to European specialists both by parties, parliament and by public opinion. Not only back-benchers, but men of influence (e.g. Hr Brouwer [Christian Democrat] or Hr Oele [Socialist]) are nominated and are exempted from national parliamentary responsibilities. The list system of election on a national basis tends to assure their re-election.

As we have seen, the bureau of the group is given general responsibility for assuring contact with the national parties, the office of the Social Democratic parties in the European community and with the Socialist International. In addition, certain organisations have been set up to ensure co-operation and co-ordination between the parties and the group. As early as 1957, at the First Congress of the Socialist Parties in the ECSC, the desire was expressed to institutionalise future contact between the Socialist parties of the member states. At the congress held in 1958, a resolution was passed establishing a liaison bureau.[6] The liaison bureau, whose name was changed at the 1971 congress to 'Office of the Social Democratic Parties in the European Community', is composed of a representative from each of the affiliated national parties, of the Socialist International and of the Socialist group in the consultative assembly of the Council of Europe. The office shares the same secretary general as the group in the European parliament and the group in the consultative assembly. This person union, as well as the wide representative character of the office, lays the basis for the effective co-operation of the Socialists from all the European assemblies and the national parliaments. The office meets at least twice per year, usually jointly with the bureau of the group. The Conference of the Social Democratic Parties in the European Community now meets biennially, and the Eighth Congress was held from 28-30 June 1971. At this congress, the delegates from the national parties (48) and the whole of the Socialist group attend. Other representatives may be invited (from parties outside the community) and it is usual for the Socialist members of the commission to attend. The congress is a forum for the development of a coherent European policy, accepted by all the national parties as well as by the group and to work out the means whereby that policy can be implemented. As befits their connection with the working class, the Socialist group has maintained links with the International Federation of Free Trade Unions. This federation contains the Socialist (as distinct from the Christian and Communist) trade unions. This body has a European section with an office in Brussels, which maintains close and regular contact with community institutions.

The German SPD members of the European parliament have, in addition, the assistance of an official of the Arbeitskeis I (Auswärtige und Innendeutsche Beziehungen), whose task it is to attend the sessions of the parliament and ensure effective discussion and dissemination of information on the work of the parliament in the Socialist group and party in Germany.

5.2 Policy

Having completed our study of the organisation and working of the Socialist group, we shall survey the political position of the group. The group has gone farther than the other groups in seeking to elaborate a general political programme for execution on the European level. The first evidence of this intention came at the Fourth Congress of the Socialist parties in the European communities. The congress heard a report from the group leader, which was sufficiently comprehensive to serve as a general programme. The main concerns of this report were for social and economic planning at the community level, with the maximum element of supranationality; social policy was to serve both workers and consumers and the community was to be open to the outside world — in its policy of association, admission of new members and in its trading policy.[7] In view of the possibility of direct elections to the parliament within the near future (it was in 1960 that the parliament adopted the convention in application of article 138[3] of the EEC treaty, to provide for direct elections to the parliament), the same congress instructed the liaison bureau to draw up a draft programme for European elections. The liaison bureau established a committee to draft the programme and consulted extensively with the national parties and the trade unions. As a first stage the agrarian programme was issued on 20 April 1961.[8] The main theme of this programme was that the agricultural community should share in, as well as contribute to, the increasing prosperity, arising in part from the establishment of the community. At the fifth congress, held in Paris from 5-6 November 1962, the draft programme was adopted. The main headings of this programme were: European political structure; economic organisation; social policy; cultural activity; international law.[9] This programme did not fulfil its intended purpose because there were no direct elections to the European parliament, but the fact that the attempt was made shows something about the progress towards cohesion on the European scale which had been made by the Socialists. Indeed, the programme was a significant step, serving to clarify differences and reach compromises which would have value for the future, quite apart from the question of European elections (which the Socialist group continues to support).

Like Christian Democracy, Social Democracy is one of the discernible political currents on the European continent. At times it may be difficult to differentiate Social Democracy from more Marxist positions, with which it maintains at times an uneasy co-existence, but nonetheless there can be said to be a distinctly Social Democratic outlook. It is this fact which has enabled the Socialist group to attain cohesion and a common position of a much more coherent and detailed character than has been the case for the other groups, particularly the Liberal group. Unlike the other groups (except the Communist members), which accept free enterprise and the market economy as the ideal, only to be interfered with in special circumstances, when the market has been shown either to be inadequate to meet the need or to have produced grossly inequitable results, the Socialist group seems to start from the reverse premise. The market economy is accepted only because it exists, not because it is in any sense ideal. The Socialists are thus seeking to reduce the role of the market economy whenever this is politically possible and replace it by public provision or intervention or, at the very least, public control. The Socialists pursue this objective by pragmatic and democratic means, which means that in practice they have to accept a considerable role for the market economy, but at all times the burden of proof lies with the free enterprise system which is watched with scepticism by the Socialists.

At the European level, this means that the Socialists support planning and control by community institutions. The group tends to seek dirigiste solutions, but on a community level. Since the early difficulties over European integration which the group experienced on account of the reservations held by the German SPD have now been smoothed away, the group is an ardent advocate of integration and supranational institutional structures. However, democratic control is not to be sacrificed in the process. This has caused the group certain difficulties and even led to contradictions, because it has not always been possible to advance both integration and democratic control in parallel and choices have had to be made. Usually, the Socialist group has nonetheless found a coherent position and has never abdicated its support of either principle and has always insisted on making full use of the (limited) powers that the parliament does possess. The Socialist group does not consider the common market in itself to be a capitalistic device; free trade is not capitalistic – only the uses which may be made of it. The common market will not of itself ensure social progress. An activist policy of intervention will be required of the community, to ensure that the interests of workers and consumers are safeguarded. These matters have been of general concern but there have been specialised interests within the group. Hr Vredeling has made the written question his speciality, at times asking as much as 60 per cent of the total number of questions in any one year. He concentrates on issues in agriculture and foreign trade. His object is to impose control on the commission and on the council and to sensibilise public opinion to European issues.[10] In the work of the parliament and its committees, Hr Vredeling concentrates on issues involving agriculture. When he was a member of the parliament, the Belgian, Monsieur Dehousse, was the specialist for the question of direct elections to the parliament. For the question of budgetary powers and the 'Ressources propres' of the community the experts were two French Socialists, Messieurs Vals and Spénale. In general terms the Dutch members have concentrated on institutional issues; the Belgian members have tended to concentrate on questions of social policy; the German members have been particularly interested in general economic matters, such as planning and anti-trust measures. One can also discern two 'ideological' lines of force within the group: the Italian party is more Marxist in its approach (notwithstanding its participation with non-Socialist parties in the centre-left coalition from 1963 to 1972) and, in keeping with the historical traditions of Italy, represents a more 'statist' approach than is usual in other European countries. On the other hand, the German SPD, especially since the 'reform' congress held at Bad Godesberg (1958), has adopted a more pragmatic, social engineering approach. It should not be assumed that these differences have hindered the group in attaining a common viewpoint − or at any rate not to a very great extent − but it has at times been noticeable.

To turn to the position of the group and Social Democratic parties in the community, the cornerstone of their outlook is a belief in effective transnational political action; a belief that modern problems can only be solved by action on a broader basis than that provided by the nation state. In general terms the Socialist parties seem less afraid of supranationalism and less equivocal in their advocacy of that ideal. The General Resolution[11] states at the outset:

> . . . the ideas and practical objectives shared by the Social Democratic Parties of the European Community can best be carried into effect through the most comprehensive form of European integration.

Whatever the contradictions and uncertainties of short-term political action, the Socialists have ever present in their minds what should be the ultimate goal of the process. The communities are by no means an end in themselves, a resting place, but rather a step upon the road to a united Europe. Referring to the integration process the general resolution states: '. . . must be continued to . . . its ultimate completion in the United States of Europe in the form of a federal state.' In addition (here is a reference to the notions of President Pompidou) the parties 'reject integration aiming merely at a confederation of states'. This resolute internationalism and realism, coupled with idealism, must go hand in hand with support for a more democratic approach − for this too is a traditional concern of Socialists. There is concern that the present development of the community is too bureaucratic and based upon the intergovernmental methods of the permanent representatives. The fear is expressed that the role of the commission is being eroded and that the commission is concealing, rather than bringing into the glare of public opinion, the inevitable conflicts associated with such a vast and novel enterprise as the building of Europe. The general resolution warns: 'The Commission must not be reduced to a secretariat of the Council.' In the same way, the obstructive behaviour of member governments is condemned, especially: 'The efforts of member governments (clearly reflected in the Council's proceedings) to withhold as many powers as they can from the Community for as long as possible.' Efforts are to be made by the Socialist members in the European parliament and in the national parliaments to persuade the council to act as a community body in line with the treaties. More crucial than this is the question of democratic control and popular legitimisation of community action, vital if the communities are to follow the path which the Socialists require. Here both the future of the European parliament and effective co-operation among the Social Democratic parties are key elements. On this point the general resolution states:

> The parties underline their conviction that the Community can only exist and develop if all the activities of the Community are subject to the effective control of a Parliament with the most democratic foundation it is possible to provide and elected as soon as possible by direct universal suffrage.

This parliament would have to have control of the appointment of the commission and legislative power, but the main emphasis is on total control of the budget of the communities as the most effective means of assuring adequate control. However, it is clear to the Socialists that, without the co-operation of progressive political forces on a transnational basis, subinstitutional structures would be hollow. Indeed, such co-operation is needed to bring about such changes, as well as to make them effective once attained. For these reasons the Socialists propose close co-operation between the Social Democratic parties wherever they hold political responsibilities and the creation of a framework within which decisions binding upon all the national parties can be taken. The Socialists do not support the need for a supranational and democratic community solely for reasons of justice, equity or ideological preference, but because of them – such is the inexorable logic of events. The nation state is dead and the 'mixed' compromise procedures so often adopted by the community are seen as no long-term solution (referring to the Economic and Monetary Union):

> Events of recent months have shown that the achievement of such a Union is as difficult as it is necessary. Our parties wish to solve these difficulties by transferring power to a common authority, functioning under democratic control, with a view to the ultimate formation

of a federation of the United States of Europe . . . Unless the Community is completed in this way and granted the necessary powers, all that has been laboriously and partially achieved so far will be in constant danger. The Social Democrats formally accept the consequences of the necessary development.

The Socialists are not indifferent to the sort of society which would come about in an integrated Europe. They have not lost sight of the needs of that section of the community which is their primary concern. The Socialist parties avow 'their special responsibility for the social content of the Community'.[12] The Socialists consider an improvement in the social order of the community to be of paramount importance:

> For the Social Democrats this takes precedence over all economic, technical and other considerations . . . the social objectives of the Community must be freed as quickly as possible from their present dependence on economic objectives and social policy must in no case be a mere appendage of other more technical and economic forms of common policy.[13]

In specific terms the main plank of the Social Democratic parties' economic policy is the programme for economic and monetary union. The objectives of this policy must be to secure economic stability and growth, to harmonise systems of taxation and budgetary structures in such a way as to give priority to the interests of the working class; and a common industrial policy. That common industrial policy should be shaped to 'control the formation of economic power in the Community' by active policy on competition, mergers and monopolistic tendencies; by a policy to control multi-national companies and to encourage public authorities. In addition, industrial policy must have wider horizons than narrow economic concerns. In the words of the Notes[14]: 'The social and economic interests of society, with particular reference to environmental protection, must be considered at least on an equal footing with the interests of private industry.' This is amplified to indicate that the community is responsible for ensuring a balanced policy of economic development: 'Special importance must be attached to industrial policy as a means of ensuring balanced development of a new economic structure in regions in which traditional jobs are being sacrificed to relatively sudden structural changes.'

In the interests of the workers of the community, the Socialists seek to see implemented an incomes policy which would enable wage and salary earners to build up capital, but that without restricting the freedom of collective bargaining. It is considered necessary to democratise the exercise of economic power by giving to the workers in an enterprise a right of co-decision with the traditional management: '. . . to democratise the exercise of economic power, in particular at company level, through legal provisions for the participation of workers and their Unions in accordance with the most advanced provisions already in force in various member states.'

The Social Democrats' support and welcome the use of medium term programmes and in particular the quantified nature of the third programme (1971 – 75) setting binding principles for both domestic and community policy. On this the party spokesman, Arndt, said:

> The socialist group considers it correct that there should be a planning body under the aegis of the Commission. The specific economic decisions of the Commission should be numerically evaluated. This must be rapidly put in hand.[15]

Although favourable to state intervention in economic matters and to a certain degree of economic planning, there are severe limits to the dirigisme of the Social Democrats; for example, in the debate on a document published by the commission, 'Orientations préliminaires pour un programme de politique sociale communautaire', Mlle Lulling (Socialist spokesman) was critical of efforts to give a legal form to wage guideline in the third medium term programme

> Does this mean going beyond a merely indicative character for the norms that are to guide the various economic actors: governments, firms, organisations of firms' trade unions and professional organisations?

Naturally in their concern for the social content of community policy and their desire to give industry a human face, the Socialists see a very close link between economic, industrial, social and regional policies. As we have seen, human, and therefore social, concerns are an integral part of economic policy. To the Socialists a community social policy must form part of economic and monetary union, both because it will ensure greater social justice and because, in the view of the Socialists, large-scale economic change will provoke human consequences which the market will be powerless to remedy without direct and purposeful public policy. Here again Mlle Lulling:

> Economic and monetary union, will it finally advance the

community's social policy? We hope so, because the correlation between the achievement of EMU and the social policy cannot be sufficiently underlined. We underline this not so much because we know that without a coordinated social policy economic and monetary union cannot succeed, but because for us the guaranteeing of social progress, the raising of the standard and quality of life remains the basic objective of European cooperation and that starting from the stage on the way represented by economic and monetary union.[16]

In the Notes[17] we read:

Social policy is more than an instrument to remedy or alleviate the damage caused by modern technical and economic development . . . it represents the totality of efforts to ensure greater respect for human dignity in the Community as well as greater equality of opportunity, more social justice.

The Socialists admit that the instruments provided by the treaties are limited, but seek as extensive an interpretation of the treaties as possible and treaty amendments to move beyond their limited scope. The general resolution calls for action in a whole range of fields. There must be more and better public provision; there must be a more effective educational and cultural policy to increase equality of opportunity for all; there should be harmonisation of social security arrangements, particularly to aid those who are handicapped or most affected by rapid structural change. The free movement of labour must be made more effective by harmonising laws on citizenship and the exercise of specific political rights by nationals of one EEC country resident in another. The resolution points out that social provisions in general — benefits, pensions, public provision of housing, educational and cultural facilities — clearly affect the movement of labour or restrict it. Without major treaty revision the Socialists consider that much could be achieved by making more extensive use of the existing machinery — if the political will exists. The reformed Social fund might become not only an effective instrument for a common employment policy, but also act to stimulate and guide social policy in general. The Standing Committee on Employment (set up in April 1970) should assume a more active role in co-ordinating action between the council, commission and the two sides of industry. In addition, each branch of the economy should have a joint committee of employers and workers in that branch to draw up communitywide agreements on wages, salaries and working conditions.

The Socialists consider that the economic development of the community has been uneven. Certain areas have benefited less than others from the perspectives opened up by the common market, as have certain industries. Indeed, certain community policies, such as the common market for coal, the common market for industrial goods and the free movement of labour, have contributed directly to the relative depression of certain areas which have been dependent on particular industries. In addition, plans to modernise agriculture within the framework of the common agricultural policy would lead to a reduction in the manpower employed on the land, creating difficulties in certain areas. It goes without saying that from their standpoint the Socialists are concerned about the victims of these changes and seek public policy interventions to assist them. The general resolution demands that the community: 'pursue an industrial policy and a policy of freedom of establishment which will help (on the basis of common criteria) to develop the retarded regions of the Community.' In the Notes on the General Resolution,[18] this view is more carefully explained:

> Because of grave shortcomings, especially in the development of infrastructures, millions of citizens in the less developed regions of the Community are at a serious disadvantage. The Socialists believe that it is a Community task of vital importance to overcome economic and social disparities. Arrangements for financial compensation within the Community must be worked out for this purpose.

On account of their size, importance or on account of their particular difficulties or complexities, certain sectors of the economy of the community have been singled out by the treaties for special treatment. Of these sectors agriculture is the most important and has caused the most political and technical difficulty and dispute. The Socialists are naturally concerned about the future of agriculture in the community, both for human and economic reasons, but tend to see the whole problem from a wider and more general standpoint − the economy as a whole and the interests of other social groups. For the Socialists, the farmer is not a special interest. In the General Resolution[19] their view is clearly stated:

> The Social Democratic parties regret that in spite of expenditure of public funds running into several thousand million units of account and the heavy taxes borne by the consumers and the economy as a whole, no progress has been made towards the solving of the economic and social problems of agriculture and the farming community within the framework of the common agricultural policy.

The Socialists oppose transferring the burden of the support of agriculture on to the community consumer (largely the urban working class) through high prices or on to the outside world (particularly the developing nations) through excessive protectionism. On this, Dröscher[20] states:

> Through the agricultural policy, not only the fate of millions of farmers will be determined, but also, and that must be said for reasons of political responsibility, that of the consumers of this Community.

The notes on the general resolution make an attack on unwarranted protectionism and autarchy in the approach to agricultural problems:

> The Community must not disturb the world market by producing surpluses. On the contrary, it must make a substantial contribution to the normalisation and consolidation of those markets by importing agricultural produce as an association of modern industrial states of ever increasing importance. Its protectionism must be reduced to ensure that an adequate volume of imports is obtained.

It is clear that if protectionism and a high price system are rejected other policies will be required to ensure an orderly reduction of those involved in agriculture and to ensure an adequate income on efficient holdings for those who remain. Here Dröscher states[21]:

> On account of the current economic developments, the salvation cannot come from price policy alone, even after the recent increases. It must again and again be repeated that it is only one part of the policy. The other part, structural policy, must follow immediately, or else the whole policy will fail.

The structural policy should be designed to promote larger and more efficient holdings and avoid the need for excessive prices, which would then be based on the income requirements of the efficient farmer. Others would, in the words of the notes on the general resolution:

> As regards those considerable number of people who cannot be helped by an economically viable agricultural policy, the Social Democrats will advocate the adoption of suitable social measures on a generous scale.

Energy policy is another field which has been singled out for special attention. Energy is the basis of all industrial activity and thus conditions economic development in the community, especially as Europe is a net energy importing area on a large scale. In addition, the coal industry has faced (and still faces) important social and economic problems over the whole life of the communities. Naturally, therefore, this sector has attracted considerable interest. The general resolution[22] places emphasis on the need to arrive at a common energy policy and sees this as a vital part of the economic policy of the community in the economic and monetary union. It is stated that one of the objectives of the common energy policy must be: 'to implement a common energy policy as a precondition for ensuring the supply of coal, petroleum, natural gas and nuclear energy to the Community at the lowest possible prices.' The Socialist spokesman Hr Dröscher[23] sums up his group's view:

> The situation in the energy market, and with it a particularly important area of our economic and social policy, has changed over the last few years. We can never again act as we did with oil policy, increasing without restraint our consumption and will never again have that cheap supply, but will rather have to contend with rising costs.

It is just these perspectives for the future which make a common energy policy of such pressing importance.[24] Hr Wolfram takes up the issue of coal production:

> If one has followed the short 20 years' life of the Communities, one will have seen highs and lows and will have got the impression that thought, action and decision have always been based on short-term considerations.

And:

> . . . there must be medium and long-term energy policy which takes account of the structure of the energy market and which defines and limits the role of indigenous energy.

Referring to the proposals of the commission in this field:

> The goal of the Commission's proposals, to create and maintain a nucleus of coal production in order to secure energy supplies for the community and the intention of creating a valid reserve, deserve full support.

Transport policy too has caused special problems. It has been subject to special rules due to the difficulty of reconciling the different approaches to the problem in the member states. Here too the Socialists are concerned at the lack of progress towards a common policy. The notes on the general resolution criticise the delays in implementing the common transport policy and demand that the council should draw up a rapid timetable for the implementation of such a policy. As to the lines on which the policy should be developed, the notes have the following to say:

> Co-operation between national railway companies, post offices, telecommunications organisations and airlines, over and above the normal level of international co-operation, must be developed more purposefully than in the past as a contribution to economic integration. Transport costs must be balanced out by harmonising vehicular and excise taxes on petroleum.

Since the disappearance of the early reservations of the SPD and French SFIO, the group has been at least as strong a proponent of integration as the Christian Democrats and for the Socialists integration has not been a necessary cement for disunity on other issues. For the group the path towards the goal of social democracy lies logically and ineluctably in the European field, in the second half of the twentieth century. For them greater 'dirigisme' at the European level is not merely acceptable because it serves a long term political goal, but because it at the same time serves economic and social aims for which Socialists came into politics, but which increasingly cannot be attained through national action alone. This has given the Socialist group the basis for a strong and coherent approach to policy problems and has led to easy co-operation between what are, after all, very similar national parties. Even if certain sub groups such as the Danish Social Democrats and the SPD can be discerned, the Socialist group gives the appearance of a cohesive and effective group.

Notes

1   Article 2
2   Finn Christensen, Debates, Special Session, 4/5 October 1973.
3   M. Dehousse, 11 May 1967, P. E. Débats VI/67, no. 91, p. 119.
4   Resolution on the reform of the liaison office of the Social Democratic parties in the European community — 8th Congress of the Social Democratic parties in the European community, 28-30 June 1971.

5   Information supplied to the author by Hr Vredeling.

6   F. Georges, 'Résolution sur l'activité du Bureau de Liaison des Partis Socialistes des pays-membres des Communautés européennes', Document PS/CE/32/60.

7   Birkelbach Report, 7 May 1960, Document PS/CE/31/60.

8   See *Courrier socialiste européen* no. 29, 23 November 1961.

9   See *Courrier socialiste européen* no. 24, 1962.

10 Hr Vredeling in conversation with the author.

11 Of the 8th Congress of the Social Democratic Parties in the European Community.

12 General Resolution, section 2.

13 General Resolution, section 8.

14 On the General Resolution.

15 Debate on the economic position of the community 1971, *Débats*, 21 April 1971.

16 *Débats*, 13 June 1972.

17 On the General Resolution of the 8th Congress of the Social Democratic Parties in the European Community (Paragraph 9).

18 Paragraph 8.

19 Paragraph 10.

20 In the Debate on Agricultural Price and Structural Policy, *Débats*, 22 April 1972.

21 In the same *Débats* of 22 April 1972.

22 Of the 8th Congress of the Social Democratic Parties in the European Community.

23 In the Debate on Energy policy of 21 April 1971, p. 150.

24 *Débats*, 21 April 1971, p. 159.

6 The Liberal and Allies Group

6.1 Membership and organisation

The Liberal group was, with the Christian Democrats and the Socialists one of the original groups, though it is (as it mostly has been) considerably smaller. However from the 1958 election in France until 1963 when the Gaullist members left the group, it was the second largest group in parliament. Its present composition is:

	Bureau	Group	Affiliated parties
Belgium	1	2	PLP/PVV
Denmark	1	2	Venstre & Radikale Venstre
Germany	1	3	FDP
France	2	12	4 centre-right parties
Italy	1		PLI
Ireland	–	–	–
Luxemburg	1	1	Parti democratique
Netherlands	1	2	VVD
Great Britain	1	2	Liberal party
Total	9	24	12 parties

Enlargement brought only minor changes to the group, but did lead to a change in the equilibrium of the membership of the group. At first there were five new members from three parties (no Liberals came from Ireland) in Denmark and Britain. The group remains dominated by the French parties, but this is now less evident; immediately before enlargement French members accounted for 11 out of 20 members. What may be loosely called 'liberal' or moderate groups are very strong in the indirectly elected senate, but have little or no national party organisation; indeed the 'Gauche democratique' and REAS are not national parties, but mere parliamentary labels in the senate or survivals from the Fourth Republic. Only the independant Republicans are a genuine national party. They sit as Liberals at the European level in order to show their independance of the UDR (Gaullists) on community policy matters and because traditionally they have not been Christian Democrats. Six of the French members come from the senate. All the parties in the group are small, only the FDP has three members.

As far as the ideological strands within the group are concerned diversity is the rule. Only the Dutch, German, Belgian and Italian parties are genuine liberal parties in the continental tradition. Even here there are variations: since 1969 the character of the German party has radically changed and it has been in coalition with the SPD. Until enlargement these groups formed the core of the group and the other members were either in effect 'apparentes' or else their membership might appear incongruous. Enlargement has brought in the British and Scandinavian Liberal parties, which do not fit into the pattern of continental liberalism which is individualist politically, but increasingly appears 'right-wing' or 'laissez faire' in economic matters, strongly European (after early free-trade scruples in the FDP) and Atlanticist. The British and Scandinavian parties are much more centre parties, even centre-left parties. The Danish Radical party has frequently been in coalition with the Social Democrats, opposed NATO membership in the early 1950s and contained within its ranks a small anti-EEC faction. Apart from these two wings of the group it is hard to find any real principle behind membership of the group. The ideological diversity in the group is considerable and it could be said that the criterion for membership is the negative one of not being naturally at home in one of the other groups, which is reflected in the title of the group – Liberals and Allies. The adherence of certain French parties to the Liberal group is determined by largely domestic considerations: as indicated, the Independent Republicans are in the government majority, but wish to show their independence, at least their difference of approach to European questions. Some of the other 'centriste' parties which adhere to the group (PDM/Reformateurs/senate groups) are the heirs of the old MRP (Mouvement populaire républicaine) which left the government in 1962 partly in protest against the negative European policy of General de Gaulle and whose early leaders such as Schuman and Bidault had played leading roles in establishing the communities. Thus, in some sense both sides of the argument on Europe find themselves within the same group at the European level. The group contained members from the Italian extreme right: the PDIUM (Partito democratico italiano di unita monarchia) and MSI (Movimento sociale italiano), a neo-fascist party. After the 1972 Italian elections, which these parties fought in alliance (the Destra nazionale – National Right), these parties were excluded from the Liberal group in which they had long been a somewhat incongruous element. This, together with the arrival of the British and Scandinavian Liberals, has shifted the centre of gravity of the group to the left. Until the 1973 French elections the Radicals sat in the group; from 1966-69 they formed part of the Federation of the left (FDGS), which was in electoral if not political alliance with the PCF, indeed, immediately before the break up of the Federation talks on a common programme were in progress between the Radicals, SFIO and PCF. This process was completed with the signature of the Common Programme in 1972, but not before the Radical party had split into 'Radicaux de Gauche' (now allied to the Socialist group) and 'Reformateurs'. The Liberal group as a whole thus possesses a progressive element, a traditional liberal element, a conservative element and to some extent a right-wing element.

As a consequence, both of the smallness of the Group and of its diversity, organisation is minimal and as fluid as possible, a position which is in any case in accord with the individualistic outlook of Liberals. Membership is largely a matter of choice. The idea of an established list of eligible parties is considered inimical to the Liberal principle. The group can refuse a member, but is very open-minded on this question. There has, let it be said, been sporadic discussion of the expulsion of the MSI, but this party has been in the group since 1958 and still remains as of now. Thus anyone who wants to join may apply and is subject to an ad hoc decision, to which no very stringent criteria are applied.[1]

Most of the work of the group is carried out informally. The group meeting itself is the main forum for decision-making. Much responsibility for preparation and co-ordination lies with the secretariat and in informal contact between members of the group. The bureau consists of one member from each member state. In the bureau there is only a president and one vice-president who acts as treasurer, as well as four ordinary members. The bureau is not important and does not meet at all often. There are no specialised committees as in the other groups. A key role in the work of the group is played by the president of the group in conjunction with the secretariat. The secretariat plays an overtly political role. It is politically committed and can thus influence and co-ordinate the work of the group, where co-ordination would otherwise be difficult. The secretariat of the Liberal group is smaller than that of the other groups we have examined and was only granted one extra post at A 7/6 in the 1973 budget. The decisions of the group are made in the plenary meeting, without any preparation, except the work that the secretariat may have put in. It will suggest a line to the group, which must then decide its position. A member of the group who sits in the competent committee of the parliament wil lead the discussion: this will be the rapporteur if he is a Liberal. This member will explain the background to the group and may indicate how he will vote himself. In the group meetings (26 in 1970) there are few formal votes; indeed, the author was informed that there were none during 1972. There is no attempt to arrive at a 'consigne de vote'. The group must first of all decide whether it can reach a common position, which is frequently impossible, and then, if this is possible, whether it should appoint an official spokesman. At times the group has had to resort to the device of appointing two spokesmen in order to represent the diversity of views which exists within the group. This means that the Liberal group less frequently presents a group standpoint than the other groups. For example, in the December 1971 session the Liberals presented statements on only two of the nine issues.

The Liberal group does not have the same network of formal outside contacts as the other groups; nor is the same effort made to co-ordinate the positions of the groups and the national parties. The group is affiliated to the Liberal International and to the Liberal group for a united Europe, but neither of these bodies has the same strength and unity as the Socialist International or the Congress of the Socialist Parties of the European Communities, or even the European Union of Christian Democrats. The group has no formal contact with the council or commission, but the Liberal members of the commission do participate informally in the work of the group. The group meets from time to time for 'Journées d'études' at which resolutions are adopted. These are useful forums for wider ranging discussions about the attitude of the group in the long term.

6.2 Policy

As far as policy is concerned, it seems difficult to define the basic philosophy of the Liberal group with any degree of detail. The position of the group must be defined largely by negative criteria — that is by reference to the other groups. In some sense, a Liberal is one who is not a Christian Democrat or a Socialist. This is definition by exclusion. The group defines itself in opposition to the two other main groups.[2] The Liberals are the heirs to the individualistic and economic 'laissez-faire' doctrines of the last century; they naturally reject state intervention and dirigisme in economic affairs, believing in the value of the market forces, of the value of individualism and free enterprise. Indeed, they could be said to support freedom as an absolute good, even to the point at which it hurts the weaker individuals. In reality, they do not exclude all state intervention, but certainly see it as a necesary evil, to be watched, limited and contained and even reduced if the opportunity should present itself. It hardly needs to be said that this approach effectively delineates the Liberals from the Socialist group. The Liberals have a fair amount in common with the Christian Democrats, but in principle consider themselves more 'purist', since the Christian Democrats have adopted some of the tenets of Christian Socialism and believe in the necessity of a greater degree of collective responsibility. The historic divide of clericals versus anti-clericals also has some influence at this point. This analysis holds good for those elements within the group who are more or less 'traditional' Liberals. Beyond that, the group appears to be a repository for those who have no alternative ideological home and – this is important – feel themselves to be to the right of centre in the political spectrum. It was in this way that the UNR members first joined the group as 'apparentes' after the 1958 elections in France. The UNR thus gained the administrative facilities of group membership without ideological commitment. The main centre of concern for the group is the individual. His freedom must be protected, his individualism respected and his enterprise fostered. The small economic unit must be protected. The group, and here particularly the Belgian Hougardy, is concerned to inject the liberal idea into the morass of technical work of the European parliament.

The Liberal group takes a realistic position on the institutional question. The group recognises the reality of the Luxemburg agreement, but at the same time makes clear the practical difficulties and delays which arise from that agreement. The group accepts that the council must for the foreseeable future remain the most important institution in the community and that it cannot be relegated to the role of a revising chamber. The commission and the parliament should naturally be strengthened, but should also use the powers they already have in a more effective way. The right of initiative, possessed both by the commission and, in a more indirect way, by the parliament, should be used to the full. The existing powers of control possessed by the parliament should be employed more extensively than has hitherto been the case and here one could cite the motion of censure. The members of the European parliament are also members of their national parliaments – this is the double mandate system. Whatever one's views on this in principle, it exists and its possibilities should be more fully exploited. Hr Berkhouver (president of the group until his election as President of the Parliament in 1973) has developed this line. He considers that members should be more active in raising European questions in the national parliaments, for example, during the debates on the adhesion treaties for the candidate countries. The powers of the community should be extended by more extensive use of Article 235 of the Rome Treaty. It is clear that full implementation of economic and monetary union will require more power for the community, but this will be automatic; it must and will come.

There are two distinct tendencies in the group as far as general economic policy is concerned. The one considers it vital to create a climate in which European industry can compete with the United States and Japan:

The will to create a coordinated economic policy must imply a common macro-economic policy. All the more so in that the EEC has to compete in an international market, with Japan, with its constant economic growth, and the United States . . .[3]

The other tendency is concerned with the danger that large, overmighty companies with monopolistic tendencies present for freedom and democracy. These companies are a danger to political liberty and individualism. This view is mostly found in the German FDP. In view of the record of German trusts this fear is understandable.[4] The group supports economic and monetary union, seeing its long-term success as a matter of perseverence. However, the group is concerned that immediate measures should be taken to make Europe real to the man in the street, to make him aware that Europe is being built and to make the process of direct concern and interest to him. The individual and the small business must not be neglected in the building of Europe. For the group the key economic problem facing the community at the present time is inflation, which endangers all economic progress and hurts certain social groups to a disproportionate extent:

Today the whole world is dominated by the inflationary pressure which it seems difficult to arrest or to ascertain its cause. The international monetary system on which we have relied, seems likely to suffer profound change.[5]

The cause of this inflation is held to be the continual pressure on the enterprise, both state and private, from the trade unions, backed up by unjustified and prolonged strikes and motivated as much by political aims as by economic aims:

What is the main cause of recession and inflation? I can answer that at once: the capitulation of the employers, who, faced with the excessive pressures from the unions, no longer have any chance to resist and who are ready to abandon their position in favour of American capital, which seems prepared to operate at a loss in some sectors in order to eliminate European competition.[6]

The only remedy is a co-ordinated economic policy which will take the necessary measures, such as a reduction in excessive state expenditures and act decisively against trade union pressure:

Substantial and immediate European unity is an urgent necessity. We can no longer continue with our diverse political and economic systems. The very existence of the world economic system should impose on the community a political coordination and harmonisation, not in the long-term or medium-term, but an immediate united economic policy. In this particularly difficult period, with its symptoms of recession, it is above all necessary to avoid the danger of divergent national solutions.[7]

In addition, the speaker says:

I ask this particularly to the competent parliamentary committee and to the Commission: isn't it time to take an initiative, to stop thinking only in the medium and long-term. Europe, and Italy in particular, need social peace. Why doesn't the Commission make proposals limiting the right to strike?[8]

The Liberal group is concerned with social policy and regional policy, policies which are themselves closely allied, but which are also closely associated with the problems of marginal agriculture. The group finds many of its members from deprived regions of the community, such as the rural areas of France and Germany. Here one detects a minor conflict, which is not overt, between those who feel that in some way the object of policy should be to preserve these regions in their present state — and to make the status quo viable — and those who look to the community policies to effect much needed changes both in structures and attitudes which, for one reason or another, the national governments either could not or would not effect:

There is talk of a Community regional policy. In Hr Oele's report it is reaffirmed that there should be a coordinated and united regional policy. The reality is, however, that each state pursues its own regional policy, in accordance with its own aims and to maintain old and outmoded structures.[9]

In the debate on the first orientations for a programme of social policy, the spokesman for the Liberal group indicated what were for his group the main priorities:

However, up to now the measures adopted by the Council and other organs of the Community have mostly been designed to assist in the solution of open crisis. These have without doubt been very useful initiatives, such as subsidies for the reconversion of regions hit by economic change. None the less, for the future it is more and more indispensable to seek to prevent such crises rather than curing them when they have already produced their bad effects, which are so keenly felt in the working world. That should be the major priority of a community social policy.[10]

Other key objectives for the group are professional training, which should be more fully developed; more aid to the handicapped to enable them to pursue a job; an end to discrimination against women at work. There should be harmonisation of social welfare provision, but competition must not suffer:

> As far as a European social budget goes, we demand a regular and thorough examination of the social costs in each country in order to compare their development and ensure their harmonisation in, naturally, the interests of their recipients, without affecting fair competition.[11]

As has already been indicated, the Liberal group obtains many of its members from the rural areas of the community, and in particular from those rural areas with agricultural and regional problems. The agriculture committee has been a stronghold of the Liberals, and particularly those from the rural areas. There are currently five Liberal members of the committee (there have been more), of which three are French senators, one a Belgian and the other a Dutchman. The chairman of the committee has by tradition been a French Liberal. Until recently the post had been held for over some ten years by Monsieur Boscary-Monsservin, who was influential and activist; he has been replaced by another French Liberal, Monsieur Houdet. The group may have a strong interest in agricultural policy, but not to the exclusion of other matters, nor to the general interest. There is a strong attachment in the group to the smaller farmers of the community and a belief that the commission has in part lost touch with reality in the proposals it makes, especially on the question of rising costs and on the possibility of violently reducing the number of people employed in agriculture within the space of a few years; some doubt the desirability (let alone the practicality) of such an approach. The group sees the need for an overall concept in agricultural policy. It believes in the use of price policy, rather than seeking to apply a policy of income guarantees. Any structural policy must take account of human factors and not become a blunt, bureaucratic instrument. In the debate on the decisions of the council of 25 March 1971, Hr Baas[12] makes it clear that his group has very great reservations about decisions of the council

114

which are reached in an atmosphere of secrecy and under the unanimity rule and demands to know who is to take political responsibility for the decisions reached. He stresses the need for a fair price policy which will take account of the rising costs and investment in land.

In their energy policy, the Liberal group diagnoses a potential energy crisis in the near future. Even by 1980 well below half the needs of the community will come from within the community — a figure which falls to 10 per cent for oil. In this situation rapid action is needed; the group does not oppose a common policy but considers it too slow a remedy, preferring to rely on the action of the individual governments and of the companies involved. The commission and the governments should encourage greater stocks, assist the building of more tanker capacity, diversify sources of energy, maintain a level of coal production, assist (by fiscal and other means) and encourage prospecting for oil within the community. Both in their research and their negotiations with the overseas producer countries the petroleum companies should be allowed the maximum of freedom and the minimum of government interference:

> .... to pay tribute to the Commission which has understood that the difficult negotiations of Tripoli and Tehran had to be conducted between the oil companies and the producer countries, without any outside involvement.[13]

and:

> However, I would draw the attention of the Commission to the fallacy of waiting for the adoption of a common policy in this area. There must be immediate action in each country at the national level; unfortunately a European harmonisation is in danger of taking too long, thus hurting research efforts. In order to arrive at the necessary diversification, any measure reducing the viability of drilling and research must be avoided, and that because any measures taken will benefit the governments in the first instance.[14]

Certainly the doctrine of the Liberal group is the least clear and least easily comprehended of all the groups. With the considerable increase in available positions (now including Gaullists, Communists, and Independents) for members, the position must be more subtle than Van Oudenhouve's suggestion that the Liberals be defined negatively by reference to the Socialists and Christian Democrats — in fact the rump. This is both less logically clear and too negative; the Liberals, in spite of the wide range of views found in the group and the looseness of their organisation, do have some positive characteristics. Certainly they are not Socialists nor are they (though they may be Conservatives) Christian Democrats, but individualism is their positive philosophy. They are not totally against state intervention — no party can be that in modern times — but they are anti-Socialist and, above all, anti-Communist. They are, let us say, *a priori,* against state intervention and have a preference for 'laissez-faire'. One might be forced to exclude the Italian extreme right from this generalisation, since they have views rooted more in corporatism and resolute anti-Communism. The group is contradictory and complex, hard to categorise, but it does have a positive quality.

Notes

1   Both sides of the Great Clerical-anti-clerical divide sit in the group.

2   Van Dijk, 'De plaats van de liberale Fractievormning in de Europese democratie' *Liberale Gedachten,* Nijgh en Van Ditmar, Rotterdam 1963.

3   Romeo in the debate on the economic situation 1971; *Débats,* 21 April 1971, p. 93.

4   Borm, in conversation with the author.

5   Romeo, loc. cit., p. 93.

6   Romeo, loc.cit., p. 94.

7   Romeo, loc. cit., p. 93.

8   Romeo, loc. cit., p. 94.

9   Romeo, loc. cit., p. 95.

10   Monsieur Berthoin in *Débats,* 13 June 1972, p. 39.

11   Berthoin, loc. cit.

12   The Liberal spokesman, *Débats,* 22 April 1971, pp. 183-4.

13   Monsieur Hougardy in the Debate on the Energy Situation 1971.

14   Hougardy, loc. cit.

7 The European Progressive Democrats Group

The group was only formed in July 1973 after the French elections had led to a sizeable reduction in the number of UDR members in the French delegation, with the result that they could no longer form a group on their own. The five Irish Fine Fáil members had sat as independents and were thus available to join the UDR in the new group — the EDP, with the following composition:

	Bureau	Group	Party
France	2	12	UDR
Ireland	1	5	Fine Fáil

The group has only a small bureau: M. Bourges (president), Mr Yeats (vice president), M. Laudrin (treasurer). From its foundation to the end of 1973 it held twelve meetings and two study days. In 1973 the group had 5 Grade A officials in its secretariat, which has been increased to 9 for 1974.

It is clearly too early to judge the new group. However no great difficulties seem to have arisen as between the two parties which form it. The main positive cement of the group is common support for the CAP, with the Irish members taking the lead in emphasising certain areas of special concern to Ireland (Mr Gibbons tabled an oral question on policy towards mutton and lamb), but with common insistence on fair prices for producers, particularly in the case of meat and milk. In other fields, except regional policy, the UDR members have been predominant. On institutional questions the minimalist position of the UDR appears to have caused no problems for the group. It is therefore clear that we must examine the old UDE (Gaullist) group in order to understand the standpoint of the new group.

7.1 Membership and organisation

In the early days of the common assembly the French members of the various parties which supported the return to power of General de Gaulle

E

sat as independent, but took an active part in the work of the assembly, even acting as rapporteurs on several occasions. In the first session of the assembly there were four such members, but this was reduced to the lone presence of Monsieur Debré by 1958. In the first Session of the European parliament there were two 'Gaullist' members (Monsieur Debré, a senator and Monsieur Estève, Républicain social from the National Assembly), who sat as independents. Then came the events of May 1958 and the return to power of General de Gaulle after the 'traversée du désert' and the election of October 1958, which brought to the national assembly a mass 'Gaullist' party, the 'Union pour la Nouvelle République' (UNR), of which eight members initially came to the European parliament. These members joined the Liberal group as 'apparentes', which gave them administrative facilities, such as the right to be named rapporteur, the assistance of the group secretariat and a greater weight to questions and interpellations. This status did not bind the UNR members politically, nor could it have done, bearing in mind the diversity of the Liberal group, to which it merely added yet another divergent dimension, whilst lifting the Liberals to the second largest group.

The fact of their common nationality, their political unity, gave the UNR members an exclusive position within the Liberal group, almost the position of a group within a group, with ample unofficial opportunity to seek a common line irrespective of the position of the Liberal group as a whole. Furthermore, their negative attitude in the common assembly had not been forgotten. It gradually became apparent that the European policy of President de Gaulle was profoundly out of keeping with the views of the majority of the members of the parliament. All these factors led to mutual dissatisfaction within the Liberal group and a desire on the part of the UNR to form a group on its own. This required a change in the rules of procedure, since the UNR alone could not then hope to attain 17 seats in the parliament. There were mixed feelings on this point; some opposed in principle the formation of national groups, but after the veto on British entry to the community at the press conference of 14 January 1963, relations between the UNR and the other members deteriorated to the point where the solution desired by the UNR was accepted. Indeed, the UNR at that point felt itself unable to sit in a group which was openly opposed to French policy.

It is against this background that we must view the UDE group. Initially, the group was just large enough to form a group under the revised rule (requiring 14 members at least, as opposed to 17). Since the elections of June 1968 the group has sent 19 members, an absolute majority of the French delegation. Of these, 17 are from the national assembly and 2 from the senate in the whole delegation. The members of the group are all from the UDR, with the sole exception of Monsieur Cousté, who is elected to the national assembly as an independent and affiliates to the UDR as an 'apparente'. All the members of the UDE group are French.

Membership is open to all UDR and 'apparente' members of the French delegation to the European parliament, but is not exclusive to those members; others may apply to join the group. There is no exclusion on the grounds of nationality. Under these conditions, the group as a whole would decide on any application and naturally has the right to refuse, and, in principle, to exclude a member. The group would readily accept both non-UDR and non-French members if they were acceptable on political grounds. For reasons of domestic politics, the two Belgian members of the FDF-RW ('Front démocratique des Francophones-Rassemblement wallon'), and the French minority parties (Messieurs Outers and Thiry) have not affiliated themselves to the UDE, although it is possible that they would do so after the enlargement of the community if other nationalities joined the UDE.

Being the smallest of the recognised groups, of one nationality and to all intents and purposes of one party, formal organisation can be minimal. The bureau consists of a president, vice-president and treasurer, plus the UDE vice-president of the parliament and the UDE presidents of the standing committees (at present two). The bureau as such has little importance and the real work is done by the president in consultation with other members and the secretariat of the group. There are no institutionalised working groups, but for special matters ad hoc groups have been formed. Meetings were held between experts and the UDE members of the agriculture committee to discuss the Mansholt Plan and between experts and the UDE members of the economic affairs committee to consider the proposal for economic and monetary union. The group meets both in and out of session, usually some eight to ten days before the session and then during the session. In 1970, the group held 15 meetings, that is substantially less than the other groups. It should be realised that the problems of reaching a common position are nowhere near as severe for the UDE; indeed, much of the work of the group in reality occurs on the national plane, in the corridors of the national assembly, in its committees and in the organs of the UDR itself. The group discusses each question on the agenda of the session and hears a report from a member of the competent committee of the parliament. It is difficult to assess how active the group is. Some authors[1] imply that the group is passive and inert. Any objective indicators of the group's activity tend to give a different, but inconclusive, result. As we have seen, there are fewer group meetings held, but this would seem reasonable in view of the composition of the group; the group does appoint a number of rapporteurs, but their number does seem smaller than one might expect and the group rarely seems to gain the rapporteurship on 'sensitive' issues, where the question of integration and institutional matters is involved. If the sessions of May and June 1971 are taken as a random example, then only 5 out of 30 reports were presented by UDE rapporteurs. Take the June session of 1972: here one report out of 19 was presented by a UDE rapporteur and that on a minor technical question of restitution payments for certain meat. The members of the group appear to ask a relatively small number of written and oral questions of the council and the commission. Indeed, the number averages about ten to fifteen per year. For example, at the meeting of the 'Groupe des Affaires Générales' of 22 July 1971, taken at random (GAG is a group of the council at which the council and commission discuss draft replies to written and oral questions addressed to both institutions), of 19 questions on the agenda only one came from a UDE member. Yet the group appoints a large number of spokesmen. For example, in the February session of 1972, the group appointed spokesmen for eight of eleven matters on the agenda, which compared with the same figure (but not on the same matters) for the Christian Democrats and the Socialists, five Liberal spokesmen and three from the Independent Italian members (Communists).[2]

As is to be expected, the outside contacts of the UDE group are with the 'mother' group in France, the UDR. Both the president of the group and the UDE vice-president of the parliament (Messieurs Bourges and Cousté) are members *ex-officio* of the bureau 'politique' of the UDR. Monsieur Habib-Deloncle is assistant secretary of the UDR for external relations; thus the views of the group are known both in the inner council and day to day work of the UDR and the positions taken by the organs of the UDR can be reflected in the work of the group. The 'Règlement des Assemblées' requires that the French delegation to the European parliament make a report to the two houses; the current rapporteur comes from the UDE and the rapporteur for the ratification of the treaty on budgetary procedure (1970) was Monsieur de la Malene (UDE/UDR). The group is the prime mover in an organisation called 'Le Mouvement pour l'indépendance de l'Europe', whose aim is to see a 'Europe des Patries' freed from American domination; this organisation does include other groups, but it is mainly French and UDR. Recently the UDR has held party to party talks with both the CDU and the SPD in Germany at which European affairs were discussed at some length. The UDR attends conferences of the Union of European Conservatives (1972 meeting in Oslo) to which a wide range of parties is loosely affiliated: the German CDU/CSU, the British Conservative party, Scandinavian

Conservative and moderate parties. This group has no pretensions beyond a useful exchange of views and in any case extends beyond the geographical scope of the present or enlarged community.

7.2 Policy

The policies of the group could be said to be 'Gaullism writ large'. At least while General de Gaulle was in power in France, the role of the UDR in France and the UDE in the European parliament was to support and promote his vision of France and Europe. In the field of European politics, the group was dedicated to the defence of French interests and followed at one remove the policy line which emanated from Paris. The basis of that policy was, and to a lesser extent still is, that the nation is the basic unit of international affairs, the basic building brick. National sovereignty has to be protected and common action organised on the basis of co-operation as equals between nations. The group accepts, as have successive French governments, the Treaty of Rome, but as a limit, not as a point of departure. The treaty must be interpreted in a limitative manner and certain aspects even of the treaty must be subject to political realities. These views, together with the long opposition to the enlargement of the community, meant that, within the context of parliamentary politics in the European parliament, the UDE group became an opposition group, the sole opposition group in a period when the other groups were tending to sink differences in order to present a united front to the other community institutions and to public opinion, in favour of more integration – that is, the extension of the powers of the community to new fields and an increase in the powers of the supranational institutions – the commission and the parliament. The UDE main role within the framework of the European parliament was to oppose the (as they saw it) unrealistic pretentions of the other groups on the integration issue. When such matters were not at issue, it is hard to place the UDE in the political spectrum. The group defended the interests of France, which in some sectors involved more public intervention and even more community action than was desired, for example, by the Liberals; then again the group does not consider itself to belong to the right or conservative wing in social and economic matters. Naturally there are variations within the UDR and, hence, within the UDE. Some members are more in the mould of traditional conservatives, whilst others could, if the term had not become debased and perverted, be called 'national socialists'.

The UDE group does not believe in supranational institutions. It accepts the Treaty of Rome and within its framework desires an intense co-operation between nations, which might well lead to some loss of 'sovereignty'. It emphasises a pragmatic approach and believes that co-operation should be between nations, the only real elements in international relations; that supranationalism is unrealistic. The group insists that solutions to outstanding problems and solid agreement among the enlarged community member states should precede institutional development. The group considers that institutions should follow on action, should follow after the facts. One should decide first what one wants to do and then devise the means to do it. The group considers itself 'un élément modérateur dans le consensus européen de l'Assemblée.[3] The group is always ready to approve of proposals which will lead to real solid progress, but looks askance at those, such as the Dutch government, who make far reaching general proposals but are reticent about accepting current, concrete proposals. The group wishes to remain within the framework of the Treaty of Rome and considers that any proposals which would require radical treaty revision, amounting to a new treaty, are unrealistic. The *Vedel Report* is commended with reservations, because it remains within the framework of the Treaty of Rome. The group considers that the European parliament should remain 'delegated' by the national parliaments, in order to avoid a crisis between the two types of body. The group is prepared to see the budgetary powers of the parliament increased to provide for a greater right of amendment of budgetary proposals. The legislative powers of the parliament can be increased, but only to the extent that this would not fundamentally alter the equilibrium between the institutions. In this sense the *Vedel Report* proposals for a 'suspensive veto' on certain council decisions is valuable, but the proposals of the same *Report* to establish a power of co-decision would have to be limited to a much greater extent than that envisaged in the *Report.*

The UDE is not doctrinaire in economic matters; it should be borne in mind that the governments of General de Gaulle (1944-46 and 1958-69) never shrank from 'dirigiste' and interventionist solutions to economic problems. The paradox of the group's position is that it demands increased integration in the economic field, and, here particularly, the co-ordination of economic policies and the full establishment of an economic and monetary union on the basis of fixed exchange rates as between the currencies of the community in order to protect the ground already gained, notably the common agricultural policy, which must be completed and strengthened. At the same time, however, these developments must be achieved with the minimum of institutional development — by unanimous agreement and by the use of such legally obscure formulae as 'Agreements between the Representatives of the Governments of the

Member States meeeting in the Council', a hybrid of community and normal intergovernmental procedures. In the economic debate of 1971, the group spokesman (Monsieur Cousté) outlined the viewpoint of his group, indicating, as had other speakers, that inflation was a major and world wide problem:

> The first and fundamental point is that we are in an inflationary spiral in practically all six countries. Nor is it a phenomenon unique to the six, but a world phenomenon . . . I want to make myself clear that we do not consider the inflation that we are talking about here is solely the result of external causes alone . . . there are causes which result from the relaxing of certain discipline in the management of public and private affairs in our six countries.[4]

What is implied here is an acceptance of inflation by many social groups, who find that not only are they not harmed by inflation but even gain from it:

> When I think of the effects of inflation, I am clearly thinking of the effects on the workers, those of industry, commerce and specially those of agriculture, when he found that the increase in his real standard of living is in fact higher in periods of inflation than in periods of stability and certainly deflation; clearly then there is a consensus, unwritten perhaps but none the less real, among the economic actors . . .[5]

In contrast to some speakers in the same debate (for example, Signor Romeo, the Liberal spokesman) Monsieur Cousté and his group consider that the situation is not over-dramatic and indeed is mildly encouraging:

> The situation is not dramatic nor is it bad. There are some dangerous signs, but let us see things as they are: overall industrial production is growing in all European countries. For 1970, agricultural production too has been quite acceptable.

The main question therefore becomes that of the development of incomes and salaries, a matter that, insists the speaker, has a social aspect which cannot be ignored:

> The real problem is that of incomes policy. It is in fact there that we find the link between the economic situation and its social results. It is here that, in our opinion, we should insist on one of the positive

elements — a more active employment policy.

In spite of the avowed need for more co-ordination of economic policies and a more active employment policy, the speaker makes a characteristic observation against the establishment of a European economic planning office, since this would erode national prerogatives.

In the field of social policy the group is at pains to point out that the community is not a kind of Liberal International; the group is in favour of a stronger and more effective social policy. In this area the group considers itself to be close to the Socialists. As can be seen from the Declaration of Monsieur Laudrin,[6] the group seeks greater resources for the fund and that it should be given a greater role in regional policy so that the differences between the community average and the less favoured regions of the community can be equalised. The group is also concerned that workers and other interested groups should have a greater share in the formation of policy, both within the firm and at regional level. The group is, however, opposed to the creation of new institutions which would impose a regional policy from the top. At the same time, the group is concerned to protect the 'integrity' of the member states; it is opposed to opening direct channels of communication and application for assistance from the fund to local bodies and quasi-private organisations, which would thus be able to bypass (and even oppose) their national governments. In the debate on the *Lulling Report*[7] in the Committee of Social Affairs and Public Health of 4 June 1971, this was clearly stated by Monsieur Liogier, who opposed a paragraph in the *Report* and resolution which would have allowed bodies whose applications were not supported by their governments to approach the commission directly. In the debate on the *Vredeling Report* on the 'Preliminary Orientation for a Community Social Policy' (13 June 1972), the group spokesman (Monsieur Liogier) made clear the concern of the group that the social policy of the community should take into account the 'Petits indépendants' and their needs; at the insistence of the group, the committee had added a section to the report to that effect. On this he declared:

> . . . it would be dangerous to foresee the disappearance of all the small family farms, as well as almost all small businesses and craftsmen. Many of them are needed to ensure a certain equilibrium in the distributive trade, especially in some regions — the least favoured ones in particular. It is therefore essential to ensure their survival and even their competitiveness by special policies.[8]

Social policy should be given a high priority and its influence should be

124

felt in all fields. Referring to the *Van der Gun Report* on a co-ordinated incomes policy, Monsieur Laudrin stated:

> At the Community level we have found satisfactory solutions to the problems of many large sectors of economic life, particularly agriculture. We will soon do the same for transport, I hope, and for monetary problems. I would like to see a greater consciousness of the fact that social problems will from now on be the first priority in all our countries and that we must find common solutions . . .[9]

Agriculture has been a major interest of France since the founding of the community; the common agricultural policy has been the *sine qua non* of French participation in the community and acceptance of progress in other areas. The UDE has consistently supported the extension of the CAP to all products with full 'rigueur'; it has supported the basic system of the policy and the implied system of community preference and quasi-autarchy in some products. It has argued for the extension of the system *in toto* to the applicant countries and has seen, at least in the case of Britain, acceptance of the CAP as a test of 'European will'. The group does not oppose modernisation as such, nor indeed the structural policies of the Mansholt Plan, but has sought to moderate the 'supranational' aspects of the proposals and to defend the French farmers, many of whom are 'marginal' in economic terms, but utterly reject the Mansholt Plan:

> It was suggested just now that agricultural prices should be kept down to avoid inflation. But do agricultural prices have a monopoly on causing inflation? If one looks at what has happened since the so called freeze of 1967, it is clear that increases in salaries and wages and costs of all kinds have hit agriculture.[10]

Structural policy is seen as useful, but too limited and too long-term in its effect to be able to help farmers faced with rising costs or those forced to leave agriculture, but too young to obtain the aid laid down in the decisions of the council. On this point, Monsieur Briot states:

> This shows how difficult it is to give real advantages to agriculture. Structural policy will come along, but this is only more or less long-term remedy.[11]

The group shares the concern of other groups for the security of energy supplies at the lowest possible prices. In the debate on the energy situation, the spokesman for the group (Monsieur Bousch) accused the commission of 'attentisme' and attacked the fact that in a number of reports the commission had accepted with equanimity that the proportion of imported energy should continue to rise at an even faster rate, particularly in the coal and coke sectors:

> One may have reason to doubt whether the requirements of a sure supply, so important in this sector, will be respected, in view of the fact that current plans reduce to 22 per cent in 1975, as against some 40 per cent at present the share of coal in energy requirements of power stations and will reduce to some 50 per cent, as against the current 75 per cent the share of indigenous energy in the requirements of these same power stations.[12]

The UDE group is particularly interesting in that it would appear (until the arrival of the Italian Communists in 1969) to constitute the only opposition group within an assembly whose most noteworthy feature is its unnatural political consensus. The early polarisation of the common assembly into Socialist and non-Socialist groupings had disappeared by the time the European parliament came into being and it was only with the formation of the UDE that one could again detect the germ of an opposition. The UDE may appear to have a diverse ideological standpoint and no fixed position in the political spectrum, but it has two constant positions: defence of the interests of France as seen by the successive (Gaullist) governments which have held power since 1958; and, secondly, overt opposition to the 'supranationalist' concept, to the 'federalist' vision of Europe, in which the individual states would have disappeared. To the UDE this view is not only not practical — it is not even desirable. Both these positions — that of a national group, defending purely national interests, and in its opposition to 'federalism' — the group places itself in counterdistinction and opposition to the other groups. It is the defence of French interests which may explain the paradoxes of the UDE in the day to day work of the assembly, where on specific issues it may advocate a more European position than other groups and appear as dirigiste as the Socialist group; it does so for France and not for the integration of Europe.

Notes

1   E.g., M. Forsyth, *The Parliament of the European Communities* (PEP).

2   Sources for this section: P.E., Comité des Presidents, Relevé des

126

travaux en cours dans les commissions parlementaires, May-June 1971.

3   President Triboulet in conversation with the author.

4   Cousté, *Débats*, 21 April 1971, p. 96.

5   Cousté, loc. cit.

6   In the debate on the European social fund.

7   On Regulation applying to the decision of the council (71/66/CEE) concerning the reform of the European social fund.

8   Monsieur Liogier, *Débats*, 13 June 1972.

9   Laudrin, *Débats,* p. 52.

10   Briot, Debate on Agricultural Prices and Structures, *Débats*, 22 April 1971.

11   Briot, loc. cit.

12   Monsieur Bousch, *Débats*, 21 April 1972, p. 153.

8 The Communist and Allies Group

8.1 Membership and organisation

The Communist and allies group was only officially formed in the December part session (1973). However, there had been Communist members in parliament since March 1969 when the Italian parliament broke away from its earlier principle of exclusion and nominated a totally representative delegation. It was the change in Rule 36 of the rules of procedure to permit any ten members from three members states or any fourteen members to form a group,[1] which enabled the Communists to form a new group.

Hitherto, the group had not had the official status of a group within the meaning of Article 36. The fact that its members had a political affinity and chose to function as a group was taken into account and certain 'facilities' were accorded. Members were appointed to committees on the basis of one per committee. In the plenary session it was treated as a group, being given priority over individual speakers and receiving the same speaking time as the other groups. The group was also allowed a small secretariat, with one A grade official and a secretary and was able to hold 'group' meetings. Its status was similar to that of 'Gruppen' as distinct from 'Fraktionen' in the German Bundestag. In spite of these facilities, the group suffered from some serious disabilities; its members could not become president or vice-president of the parliament nor sit in the bureau of committees nor be rapporteurs. Nor did it have a seat in the bureau, enlarged bureau or committee of presidents. Thus it was excluded from influence over the agenda, the reports to be made and administrative questions including the budget of parliament.

From its early isolation the group has gradually developed its position. At first it was entirely Italian, but not entirely Communist, since there were members from the PSIUP[2] and 'Independente di Sinistra' in the group. From enlargement the group was joined by one Danish Socialist People's Party member (Per Dich, and after the Danish election of 1973, Jens Maigaard).[3] After the French general elections of March 1973, the national assembly nominated three Communist members as part of the French delegation. This brought the total membership up to 14 from three countries, with 4 constituent parties:

Italian PCI	8
Independente di Sinistra	1
French PCF	4
Socialist Peoples Party	1
Total[4]	14 from four parties

In spite of its small size and isolation, the group, which at that time consisted almost exclusively of Italian communists, always had a wider, European vocation. At the European level 'Communist' seems to mean a tendency more than a party; it seems to signify an attitude towards the community. In his opening address to the Colloque on 'The Italian Communists and Europe' held under the auspices of CESPE in November 1971, Signor Amendola said:

It is essential that the large political forces that to varying degrees orient and organise the popular masses of the community countries, communists, socialists, christian democrats, be represented in the parliament with the strength that they really have, so that through their convergence or divergence they can effectively decide community policy. Today there are multi-national socialist and christian democrat groups, but although the Italian communists are represented there is no multi-national communist group.[5]

The group has always considered itself a vanguard, representing the absent parties. To the extent that the French party is under-represented and other parties not at all this vocation continues even now:

Our role is representing the Communists of the other countries or at least a current of ideas which is an essential part of European and world political reality.[6]

Before becoming an official group no formal organisation was needed. In any case the group was uninational, small and dominated by the PCI and therefore followed the line defined by the mother party. Amendola was the group leader and different members held special responsibilities according to their expertise: Cipolla (agriculture), Leonardi (economic questions and energy policy), Iotti (institutional questions), D'Angelosante (legal issues). The party has somewhat departed from normal practice in respect of its 'European' MPs. Normally rank and file senators and deputies sit for only one or two legislative periods. In the case of the members of the European parliament they were all allowed to be candidates in the 1972 election and their re-election was ensured and they were all reappointed to the European parliament.

Since forming a group a bureau has been elected, consisting of one member from each country (Amendola as president, Ansart as vice-president and Jens Maigaard). The group has held three meetings in 1973 and one study day. In addition to the wide-ranging outside contact of a general nature carried on by the PCI and the PCF — such as the mutual sending of delegates to each other's conferences, bi-lateral discussions with other parties, consultations within the framework of the world communist movement — some direct steps have been taken in the context of European policy. The PCI and the PCF hold an annual meeting. Communist members of the European parliament have travelled widely in Europe, both in the community of the six and in the new member states (including a visit by S. Amendola to England, where he criticised the attitude of both the Labour and Communist parties). A conference was held in Rome in November 1971, under the auspices of CESPE, devoted to the theme 'the Italian Communists and Europe'.[7] There were both Communist and non-Communist participants, Italian and foreign visitors. Reports were given on a wide variety of issues. Of even greater importance was the first conference of Western European Communist parties held in January 1971 and devoted to the working class struggle in the face of the multi-national companies. Such meetings were to become a regular forum for the exchange of ideas and views, as well as for co-ordinating action in response to particular problems.[8] The second such meeting was held in Brussels in January 1974. The title of the meeting was 'Conference of the Communist Parties of Capitalist Europe'. The format was somewhat different from the earlier meeting, in that 19 parties were represented and that at the highest level (secretaries-general), and in that the theme was wider, leading to a general political declaration. There was no clear unanimity about the Italian thesis, particularly the French party and those from non-community countries were critical. No machinery such as a regional secretariat was set up either at the level of the 'nineteen' or of the 'nine'. It is clear that the time is not ripe for such a development, although the conference was itself an important progress. One difficulty remains. Soviet hostility is still evident towards independent regional groupings of Communists, even if in regard to the community itself Soviet attitudes have evolved considerably.[9]

At all events it is clear that the Communist parties place considerable importance on the community. The conference and colloques referred to illustrate that. Furthermore the quality of the MPs sent to the European parliament both by the PCI and the PCF has been above average, and as we have seen the PCI has sought continuity and experience. Both S.

Amendola and Mr Ansart are in the central committees and praesidium of their respective parties and on the Italian side Signora Iotti is vice-chairman of the chamber group and D'Angelosante is vice-chairman of the senate committee of European affairs.

8.2   Policy

The development of Communist attitudes towards the community has broadly been one of movement from negative externalised opposition towards internalised and constructive opposition. The evolution has, however, been contradictory and at times difficult to follow, after the pattern of two steps forward and one step back, with the Italian party always in the lead. At the outset, European integration was opposed as an emanation of the cold war, an economic NATO under American hegemony, directed against the Socialist countries, definitely dividing Europe into blocs. Initially the Communist parties opposed ratification of the community treaties and Soviet diplomacy attempted to prevent the birth of the communities by proposing wider co-operation within the framework of the United Nations Economic Committee for Europe (ECE). This having failed the Communists denied the reality of the communities, sought to destroy them and predicted their collapse, as part of an objective Marxist analysis of what was considered to be an example of the contradictions within the capitalist system. This was the purport of the original '18 Theses on the Common Market'.[10]

By 1962 Communist economists meeting in Moscow adopted a more nuanced position which recognised the reality of the EEC, but expected its collapse (The 32 Theses). Already the Italians were dissident; they opposed this negative line. As early as 1960, Longo (general secretary of the PCI) had declared: 'European integration was an essential element in the Italian great leap forward'. The PCI recognised that the community had produced benefits for Italy, that its collapse would be economically dangerous and was in any case unlikely. A more flexible response was required placing the accent on a democratic transformation from within. This led to an offensive for representation in community institutions, opened by Longo at the 11th Congress of the PCI in January 1966 and led to the representation of the CGIL in the economic and social committee in 1966 and the PCI in the parliament in March 1969.[11]

An early statement of the objectives of this action was found at the PCI-PCF Conference at San Remo of 1966. This was noteworthy because it led to a common position with the PCF, even if only at the highest level of abstraction and generality. The statements by Longo and Therval at the conference indicated what the policy aims would be: the revision of the treaties; elimination of discrimination in East-West trade; an end to the neo-colonialist policy of association; the replacement of supranationalism by co-operation based on equal rights, at least so long as the community retained its present economic character. This represented an evolution of the French position, but was minimal as far as the PCI was concerned.

In parallel, but even more haltingly there has been an evolution in the Soviet attitude. This has come about under the impact of the general 'détente' policy, Brandt's 'Ostpolitik', the opening of the Conference on Co-operation and Security in Europe and the desire of Russia to increase trade with western Europe. The year 1973 was marked by indications of the new attitude. In a foreign policy speech, Brezhnev recognised the community openly for the first time; on a visit to Moscow, Nørgaard, at that time president in office of the council, was given indications that talks between COMECON and EEC might be held.

The Italian attitude has moved considerably. The aim is no longer to undermine the Community, which is recognised as having benefited Italy and the other member states. It is not only recognised as an objective reality but as a feature of the political landscape, a source of important political decisions and a development which is now irreversible except at an unacceptable cost. Accordingly the PCI seeks to work from within the framework of the community in order to transform the system and democratise it. The PCI sees itself as the representative of an important political force and has the goal of acting as a pole of attraction to the Left at the European level. At his press conference of March 1969, Amendola stated that the aim of the party in entering the parliament was to end the discrimination against them, to learn about the community, to establish contact with the European Left and to defend the interests of the Italian working class.[12]

Feld, in the article already quoted, shows some concern at the apparent contradiction in the PCI position. He considers that a genuine 'learning process' has occurred and that this has led to some revisionism. In his analysis he indicates that the ideological approach to the community would seem to be in contradiction with the desire to participate in a forum where decisions are in fact taken and thus no doubt contribute to the objective reality of the community. In addition, the desire to democratise the community, at least in the way that the PCI has given this policy concrete expression would seem to contradict the apparent rejection of supranationality. This view would seem, even now, to apply more to the PCF and to be diminished in force at least in its ideological aspect by the evolution of the CSPU position. It might, too, be argued that once a new reality is established it becomes for Communists a higher reality (it must be remembered that for Marx capitalism was vaunted as a higher stage of development than feudalism). It must be admitted that the contradiction remains and comes out again and again in careful examination of PCI statements and may in part result from the conflict of unresolved differences with the PCI and in part from the requirement of a minimum of cohesion of the international movement.

It would seem that the party is acting (as is the PCF) on the basis of unspecified objectives of a domestic nature. Representation in the European parliament, together with a strong and at times violent defence of Italian national interests and those of certain groups under economic pressure enhances the respectability and electoral popularity of the party among traditionally unfavourable sections of the population and makes co-operation with other pro-European parties of the Italian left more feasible.[13]

At the conference of Communist parties in Western Europe held in Brussels in late January 1974, Amendola confirmed the thesis of the PCI. He stated: 'The Community has proved itself incapable of giving a unified response to the great problems posed by the world economic crisis . . . such a crisis can only be overcome by a profound democratic transformation. We are struggling for such a transformation because we consider useful the existence of a democratic and multi-national organisation to meet the problems which the individual countries are manifestly incapable of resolving: monetary problems, capital movements, control of the multi-nationals, the energy crisis.'[14]

Naturally the group is no longer dominated by the PCI alone. In spite of the evolution of the PCF, a fact evident in the signature of the Common Programme of the Left with the Socialist party and the left-wing Radicals, which would form the basis for a left-wing government, which would remain a member of the EEC, there remain differences between the two parties, and the Danish party is not a Communist party. It has become more difficult to maintain a coherent line. The French Communists sometimes put up a spokesman who will present a somewhat different view from that of the main group spokesman (usually an Italian). This has been particularly noticeable on institutional matters, such as the budgetary powers of the parliament. In more general terms Mr Ansart stated by way of an opening declaration in the parliament:

We can not sanction any surrender of national sovereignty to a supra-national body, nor do we accept attempts at political unification which accentuate the already noticeable movement towards 'atlanticism' . . . Our frank criticism of the Community does not mean that we refuse any European organisation at all . . . It is a fact that the EEC is dominated by the large financial and multinational companies. The Community must be given a new economic and social content in the interest of all the workers of Europe who have the same basic interests . . . It is essential to remove from the Council and the Commission their present exorbitant powers.[15]

A statement by M. Marchais to the central committee of the PCF somewhat attenuates the rigour of Mr Ansart: '(We accept) . . . delegation of certain competences under the conditions provided for in the Treaty of Rome a precise situation makes it useful.' The Danish SF does not cause any great difficulties within the group. It has its own preoccupations in defending the national interest as it conceives it: to oppose transfers of sovereignty and to limit the impact of the community on Denmark. It pursues this aim, which could be considered to be in conflict with its partners in the group by minimal methods — minimum participation in the work of the institution — a kind of watching brief coupled with statements of principle on major issues. On any issue Mr Dich took the standpoint that he was the representative of the 32 per cent of the Danish electorate who voted 'No' in the referendum. He thus did not provoke dispute within the group, since his aims were purely limited and concentrated on a specific problem.[16]

In the matter of institutional problems the Italian party affirms categorically its acceptance of Article 11 of the Italian constitution which permits the limitation of national sovereignty in favour of international organisations. The party's analysis takes a pragmatic view of the matter in accepting that sovereignty should be limited provided that the content of the policies carried out is acceptable:

It is not therefore a matter of isolating oneself in a closed nationalism, but to see what directions European integration has taken and will take, what contradictions there are within it and how we Communists can act within these contradictions to change the nature of them.

In the same report Signora Iotti makes no effort to attack the supremacy of community law; indeed she appears to quote with approbation a report of the parliament made in 1965 upholding the principle. Her approach seems to be rather to examine the practical consequences of integration in the various sectors:

(we should examine) . . . the main areas of community intervention in order to understand their importance for the economic and social

135

life of each of the states and how far they determine the general direction of a country.

This view contrasts with the position of the PCF which, as we have seen, takes a very limited view of the possibility of delegating national sovereignty; naturally it reproaches the community for its internal contradictions, but its critique is based at a lower level of integration: the defence of national sovereignty. Control of the policies referred to by Signora Iotti: control of these policies is in the hands of the ruling forces of the member states — the monopoly capitalists — and hence the character of the policies hitherto adopted is not acceptable to the Communists. Until the nature of the policies can be changed the Communists will continue to be cautious about supranationalism. Change can only be assured through a thorough democratisation of the decision-making process of the communities. Signora Iotti points out that in the Western European countries the centre and focus of popular control lies in the parliaments. It is thus natural that the European parliament should have the same function at the community level. This view leads to a call for a parliament which will reflect the political forces of the community, including the Communists of all the member states, which would have to be elected by universal suffrage:

> It seems to us Communists that the introduction of the election of the European Parliament by direct universal suffrage, by proportional representation, in accordance with a common electoral law for the whole Community, would serve to introduce into the Community dialectic a new element, which would enable the voice of the great mass of the people to be heard.[17]

Such a body would have to be endowed with significant powers of control over the commission and the council of ministers. Referring to this development Signora Iotti states:

> This would mean the introduction into the dynamics of the community the control of popular sovereignty, all the more necessary as the scope of the communities increases and as veritable supranational powers, quite distinct from national powers, are created.[18]

Only such an introduction of democratic control and popular sovereignty at the community level can make delegation of sovereignty acceptable.[19] This democratisation would also involve other institutions of the community. The PCI recognises that in the long term the rule of unanimity in the council cannot be considered an ideal or democratic solution, but considers it a necessary protection for the smaller and economically weaker member states at the present limited stage of development of the communities. The commission is seen to have declined from its former power and, indeed, to be in practice incapable of exercising the powers of initiative conferred on it by the treaties. To regain its position vis-à-vis the council it must become more representative of the peoples of the member states, which could, in the view of the party, be attained by requiring the commissioners to be elected by the national parliaments on the proposal of their government and ratified by the European parliament. The commission and, indeed, the council must enter into a dialogue with the democratic forces of the community and, here particularly, the trade union movement, which is seen by the Communists to be an integral part of the framework of democratic control. It is interesting to note that the Communists press the responsibility of the commission even under the present incomplete structure. In the debate on the Euratom budget for 1969, Leonardi demanded the resignation of the commission on the grounds that the parliament had rejected the draft budget.[20] It appears that the Communists are no longer hostile to integration *per se,* nor do they even reject the community model as such, but rather seek to reform the concrete policies which have resulted from integration and to introduce into the process greater popular participation. Indeed, it is clear from the note by Signor Fabrinni[21] that the party accepts the major significance of measures such as the introduction of own resources and is prepared to work actively within the changed situation to ensure democratic control of the resources of a supranational character.

As far as the economic policy of the community is concerned, the Communists are in general terms sceptical as to the positive gains which have been realised through the community over its twenty-year life. To them it is unclear to what extent the economic development, intense until about 1963, which has occurred in the community is in fact due to the integration process. Clearer is the fact that the essential inequalities of development as between countries and regions within the community persist and, indeed, have in relative terms increased. The main feature of the community has been a negative integration (the removal of barriers and restrictions) in the interests of the 'free movement' ideology and the positive integration prefigured in the treaties has to a great extent either not materialised or proved to be inadequate to the problems involved: 'The EEC is an incomplete customs union, with some characteristics of an economic union.'[22] This failure has in the view of the party had serious and damaging consequences for the European economy:

In reality the necessary political autonomy is lacking, which would be the sine qua non for positive integration; this fact endangers the results of the negative integration already achieved and creates growing imbalances as between sectors and countries, whilst at the same time removing from the nation states the necessary remedial powers.[23]

The central theme, which animates all criticism of the community, and, to some extent, explains its failures and deficiencies, is the dependence of the community on the United States. The community was conceived in the interests of the United States as part of its 'bloc policy' in the cold war and has not outgrown that status; the failure of European integration lies in its central contradiction, failure to become independent of the United States in any sphere. The breakdown of positive integration can be explained through this fact; all measures being doomed to failure until the community assumes its independence. Until such a time the negative integration measures have aided solely the American multi-national companies to develop their present power and enabled them to escape government or trade union control or regulation:

The operations of American multinationals in the euro-dollar market enable them to escape from the policy of control of the money supply introduced by the member states and thus undermine their effectiveness.[24]

Only when the community accepts this conclusion and acts accordingly will it be possible to achieve genuine integration:

In order to give the community an autonomy and individuality in regard to the outside world, and thus to reduce the margins between the community currencies, it is essential above all to give effect to active common policies, which would be in the interests of the peoples and would have a direct influence on the structures, reducing the deep structural disequilibria . . .[25]

The remedy is thus to pursue a policy independent of the United States and of internal monopolistic interests, which would be acceptable to the broad popular masses. Such a policy would, as we have seen, make possible an economic and monetary union, but that would only be acceptable if it rested on the principle of absolute independence:

The various exchange rates of the Community currencies have been adapted to the exigencies of relations between the different member states and the United States of America; it is this which has led to the deterioration of the internal situation of the community . . .[26]

warns the speaker. The community must realise that the multi-national companies have been directly assisted by community policy and pose a direct threat to any coherent economic policies, either by the community or by governments. Inflation has basically the same cause; the Communists reject the view that wage increases over the last few years are responsible for inflation: indeed, in his speech in the 1971 economic debate, Fabrinni develops the thesis that increased wages lead to increased demand and hence stimulate investment and economic growth. Again the central theme is the dependence on the United States:

I consider that one of the basic causes of the inflationary tendencies which are becoming stronger inside the community, is to be found in the serious economic situation in America, in the growing American balance of payments deficit . . . arises above all from the fact that our countries continue to pay the price of this grave American economic situation.[27]

Equally the Communists reject demands (such as those made by the commission) for stringency in public expenditure, since the structural situation in Italy demands the reverse, for schools, hospitals and so on.[28]

In industrial policy, the Communists demand control of multi-national companies and of monopolies, but at the same time seek the adoption of concrete measures to assist small-scale businesses of an artisan or craft character and demand that the measures taken to fight inflation, particularly those which reduce internal liquidity, should not exclusively harm enterprises of small size.

The Communists consider that a regional policy is an absolute *sine qua non* for the economic and monetary union, without which such a policy would be both unacceptable and doomed to failure:

There is talk of a parallelism between community policy and regional policy, which in fact does not exist. In fact the community policy has widened the gap between rich and poor regions. Given this situation, we think it absurd to introduce an economic and monetary union, which will not only be unfair, but also impossible to create.[29]

139

The party is, however, sceptical about the quality of the regional policies which have been applied hitherto, holding that these have had too much 'a capitalist character, related only to economic efficiency· criteria',[30] which has been ineffective in meeting the real structural problems or improving the lot of the working people of the deprived regions.

Social policy is closely linked to considerations of general economic policy and to political structures and systems. The party seeks to link discussion of the future social policy of the community with more general themes; in its view social policy must form part of the 'parallelism' with economic union and, as with regional policy, must be a *sine qua non* of the success of that union:

> What should we think about the grave possible social consequences of the precarious economic situation of the EEC. In these conditions the social orientations probably mean very little. However, we should redefine our political vision and turn it into action, in defining a new social policy . . .[31]

The theme is that social policy is dependent on the general economic framework and that an economic union without an adequate social policy is unacceptable; therefore new economic and political conceptions are needed to attain the economic union with the necessary parallel social measures. Policy-makers must face the problem; the Communists reject a social policy which merely hides the ills of capitalism or acts to palliate them, an example being measures to aid the handicapped — these measures must not lead to a new exploitation of labour.

The position of the Communists on the agricultural policy has both nationalistic and ideological elements; nationalistic in their strong defence of the interests of Italian farmers, wine-growers and horticulturalists. An example of this is the violent attack made by Signor D'Angelosante on the *Lulling Report* on proposals for a policy for tobacco, on the grounds that the rapporteur had minimised the problem of reconversion of a number of Italian small growers.[32] The Communists' position is ideological because of their attack on the favouritism shown by the CAP to large-scale producers, the heavy and regressive weight of the price policy on the European consumer, and due to the apparent indifference to the fate of the small farmers. In their *Report* to the 'Colloque i Communisti italiani i l'Europa'[33] the authors' analysis of the agricultural policy is critical. In their view, the policy consists of a chaotic collection of regulations, structures and systems determined more by the balance of power in each sector than by principles of rationality or social justice. The overriding constant has been the excessive price policy: 'This high price policy, which the whole population of the community has had to pay, has not aided the great mass of producers.' The high price policy has served to aid only the large-scale producer who has had an efficient infrastructure; indeed, this category has made excessive profits. What is worse, in order to survive, the small farmer has been forced to demand ever higher prices:

> The larger and more developed farms with a low cost of production, adapted to international markets have received enormous subsidies and have thus been greatly strengthened both in respect of their productivity and financial position.

In addition, the price structure has provoked disequilibrium in the various sectors, stimulating excessive production in sectors such as grain and dairy produce and retarding other sectors, such as meat, vegetables, citrus fruit and wine, making necessary imports which bear the regressive levies and displacing workers from the Italian Mezzogiorno in the fruit, wine and tobacco sectors. The Mansholt Plan is not considered to offer the answer to these problems; it does nothing to attack the speculation of the middle man; it does not eliminate the excessive price system, nor does it rule out excessive protectionism, and, indeed, seeks to reinforce the tendency towards large-scale capitalistic farming:[34]

> This has operated in favour of and promoted a certain type of farming on a capitalistic scale, subordinated to the interests of financial and industrial combines.

This, the attack on the price rises and the fact that there had been discrimination as between products, indicates the dissatisfaction of the party with the policy.[35] The alternative, proposed by the Communists, is briefly sketched in the report already quoted of Cipolla and Conte; they propose that the needs of the small enterprise should be met through a wide-ranging system of co-operatives, which would leave the ownership pattern intact and thus avoid the concentration of ownership and the creation of 'capitalist' farming as proposed by the Mansholt Plan in its various versions. Such a system would give flexibility in the face of ongoing technical progress, without creating the social upheaval and expense of the alternative and without giving the advantages to large-scale producers on capitalist lines. This system would enable the small, but co-operative, units to survive without the need for the present high-price system. The system would be freely created by the farmers, but would receive ample, economic, financial and technical aid and encouragement from the state and the community.

The Communist group has shown considerable interest in energy policy. In the debate on the resolution of the committee on energy on short-term measures to meet the energy crisis, the group tabled two amendments, of which one was adopted. Signorini Leonardi and D'Angelosante have recently tabled written questions on Euratom and ECSC research and on the profits of oil companies. The group opposed the report of Signor Pisoni (December 1973 session) which rejected the proposal of the commission to increase the rate of the ECSC levy from 0.29 per cent to 0.30 per cent. In the debate on energy policy in May 1973, Leonardi had already sketched in some of the group's themes:

> The decision to place the ECSC and Euratom treaties in mothballs, when precisely these treaties offered wide scope for action to develop certain sectors of energy, should be recalled ... the real problem is the need to get out of the situation into which the member states have placed themselves, owing to their lack of political will, which can be explained by the fact that they have not seen that their real interests are different from those of the large oil companies on which they have always preferred to depend.

The Italian Communists and their allies are interesting from a number of points of view. Like the Gaullist members — and even more so — they represented an alternative scheme to that of the pro-integration parties. They were an opposition element, but were excluded, or initially desired exclusion, from the assembly. The evolution of the position of the Communists (particularly the PCI) has to an extent fulfilled the hopes of the proponents of the 'engrenage' theory; the objective changes in the European situation brought about by the existence of the communities has brought about a modification in the attitude of the Communists. Recognition of the communities has not been without paradoxes for the PCI and has led to an ambivalence in their approach to integration: at times they appear to accept the concept of integration and even, in the name of democratisation, seem to propose greater integration. At other times one detects a dislike of supranationalism; does this arise out of the capitalist-atlanticist bias of the communities alone? At all events, the Communists have taken the European parliament seriously; they have sent a delegation of high calibre and have played the parliamentary game, acting as a classic opposition — a responsible opposition.

Notes

1 See the *Vernasci Report* adopted on 16 October 1973.

2 The PSIUP (Italian Socialist Party of Proletarian Unity) held one seat in the parliament until the renewal of the Italian delegation after the 1972 election.

3 The Socialist People's party (SF) was formed by Mr Aksel Larsen (the then leader of the Communist party) in 1956 in protest against Soviet intervention in Hungary and rapidly took most of the Communist electorate. It is a non-Stalinist Marxist party, independent of Moscow. In the 1972 referendum it strongly opposed EEC membership. See my article 'Scandinavian Referenda and the EEC' in *European Review,* Spring 1973.

4 Situation as of February 1974: Bulletin of the European Parliament, list of members.

5 Amendola: *The Italian Communists* reprinted in the Foreign Bulletin of the PCI, no. 1, 1972.

6 Amendola: Journal Officiel Annexe *Debats*, no. 113, March 1969.

7 The conference was jointly sponsored by CESPE (Centre for Economic and Political Studies) and the PCI parliamentary groups from 23-25 November 1971. The reports covered integration, economic matters, agriculture, monetary policy, etc. Their authors were both from the European parliament and the national party, published by CESPE under the title *I Communisti italiani e l'Europa.*

8 Details in the *Foreign Bulletin* of the PCI, no. 1, 1972, p. 112.

9 For details of the conference see interviews with Jean Kanapa (PCF) and M. Segre (PCI) in *Le Soir,* 26 January 1974, p. 5, and *Le Monde,* 29 January 1974, pp. 1, 4. For Amendola's speech see *L'Unita,* 28 January 1974, pp. 1, 5. Outside the conference members of the commission met both Ms Marchais and Berlinguer.

10 See G. Zellentin, *Die Kommunisten und die Einigung Europas,* Athaneum Verlag 1964.

11 See Griffith, *Communism in Europe,* MIT Press 1964, pp. 301-84.

12 *L'Unita,* 22 March 1969, p. 3.

13 See J. Leich, 'The Italian Communists and the European Parliament', JCMS vol. 10.

14 *L'Unita,* 28 January 1974, p. 5.

15 Ansart: Annexe *Débats*, no. 164 of 4 July 1974, p. 111.

16 For example on the agreement with Norway, Mr Dich intervened to demand whether Denmark could herself have obtained such a favourable agreement if she had stayed outside the EEC.

17 Iotti, Sovranita Nazionale e Instituzioni Communitarie.

18 Iotti, loc. cit.

19   See Leonardi, *Un Alternativa per i Paesi del Mercato commune.*

20   Leonardi, J. O. *Débats*, no. 116, July 1969, p. 51.

21   Il Bilancio della CEE e i potari del Parlamento europeo.

22   Leonardi, Il processo d'integrazione nella CEE, Report to the CESPE Colloque, Rome, 23-25 November 1971.

23   Leonardi, loc. cit., p. 22.

24   Leonardi, loc. cit., p. 47.

25   Leonardi, in the Debate on the Economic situation of the Community, J. O. *Débats*, February 1972, no. 146, p. 115.

26   Leonardi, loc. cit., p. 114.

27   Fabrinni, *Débats*, 21 April 1971, p. 99.

28   See Fabrinni, loc. cit., p. 100.

29   Leonardi, Débat sur La Question Orale 13/71, Politique régionale des Structures, *Débats*, no. 146, p. 89.

30   G. Sabbata, Report *La politica regionale della CEE.*

31   Mme Carettoni Romagnoli, in the Debate on the Orientations for a Social Policy for the Community, 13 June 1972.

32   See J. O. *Débats*, no. 116, July 1969, p. 119 ff.

33   Cipolla and Conte, *La Crisi della politica agricola della CEE.*

34   See especially Point 3 of the Resolution adopted by PCI group in the European parliament, meeting with PCI Agricultural Experts, Rome, 27 October 1970.

35   See Cipolla, in the Debate on Agricultural Prices and Structures, *Débats*, 22 April 1971, pp. 188-90.

9 The Conservative Group

The Treaty of Accession provided for 36 British members of the European parliament, just as for the other large states. Discussions through 'the usual channels' established that there should be 18 Conservatives, 15 Labour, two Liberals and one cross-bench peer. It was also established that the delegation should include members of both Houses of Parliament. Since the Labour party at its meeting of 13 December 1973 voted against sending a delegation (134 votes to 88), the Conservative party was faced with a decision as to whether it would itself fill the Labour quota or leave them vacant. The second course was followed, both as being fairer and having a greater symbolic impact.

This decision in itself had an impact on the composition of the Conservative delegation, in that more peers had to be sent, in order to avoid situations where too many MPs would be absent from Westminster at once. Altogether the appointment of the delegation was a delicate political operation. The different regions, expertise and political nuances had to be combined within the delegation. Most regions are included: Northern Ireland (Mr Pounder), Scotland (Mr Brewis), the Midlands (Sir John Peel and Mr Normanton), East Anglia (John Hill), Wales (Sir Brandon Rhys Williams). There is a fair degree of middle-rank ministerial experience and most of the main aspects of community policy are covered: agriculture (Scott-Hopkins, Lord St Oswald), industry (Normanton), finance (Pounder), social affairs (Lady Elles), legal issues (Sir Derek Walker-Smith). The delegation contains also one anti-marketeer (Sir Derek), one sceptic (Mr Pounder) and a convinced and experienced 'European', Sir Tufton Beamish.

The other major question was to what group, if any, should the Tories affiliate. In spite of the close relations which had been established between Heath and Pompidou, the UDE could be excluded for political reasons — such a decision would not have been well received in the UK. More likely was decision to join the Christian Democrats. As the confessional aspect of Christian Democracy has receded, these parties have become more of the centre-right type of party that the Conservative party also is. However, the confessional aspect is not completely lost, especially the identification with the Catholic Church. Furthermore, the Italian party considers the Conservatives too 'laissez-faire' in economic matters. It is true that conservatism does represent a distinct political current, which did not exist in the community of the six, but which has its place in Britain and Scandinavia. Also, given the powers of group leaders in the parliament, the Conservatives would have more freedom of manoeuvre if they were not submerged in a larger group such as the Christian Democrats. Such considerations led to the formation of a Conservative group; however a 'broad' group might have been envisaged taking in some of the French Liberals but tradition and likely disagreement over agricultural policy excluded this possibility. It is clear that the time is not ripe for a regrouping exercise. This left only a 'small' Conservative group, which would be uninational or binational (without Norway). The presence of the Danes avoided the formation of a second purely national group. At first the group consisted of 18 British Conservatives and two Danish Conservatives. The present composition of the group is: [1]

British Conservative party	18
Danish Conservative People's party	1
Danish Centre-Democrats	1
Total	20

Recently there have been changes in the UK delegation. This was necessary because of the fact that after the February 1974 Election some members were no longer MPs at Westminster. Mr Pounder and Lord Chelwood (Sir Tufton Beamish) have been replaced by Mrs Peggy Fenner and Mr Howell. Labour remains unrepresented.

The group requires little formal organisation, and can work in one language. There is a four-member bureau, consisting of a president and three vice-presidents (two MPs, one peer and one Dane). The plenary group meeting is the decision-making body, but, in practice, the group leader and bureau members play a strong role. The group held 41 meetings in 1973. There are no committees or working parties. Individual members are given responsibility for an area of policy (Mr Scott Hopkins for agriculture, Sir Derek for legal matters, Sir Tufton Beamish for the work of the political committee, etc.), and the task of liaison with their Christian Democrat colleagues in the same field. Longer-term planning is carried out at the study days held by the group (3 in 1973) and through the research department of Conservative central office which has taken quite an interest in community matters.

The group does not have the wide external links that the Socialist, Christian Democrat and Communist groups have. The British and Danish Conservative parties participate in the work of the European Union of Conservatives, where links can be developed not only with Conservative parties as such, but also with the German CDU/CSU and the French UDR. As previously indicated, this union is very loose in structure and diverse in terms of membership. In the European parliament itself, the group has developed close but informal liaison with the Christian Democrats. There is a joint bureau meeting every session and there has been at least one joint plenary group meeting. At the committee level the liaison is carried out by the member responsible for the sector.

The group secretariat consists of A Grade officials (these correspond to administrative class officials in the British civil service) and B Grade officials. The staff of all the groups is to be considerably reinforced under the 1974 budget.

The group, at least its British members, arrived with a very clear brief to shake up the European parliament which was seen as over-rigid and legalistic, by an injection of Westminster methods and British pragmatism. The parliament as an institution should become more aware of itself and adopt an aggressive stance: 'We take as our motto: "silence gives consent" – that we are entitled to do anything not expressly forbidden . . . The power we have may be a negative one, but so it has always been in the formative years of parliaments. But it is a real power just the same, and there for the taking.'[2] At the first part session after enlargement the group tabled a memorandum on reform of the parliament. This was indeed a bold (and not unreservedly welcomed) move for entirely new members.[3] This memorandum proposed a 13-man committee to report on procedural changes within three months. The memorandum itself contained numerous suggestions, most of which would have brought the procedures closer to the Westminster model. It proposed a question time (which was at the time already under consideration), SO9 type debates and adjournment type debates, a simplification of the consultation procedure for minor and technical matters.

On institutional matters the group has adopted a pragmatic approach. Its line has been to 'wait and see'. It has not developed any overall blueprint for European union or plan for a European government. On the other hand it has not rejected such ideas outright. Its view of the institutions themselves is pragmatic: do they work? The group supports the commission because only the commission can provide the impulsion and the co-ordination to the community machine. If it does not do so it is attacked. Similarly, the group will attack the inaction of the council, but does not systematically attack a major cause, the unanimity rule. If the council 'delivers the goods' the procedure does not matter. The group always seems to concentrate on the content of policy, rather than on form or method. The Danish Conservative party held, at the time of the referendum on EEC entry, the most advanced position on institutional matters of any of the Danish parties. It took the logical view that political co-operation could not be separated from economic co-operation; it took a developmental view of the institutions. It might be that the Danish Conservative party is somewhat more advanced in its thinking on institutional questions than the British party. This fact does not seem to have created any difficulties within the group.

On the powers of the parliament, which have been a major issue in 1973, the group has adopted a cautious, realistic, but not negative position. An increase in the powers of the parliament is given priority over direct elections. No immediate revision of the treaty is sought, but rather in the first instance a more energetic use of the existing powers of the parliament. The memorandum states: 'The Commission should be reminded of its dependence on the Parliament by more frequent use of the motion of censure.'[4] On budgetary powers, the memorandum argues that '. . . the budgetary powers granted to the Parliament under the Treaty of Luxemburg are there to be used and may well constitute the most powerful weapon in the Parliament's armoury.'[5] When the commission presented its proposals for the extension of the budgetary powers of the parliament in June 1973,[6] it rapidly became clear that the key to parliamentary control over the budget lay not in the budget itself, but in power to approve legislation with financial consequences fixing the bulk of the budget well in advance of the annual budgetary procedure. Indeed it was just this realisation on the part of the council which lay at the base of the distinction drawn by the Treaty of Luxemburg between expenditure 'necessarily resulting' and the so-called non-obligatory expenditure. The commission proposed a vague second reading proposal for the legislation with financial consequences, against which M. Spénale proposed that the parliament should have the last word, albeit by a three-quarter majority. The Conservative group took up a middle position. It believed that the present proposals were only a first step and that some initial strengthening of the parliament's powers was vital, but that the Spénale last word proposal was at this time excessive and unrealistic, if not over-rigid and legalistic. It preferred to create an open-minded dialogue with the council, where neither party would have the last word, thus condemning them to agree if there was to be any progress. The group also considered the proposal to increase the ceiling of VAT which could go to the community budget prematurely. The right of overall rejection of the budget was considered too rigid, but was accepted when coupled with the right (in fact far more radical) of the right to reject specific chapters. Great emphasis was also laid on the creation of an audit court, which the Conservative group had first put forward as an amendment to the interim report of M. Spénale at the July 1973 session. Mr Kirk said:

'Can one imagine that at this stage of the development of the Communities, whatever guarantees might be inserted, the Council would accept and the Commission recommend to the Council, a decision which would give to the Parliament alone the final control on all legislative matters.' He went on to say, 'We are not prepared to leave the final word to the Council; if we ourselves can not expect the last word, let no one have it.' In his view this meant that 'we must find another means of co-decision'. This was stated by Mr Pounder to be 'an automatic and well-defined conciliation procedure'.[7] Sir Derek Walker-Smith however went further in taking an even more limitative position: 'In the particular context of the European Parliament, its functions must harmonise with those of the national parliaments . . . no solution is conceivable which does not have the support of the national parliaments. To have that support a solution must be found which gives them the right of participation which belongs to them.'[8]

The Conservative group (in spite of its at least nominal multi-national composition) has been closely identified with the British government, and indeed much of its concern has been directed towards the defence of the British national interest, both in a positive and a negative sense. In the negative sense it has attacked aspects of the common agricultural policy (CAP) and certain harmonisation proposals which do not take into account the British situation or which have been heavily attacked in the United Kingdom, such as proposals for harmonisation of beer and bread, driving licences, company law. In a positive sense it has advocated strongly regional policy and the research activities of ECSC in the coal field.

The CAP and its ramifications in economic and trade policy have been a constant preoccupation of the group. Defining a consistent and logical policy towards the CAP has not been without difficulties. First of all, the British government has formally accepted the CAP as part of the entry negotiations. Then there is the fact that the CAP has been a prime target of opponents of the community: it is alien to our system, bureaucratic, it has ended the 'cheap food policy', led to excessive and absurd surpluses which are destroyed. It is protectionist and harmful to the Third World, a source of friction in our relations with the USA. Britain needs no structural policy except in a few limited areas, such as hill farming and the high price policy is needed to maintain economically marginal, but politically important, small-scale agriculture on the continent. Against this, certain sectors of British agriculture stand to benefit from the price policy of the CAP and some group members have rural constituencies or have close ties with farming. Thus the group accepts the CAP in principle, attacks excessive price increase proposals, but supports price increases where cost inflation justifies them, supports structural policy, particularly

F

on the continent in the hope that in time a more rational price policy will be possible. It also supports the manipulation of price relativities in order to orientate production away from the surplus dairy sector towards meat production. In respect of two products, sugar and butter (from New Zealand) which were the cause of prolonged wrangling during the negotiations and subsequently in parliament, the group considers that it has a moral duty to ensure that the interests of the commonwealth producers are safeguarded. Thus it was that Mr Scott-Hopkins took an extremely critical view of the commission's 1973 price proposals and proposed an alternative resolution to that of the rapporteur, Mr de Koning. He demanded that the house should examine 'what the price proposals would mean in real terms, not only for the farmer, but also for the consumers, for the housewife . . . they would provoke inflation and surpluses.'[9] He did not contest that a 1 per cent price rise had only a 0.1 per cent repercussion on final prices, but reminded the house that even this was enough for pensioners and those living on fixed incomes. He said that 'only a 3 per cent rise in Community agricultural prices could be economically justified'. At the same time: 'I have absolutely no desire to destroy or damage the CAP'. The Conservative amendment, which was in fact an alternative motion, asked for the price rises to be withdrawn, an end to monetary compensations, a vigorous structural policy, a reduction of VAT on agricultural products and inputs and a change in relative prices so as to encourage beef production. Lady Elles (speaking in her own name) went as far as to indicate that the CAP had been designed at a time when in some countries almost 50 per cent of the work force was on the land, with this no longer so a new policy was needed. John Hill and Mr Brewis emphasised rather the needs of certain types of farming: hill farmers and beef producers. In the 1974 price debate, Mr Scott-Hopkins had become institutionalised: he was the general rapporteur. In any case, as he himself stated, the explosion of costs led to different considerations: even in the middle of a general election campaign he was prepared to advocate a moderate general price increase, but not as high as most of the other groups would have preferred.

The group has placed great emphasis on external relations: with the United States, with the commonwealth 'associable' countries, with the state trading countries. In his speech on the sixth general report, Mr Kirk called this aspect one of the major problems for the year: 'The importance for the Community not only of its enlargement, but of the new situation in which we find ourselves in 1973 comes in large measure from its external relations . . . These run from the renewal of the Yaoundé Convention and the invitation to be given to certain Commonwealth countries to join that Convention . . . to culminate in the negotiations with the USA

150

which will open towards the end of the year.'[10]

The group has followed carefully all proposals for harmonisation, most of which were drafted prior to enlargement. It has often attacked what Mr Kirk called, in introducing his oral question 186/73 'harmonisation mania, harmonisation for harmonisation's sake'. The group accepts harmonisation to accomplish the treaty goals of free movement of goods and services. In particular the group criticised the proposals on beer and bread. In the field of fiscal harmonisation the commission had not taken into account the UK zero rating system in proposing its VIth Directive on VAT.

On economic matters the group has placed emphasis on the fight against inflation and the realisation of economic and monetary union (Sir Brandon Rhys Williams was rapporteur on that question). However it has had to defend the continued floating of the pound. As in the UK, growth was the keystone. In the debate on the economic situation in 1973, Sir Brandon stated that the community 'should overcome the limits to growth'. There has been a strong insistence on the creation of a community regional fund as was agreed at the Paris Summit Conference (1972). Throughout the debates in parliament stretching through the summer and autumn of 1973, the group was firm that there should be a large fund, which would concentrate aid to three countries: Ireland, Italy and Britain. It was also essential that the criteria for the distribution of aid should take into account the needs of declining industrial areas. Social policy initiatives have been supported by schemes such as ECSC readaptation aid in the coal and steel industries, social fund activities and so on. All these (and the regional fund) were seen, irrespective of their own merits, as a return for the 'contribution' to the CAP. Another area to attract attention was competition policy. In this case the group developed a distinctive position. The commission presented a proposal for a regulation implementing Article 86 of the EEC treaty analogous to Regulation 17/62 implementing Article 85. This would impose a prior control of mergers, which would have to be notified to the commission if the combined turnover exceeded a certain level. This the group fought strongly. Sir Derek argued both that the legal basis for the proposal was defective and that it was economically harmful. He argued that its spirit was opposed to size and the creation of new viable firms would be blocked. He argued that mergers were often beneficial and that there should be no *a priori* prejudice against size. Furthermore the procedures were arbitrary, complicated and slow such as to create business uncertainty. In this line the group obtained the support of the DEP group which, however, went further so as to argue in the words of Mr Cousté: 'The Commission has become the accomplice of American power in preventing the formation of European scale enterprises.' This was an overtly political note avoided by the Conservative group.

The group showed great interest in energy policy, a vital subject as 1973 was to show. The group favoured more intense action to promote co-operation in the energy field and already in May 1973, Lord Bessborough was demanding 'immediate aid to coal production and in the longer term the conservation of the potential of Community coal production'. The group opposed the majority view of the parliament that the ECSC levy should be fixed at 0.29 per cent rather than at 0.30 per cent as proposed by the commission, and in fact, tabled an amendment to restore the commission's proposal.

As we have seen the group entered the parliament with 'élan' and reforming zeal. It has been active in most policy areas and has made full use of the procedural devices available in the parliament such as question time, written questions, amendments and oral questions with debate. To an extent, though, it has been absorbed in the machine: many of its reforming ideas were in part accepted, but less talk is now heard of reform. Either the present degree of reform is adequate or the group has learned to work the system. After one week in parliament, Mr Kirk already commented on the power of the groups and the influence of the group leaders. The dominance of the British in the group has been marked: rarely have the Danish members been spokesmen and policy has mostly reflected British concerns. There has been no evidence of disagreement within the group nor have Danish members as individuals brought forward a distinctive point of view (as has often been the case in the Socialist group). Mr Scott-Hopkins did indicate in his speech during the 1973 agricultural prices debate that he spoke only for the majority of his group on certain points; it may well be that this in fact meant that the Danes were not in total agreement on all points. So far, with just over one year's experience of the group, the most that can be said is that it has got the feel of the parliament, introduced some new dynamism, more cut and thrust and has developed distinctive policies on some issues, such as institutional questions and agriculture.

Notes

1 European parliament list of members.
2 Mr. Kirk, Debates, 16 January, pp. 13-14.
3 Memorandum of 16 January 1973 on the procedures and practices of the European parliament.
4 Memorandum, paragraph 35.
5 Idem, paragraph 38.

6   Document Com (73) 1000 of 6 June 1973.
7   Debates, Special Session of 4 and 5 October 1973.
8   Debates, idem.
9   Debates, 5 April 1973, p. 90.
10   Debates, February 1973.

10 Unaffiliated Members

The main topics which we are considering are the groups and their functioning. However, it is useful to consider the position of those members who do not join any group, because this can give us valuable indications about the role of the groups. In other places, some scattered information has been given about members who have not belonged to any group; at the risk of some repetition it is intended to give a full account of their position. It is certainly possible that the treaty-makers expected that the national delegations or individual members would play the major role in the functioning of the common assembly. As we have seen, though, it was not long before groups were officially recognised and came to dominate the organisation of the assembly and its debates. Within the first session the position of the groups had become so dominant that a member who did not join a group would be at a severe disadvantage in the work of the assembly. As we have seen, these principles were reintroduced and even strengthened in the European parliament after 1958.

The rules of procedure of the parliament, together with its customs, impose serious disabilities upon the individual unaffiliated member. He will never be elected president or vice-president of the parliament, nor will he be either directly or indirectly represented in the 'bureau élargi' or the 'Comité des Présidents' and thus will have no influence over the agenda of the parliament, the organisation of the debates, the drafting of the budget or the organigramn of the parliament. Unaffiliated members are not excluded from the committees of the parliament, but tend to be appointed to the less important committees and are not appointed to the bureau of a committee. In the early days it was possible for unaffiliated members to be named rapporteurs (there were, it must be admitted, only 2 cases out of 110 reports and 30 complementary reports in the common assembly). Since 1958 this does not happen. Although the rules of procedure permit any member to table a draft resolution or an amendment, it is clear that less political weight will attach to the initiatives of unaffiliated members. As far as oral questions for debate ('interpellations') are concerned, the individual is at a real disadvantage; oral questions for debate can only be tabled by a committee, political group, or by five members. Only where the question is the initiative of a group is a debate accorded as a right. As we have seen, Article 31 of the rules allows the spokesmen of the groups to claim priority in debate; in addition, Article

28 of the rules permits the regulation of the time for which members may speak. In practice this involves a smaller allotment (say ten minutes as against twenty minutes) to the individual speaker. In addition to these procedural disabilities, the unaffiliated member loses the benefit of what has been called 'ideological teamwork'.[1] The member does not have the support of like-minded colleagues; his initiatives are thus weaker and less likely to be effective, both in terms of their impact on the parliament, upon other community institutions, and upon public opinion. The member also lacks the aid of the secretariat, which is provided by the groups; this can be invaluable in researching a question and formulating a proposal. The net result is that both in political and procedural terms the unaffiliated member is weaker in influence than a member of a group. That is, the system works against him.

In view of these serious disabilities, it would seem that a member would only choose that status on the grounds of overriding political necessity, such as might arise from the incompatible relationship between his own political position and that of the existing groups. A member might not join a group because he opposed the views of the existing groups on integration or because he was unable to join any group on the grounds of more classical ideological divisions or because domestic political reasons militated against his joining the most logical group.

Here one should distinguish between pure 'individual' members and what one can call 'embryo' or aspirant groups. This means a number of members who would wish to form a new group, but are excluded from so doing by their lack of numbers. Such members will act as a group and will consider that they are the victims of discrimination. Some accommodation must be made, giving them the 'halfway' position of a 'quasi-group'. In the early days of the common assembly the small group of members of various labels (e.g. 'Républicains-sociaux') who represented the Gaullist philosophy acted as a group, even though their numbers never exceeded four (as against the nine required to form an official group). In the last period of the common assembly there were at times no more than two members: Michel Debré and Monsieur Estève (from the national assembly). For one session, Monsieur Debré was the sole Gaullist member of the assembly. In these conditions one could scarcely talk of any kind of group behaviour. After the election of 1958, at which the new Gaullist party, the UNR, made sweeping gains in the wake of General de Gaulle's return to power, the UNR members of the European parliament joined the Liberal group as 'apparentes', a position with administrative rather than political significance. Over the next five years the tension grew between the UNR members and the rest of the group and the UNR 'apparentes' came more and more to be a group within a group, finally, as we have indicated, aspiring to break away and succeeding in that aim, constituting the UDE, a new official group.

The position of the Italian PCI members who entered the parliament in March 1969 was similar, but with important differences. The PCI members were, as the UNR, a single national group (but did contain other Italian parties, such as the PSIUP), but, as we have seen, it had supranational aspirations – to join with Communists and others from other member countries if such should be appointed to the parliament. There was no possible 'apparente solution', both for reasons of views on integration and on general ideological grounds; the rejection was mutual – no group wanted the PCI. The PCI, unlike the Gaullists, was from the start militant about its position, denouncing the discrimination, of which it considered itself the victim, in its first public statement in the parliament. It was unable to obtain satisfaction in the way that the Gaullists did.[2] However, it did obtain some 'facilities' on both the administrative and procedural levels, which reduces the discrimination and gives it the status of a 'quasi-group'. In this case (as was to some extent true of the Gaullists), the problem arose over the inability and refusal of the members in question to adapt themselves to the existing group structure. The PCI and the Gaullists were in the ultimate unacceptable to any other group (it is, for example, likely that the Gaullists would in any case have been expelled from the Liberal group – if not in 1963, then in 1965 when the French boycott crisis arose).

For other members the case has been different; they did not aspire to form a new group, nor did they, as do the PCI and, to some extent, the Gaullists, consider themselves to represent a separate political 'tendency'. For these members their unaffiliated position has been merely 'negative' in the sense of being a rejection of the existing groups and not even necessarily a rejection by them. Such members have been few and there are at the present time as many as there have ever been in this category. There are three members who can be called 'genuine' unaffiliated members. After the Dutch general election of 1971, the second chamber sent Hr Engwirda, a Demokraten '66, or D'66, member to the European parliament. This party has been called technocratic in that its main aim seems to be a determination to avoid ideological classifications and sterile political disputes and to promote efficiency in government. Its dislike of ideology would tend to make it refuse to join any of the European groups, which are, after all, differentiated on ideological lines. Its critique of ideology and political confrontation would prevent alliance (through mutual distaste) with the Socialists and yet its emphasis on modernity, progress and efficiency, irrespective of political divisions, prevents alliance with Conservative elements in the parliament. Since the Belgian elections of 1971, the delegation to the European parliament has included two FDF/RW members, Messieurs Thiry (Senate) and Outers (House of Representatives). The FDF/RW is the union of the francophone groups in Wallonia and Brussels, whose main objective has been to protect the linguistic interests of French speakers in Wallonia and particularly in Brussels, a linguistically contested area, and to defend the economic interests of the declining industrial area of Wallonia. This party has no obvious counterparts in other member states and no obvious position in the ideological spectrum at the European level. In view of its interest in the defence of francophone interests it has been suggested, and considered by the party, that it should affiliate to the UDE. However, this must be excluded, as long as the UDE remains exclusively French and, it may be pointed out, that if it became supranational then its interest for a francophone party would disappear. At the present time, the FDF/RW cannot for domestic reasons join with a party so closely identified with the interests of France, since to do so would imply that the party wished to abandon Belgium in favour of annexation to France. Such might not be the intention, but such an intention would readily be inferred.

It might be argued that the FDF/RW members could have no general European interest in view of their regional base and specific, sectional policy. However, aspects of the policy of the European communities have great importance to Wallonia — the subsidies to coal mining given by the ECSC; energy policy in general, as it is this policy which determines the place given to coal production in supplying the total energy needs of the community; regional policy (or, more precisely, the lack of a policy); transport policy. One can identify clear areas of interest for a regional party within the European context. There is also some evidence that the party has a view of Europe, a regionalised Europe giving greater strength to units below the level of the nation state.

The exclusion of the Italian MSI members from the Liberal group after the 1972 Italian elections has made them involuntary and isolated non-affiliated members. They are independents because they can join no group. They have never ceased protesting about their situation, but for the rest have not been markedly active. A certain number of other members have for a short period been non-inscrit: the Irish Fianna Fáil, Dick Taverne (in this case due to the desire of the Socialist group not to anger the British Labour party), M. Muller, a French reformateur who later joined the Liberal group and Mr Nyborg from Mr Glistrup's 'Fremskridt-sparti' in Denmark. These members have been fairly inactive.

Lord O'Hagan has had a real vocation as a 'non-inscrit'. As the representative of the British cross-bench peers, his constitutional position would preclude group membership. Beyond that he has made an advantage of this: his independence is useful and enables him to play a role which would otherwise be difficult. He has, at least in the terms of questions — both written (well over half the total number asked since accession) and oral — to commission and council, become the most active member of the parliament. Given the disadvantages of a non-inscrit from a procedural point of view he has played an active role in the social affairs committee and the plenary, speaking in a wide range of debates. He has made the rights of under-privileged groups such as migrant workers his particular interest, as well as seeking to attack those aspects of community policies which lead to a bad image in Britain and to publicise the positive aspects of community membership.

As far as activity in the parliament is concerned, it seems that at least Hr Engwirda[3] and possibly also the two FDF/RW members taken together are more active than the backbench members of the groups. It is true that each member belongs only to one committee: Monsieur Outers to the legal committee, Monsieur Thiry to the committee for the association with Turkey and Herr Engwirda to the finance and budgetary committee. This would not seem to be in accordance with their interests; except in the case of the general interest of D'66 in 'efficiency' (but not with Hr Engwirda's personal interest in development policy). Both Hr Engwirda and the FDF/RW members taken together have intervened in all the important debates since their arrival (regional policy, the preparation of the summit conference, debate on the preparation of the third UNCTAD conference). For example, in the July 1972 session, Hr Engwirda intervened three times and tabled several amendments. In the debate programme of the commission for 1972, Hr Engwirda intervened to make a serious critique of the priorities of the commission. Monsieur Outers intervened in the July 1972 Session in the debate on the preparation of the summit conference. Monsieur Thiry intervened in February in the debate on the oral question to the council on regional policy.

These members have tended to concentrate on certain topics of interest either to them personally or to their party and its electors. The first speech of Monsieur Thiry was on regional policy.[4] Here he indicated the importance of the topic to Wallonia as a whole and to the Sambre-Meuse valley in particular. He sought to introduce two elements into the debate, which might be considered to arise from the outlook of his party: a greater emphasis on regional aid to non-agricultural depressed areas, which have hitherto been neglected; more autonomy for the regions in areas of policy associated with regional policy, that is, giving to them greater freedom of action and initiative in relations with the community organs without regard to the national state. In the debate on the report of

Hr Müller on the summit conference,[5] Monsieur Outers expressed a minimal view of the institutional problem; for him it was important not to get lost in a quarrel between conflicting schools of thought as to the process of integration. It would be more valuable to use the existing institutions' powers and competences more fully in order to solve the concrete problems facing the community. This would seem to be an almost Gaullist view of the institutional question.

Hr Engwirda made his maiden speech in the parliament in the debate on the programme of the commission for 1972.[6] Here he attacked the commission for the low priority accorded to what he considered two vital problems: a policy for the environment, especially in view of the pessimistic reports from the club of Rome and others; and the relations between the developing nations and the community. These themes were to recur in other interventions of Hr Engwirda. In the debate on the preparation of the third UNCTAD conference[7] he asked for a less exclusive and restrictive policy to assist those countries outside the Yaoundé Convention and, in particular, the least developed countries both within and outside the association system. In the debate on the *Müller Report*,[8] he returned to the question of priority and denounced the absolute priority which seemed to have been given to institutional progress and sought to include an amendment to strengthen the demand for an environmentally sound industrial policy and a general commitment to environmental protection, a demand he made more specific in the debate on the communication of the commission on an environmental policy for the community.[9] As to his more general approach, in his maiden speech he employs with approval the phrase 'Si L'europe sait vraiment être pragmatique . . . ' and at another point: 'In modern politics, you must have the courage to look the facts in the face and to base decisions to a great extent on the results of scientific research.' This indicates a pragmatic, technocratic style based on realism and a dislike of ideology.

It should be noted that Hr Engwirda subsequently lost his seat in the Dutch Second Chamber and was replaced by Mr Eisma, who is affiliated to the socialist group. Over time the technocratic character of D'66 has changed.

One might conclude that unaffiliated members find no bar to activism and, indeed, may be more active and that they have a tendency to make certain areas of policy their special fief.

Notes

1   Monsieur Dewulf, in conversation with the author.

2   This problem has, of course, now been solved by the change in the rules, enabling the formation of a Communist group.

3   His successor, Mr Eisma, is now affiliated to the Socialist group.

4   See: Debate on the Oral Question no. 13/71 to the Council on Regional Policy, at J.O. *Débats*, no. 146 of 9 February 1972, pp. 93-4.

5   See: J.O. *Débats*, no. 152 of 5 July 1972, pp. 167-8.

6   See: Debate on the Programme of Activity of the Commission for 1972, J.O. *Débats*, no. 146 of 10 February 1972, pp. 158-60.

7   J.O. *Débats*, no. 152 of 4 July 1972, pp. 94-6.

8   J.O. *Débats*, no. 152 of 5 July 1972, pp. 168-70.

9   J.O. *Débats*, no. 152 of 6 July 1972, pp. 240-1.

11 Comparative Cohesion of the Groups

We have up to now studied the groups individually, in order to discern their particular characteristics in respect of organisation, working methods and policy. However, no group operates in a vacuum; each reacts to what other groups do and is in its turn reacted to. Opinions and policy positions emerge through a complex process of interactions among the groups. The first comparative point we should examine about the groups is their cohesion. All political parties are in some sense coalitions, although this may be less true of the community countries with their multiplicity of parties than of the Anglo-Saxon democracies. Even if it is less true of the individual parties in the member states, it certainly is true of the political groups in the European parliament. As we have had occasion to remark, some of the groups contain a very wide spectrum of political opinion, with consequent difficulties of consistency and cohesion. Even the most cohesive group has some internal adjustment to make. It is worth remembering that the question of cohesion or unity has a rather different character than in the national parliaments. In one sense there is more pressure (or perhaps incentive would be a better word) to conform to the majority view within a group. This is due to the character of the parliament as an institution; it is weak in decision-making powers or of powers of control which have any legal sanction or finality. It is a consultative or persuasive organ, which imposes limitations upon the level of discord which can exist within it if it is to retain credibility; in other words, the pressure is towards unanimity to impress and persuade other institutions which have the power of decision, by the weight of opinion within the parliament; disunity makes the opinions of the parliament easier to ignore. With this in mind, together with the fact that a would-be dissenter can console himself with the fact that the parliament makes few final decisions, it is easier to reach unity than would be the case in national parliaments.

One could equally argue that there is less pressure to conform. A member may feel that he is more entitled to follow his own dictates than in national political decisions precisely because the decisions of the European parliament are rarely final or legally binding and so of lesser importance. To fail to toe the party line cannot have the same consequences as at the national level. The position of the government — its survival or defeat — is not at stake, hence the member is not under the same pressure to conform; nor is refusal to conform likely to render the member liable to sanctions such as loss of the whip or expulsion from the party, loss of ministerial prospects, and so on, as is often the case at the national level.

There is much force in both lines of argument. *A priori* one might expect more independence in the European parliament than in the national parliaments, but this does not in fact seem to be the case. This could be due to the basic 'Europeanness' of the groups (with the exception of the UDE, who can unite in opposition to supranationalism) and self-denying ordinance on other issues, such as social and economic questions, based on the realisation that disunity would weaken the influence of the parliament. One could imagine that issues which divide the groups on the national level (such as those which give rise to 'right' and 'left-wings' of national parties) are tacitly avoided on the European plane precisely in order to avoid conflict. However, as we shall see, the level of disunity within the groups in the European parliament is on the whole no higher than that found in the national parties.

Cohesion and unity are difficult notions to define. To a large extent any evaluation must be subjective. One can at any rate scarcely disagree with Henig and Pinder[1] that 'the Socialists have been the most cohesive of any national or supranational group'. If any group gives the appearance of a party group in a national parliament then it is the Socialists. The group has been dominated, at least since the decline of the French SFIO after 1958, by the German SPD, who at present account for 16 of the 37 members. The remaining members are divided among seven national parties, of which the Italian Republican party and the 'Parti-social Démocrate Luxembourgeois' count only one member. In the early days, as we have seen, the SPD had misgivings about the European integration movement, but these had been overcome by 1957 and the party voted for the ratification of the Treaty of Rome. Since then it has been the solid pro-integration line of the SPD which has formed the backbone of the group, reinforced by the active Dutch Socialist members (Messieurs Vredeling and Oele). The Dutch and German members who have become the main champions of integration and democratisation of the communities compose, it should be remembered, 20 of the 37 members of the group. This means that there is a constant core of the group who have a well defined line and who are used to cooperating in the national political arena. This is not to say that distinct national tendencies have not been apparent within the group, either in terms of the specialisation of members or of approach to certain issues.

164

As has already been mentioned, both the SPD and the French SFIO had in the early days some scepticism about integration in 'Little Europe', which gave them a distinctive position within the group, and led the whole SPD membership of the Ad Hoc Assembly (an enlarged common assembly formed to draw up the draft treaty for a political community) to abstain from voting on the final draft. Since then certain national attitudes have emerged; the Dutch, in common with the other Dutch members, hold a free market, and less dirigiste position on transport policy, than do the other parties, because of the special position of transport as an economic activity in the Netherlands. Specialisation on certain aspects of the communities has occurred. The Dutch members, with Hr Vredeling in the forefront, have tended to concentrate on the working of the institutions and the question of adequate democratic control. The German members of the group have in general specialised in economic aspects. They have concentrated on such areas as planning, the control of inflation and competition policy. The Belgians have interested themselves in social and regional policy, especially in the framework of the coal and steel community, often adopting more radical positions, such as demanding the nationalisation of the coal industry at the European level (e.g. members such as Messieurs Tobeau and Troclet, Wallon PSB members). Certain Socialist members have made a given policy area their own: Monsieur Dehousse on direct elections, Georges Spénale for the budgetary powers of the parliament, Vredeling on agriculture, among others. It is not that these individual specialisations in themselves decrease the cohesion of the group, but rather tend to decrease its importance, in that initiatives are taken by individuals rather than by the groups, causing the groups to lose some of their co-ordinating role.

As we have already seen, the Socialist group alone decides when a free vote of its members should be allowed. The corollary of this is that discipline is the expected norm. Indeed, Article 7 of the rules of the group makes it clear that only a member who brings forward 'weighty political reasons which make him dissent from a particular majority decision' can be released from the obligations of party discipline. As we shall see, outright opposition to the point of voting against the party line in a roll-call vote is rare in the Socialist group. Opposition which takes the form of speaking to a different line from that adopted by the group spokesman, proposing individual amendments in the plenary session, which are opposed by the group as a whole, is less rare, but is usually avoided by compromise in the group meeting; thus it is difficult to trace dissident views, as in the words of Neunreither[2]; these had been 'arranged'. There are, however, certain typical cases which can be pointed to. We have already noted the attempts by Hr Gerlach to reduce the

1972-73 budget of the European parliament. In the November 1971 debate on agricultural prices and structures one SPD member, Hr Kriedemann, voted against the draft resolution of the agriculture committee, although the resolution had been approved by the group and one of the rapporteurs had been Hr Vredeling, Dutch Socialist and vice-president of the agriculture committee. Another recent case was the censure motion introduced against the commission in the November 1972 session and debated on 12 December 1972. The motion attacked the commission for failing to make proposals for the extension of the budgetary powers of the parliament within two years of the Treaty of Luxemburg (1970).[3] This motion, the first in the history of the communities, was tabled by Monsieur Georges Spénale, president of the finance and budgetary committee. It became clear that he had tabled the motion without the approval of his group and that many Socialist members opposed the move, which was largely instrumental in the withdrawal of the motion by its author, and its replacement by a resolution.[4] Thus in large and small matters dissidence does occur, but is rare in the Socialist group.

The advent of the Danish Social Democrats has introduced a new element into the situation; as has already been indicated, the Danish political situation requires that all Danish parties adopt a restrictive view of institutional development (although this is less true for the Conservatives). Under these conditions, on issues such as the budgetary powers of the parliament and political co-operation, the Danish Social Democrats have acted as a group, distinct from the Socialist group as a whole. They thus voted against the crucial paragraph 14 of the *Spénale Report* on budgetary powers because this would have given the 'last word' to the parliament over legislative acts with financial consequences.

Both of the other supranational groups, the Christian Democrats and the Liberals, appear a great deal less cohesive than the Socialists. The Christian Democrats are able to unite on the basis of total support for integration, going well beyond the present limited structure of the communities. But even here there are differences; Signor Scelba was in complete disagreement with the remainder of his group, and in particular with Hr Müller (the rapporteur) in his approach to the resolution to be sent to the summit conference (1972) — Scelba sought to take more account of political reality, that the development of integration depended on the will of the existing states which could not be circumvented. In economic and social questions the group is distinctly less well integrated and cohesive. The group has members such as Dichgans (now no longer in the parliament) and Burgbacher who came from the doctrinaire anti-planning wing of the CDU/CSU and members who take particular interest in the protection of the high farm prices, such as Messieurs Vetrone and Richarts. These members held views largely out of key with those of the urban, trade union orientated members of the group, such as (in their time) Califice, Rubinacci, Sabatinni. Compromise is usually possible, at the risk of incisiveness of position, but potentially the losing wing might take a stand against the group. Thus views to the 'right' of 'left' of the group line are not infrequently expressed by individual speakers in the plenum.

The Liberals appear the least cohesive, both on the *a priori* grounds of their composition and on performance. The Liberals tend to apply their belief in individualism in their parliamentary action. The party line as such is weak and ill-defined. The group holds fewer group meetings than the other supranational groups and hence leaves more room for the initiative of the individual member. The group has much greater difficulties than any other group in reaching a common standpoint on issues before the parliament. The group appoints fewer spokesmen than the other larger groups. In a typical session (February 1972), 12 subjects were debated, including two major matters, the economic debate and the debate on the programme of the commission for 1972. A total of 32 spokesmen was appointed by the five groups (including the PCI). The Socialists and Christian Democrats appointed eight each, as did the UDE, but the Liberals only appointed five spokesmen. This figure would probably have been lower, but for the two major debates, in which all five groups participated. The Liberal group more often appoints two spokesmen than other groups, in order that the diverse views within the group may all be ventilated; in fact this device indicates a failure to reach a common line. The spokesmen for the Liberal group tend in any case to present a much more individual approach than is the case for the other groups. For example, it is clear that the speech made by Signor Romeo (Italian, MSI) in the economic debate of 1971 was more a personal or national party view than a group statement; this is evident in that he drew almost exclusively on the Italian situation, addressed himself to Italian problems, violently attacked the trade unions, blaming them entirely for inflation, and struck a stridently anti-Communist tone. It is by no means clear that this was the view of the whole group, particularly the German FDP or French Radical and 'centriste' members of the group. Such 'personal' statements in the guise of group statements are relatively frequent in the Liberal group.

In the case of the UDE and the PCI and allies the situation is quite different. Both these groups are uni-national (French and Italian) and are to all intents and purposes composed of one party (UDE plus one 'apparente' and PCI plus PSIUP — not since the renewal of the delegation

167

in late October 1972 — and independent left). Here the problems of cohesion do not arise in any more acute form than at national level and, since the parties are mere projections of national parties, party discipline is easier to impose. The UDE is most cohesive on the institutional questions which provoked its founding. It can rally round the banner of the defence of national sovereignty and French national interests, and opposition to supranational development of the community. It is less cohesive on social and economic policy matters, which is a reflection of the diversity of the UDR itself. It was united by loyalty to the person of General de Gaulle and support for his ideals and later by support for Gaullist continuity in the person of Georges Pompidou. It represents the assimilation of the independents, conservatives and even centristes of the Fourth Republic, plus the Gaullists of the 'first hour' and more radical elements from the RPF experiment, who rallied to the ideas of the General for 'national solidarity' and 'participation', such as Louis Vallon, René Capitant and André Malraux.

The Communists are cohesive by tradition. The members of parliament in Communist groups are tied to the party line established by the central organs of the party outside parliament. In the European parliament, the group (or earlier 'embryo-group') had only one member per committee (since the constituent session of March 1974 this has changed in the case of some committees) and hence no conflict or divergence can arise, as may be the case for the larger groups. This member will lead the discussion in the group meeting. Up to now, one spokesman (and no individual speakers) has been appointed, usually the expert on the subject (Amendola on general political issues, Cipolla on agriculture, Marras on social questions, Leonardi on economic issues). With the enlargement of the group to include PCF members and a Danish member, internal cohesion has become less easy to maintain. The Danish member has had his own preoccupations: he has rarely spoken for the group, but often in his own name. The PCF has evolved less far on community questions than the PCI, with the result that on institutional issues (such as budgetary powers), and in respect the extent to which issues can be tackled within the community framework, the PCF members have felt the need to express their own view. How far this difference of nuance will continue and what effect it will have on the work of the group it is too early to say.

The Conservative group is of course virtually uni-national and uni-party. Furthermore it has been (up until the general election of 28 February 1974) closely associated with the general aims of its home Government in European policy. In some respects too, party discipline has always been stronger in the House of Commons than in Continental parliaments. The Conservative group placed, from the start, a great premium on efficient activity in the parliament. The group had certain aims, some political, some procedural which its cohesion and political ability, as well as the strength of its arguments would enable it to attain. All of which would lead one to expect a high degree of cohesion, as has in fact been the case. Individual members were given responsibility for policy areas and these members lead group policy formation. The group has a whip, on Westminister lines (Sir Tufton Beamish) and issues three line whips on major issues for the group — for example the vote on the draft regulation on mergers. This degree of discipline has had some spillover effect on the other groups, who have realised that cohesion and voting presence can be important.

In an article in *Government and Opposition,* Gerda Zellentin develops (among other things) an objective 'cohesion index' for the groups.[5] This index is based on the percentage deviation from unanimity of the voting of a group in roll-call votes. Since the article was written, there have been virtually no roll-call votes and the PCI, new arrivals since the article, would show almost, if not total, cohesion. We can therefore use the index to draw some conclusions to the extent that it appears inherently valid. The greatest drawback is the use of the roll-call vote as the criterion. Roll-call votes are only used in a very limited number of cases: for votes requiring a special majority (censure motion, budget amendments after 1975, little revision of the ECSC treaty) or where other voting methods are not clear enough, or where ten members request it.[6] There has been only a very small number of roll-call votes and fewer in more recent years than in the common assembly. Important political issues have been decided without a roll-call vote, such as the annual agricultural prices resolution, whereas matters with no controversy attached, such as the little revision of 1960 (only two 'Noes'), were subject to roll-call votes. Bearing in mind these difficulties we can nonetheless make use of the index:

National Delegation	Percentage of seats in Parliament	Cohesion Index 1958-63	Cohesion Index 1963-66
Germany	25.35	35.9	26.5
Italy	25.35	4.4	3.2
France	25.35	11.8	24.6
Belgium	9.85	30.8	19.8
Netherlands	9.85	6.0	9.1
Luxemburg	4.25	28.0	9.6
Average of all states		19.5	15.5

Party Groups

Christian-Democrats	43.7	15.2	14.9
Socialists	24.7	1.7	2.0
Liberals	18.3	13.7	17.6
UDE	10.6	–	4.5
Average of all groups		10.2	9.7

Certain conclusions suggest themselves; on average the groups are more cohesive than the national delegations, which is what one would expect if the political groupings are to acquire any significance. But the Dutch and the Italian delegations are very cohesive; indeed, they are as cohesive as any group except the Socialists and the Italians are more cohesive than the single-nation, single-party UDE group. The Dutch and the Italian delegations have obviously found causes of national interest, bringing together the national delegation as a unit. This is clear in the united Dutch stand on the democratisation of the community in the 1965 crisis and since in the Dutch opposition to high food prices and their special position on transport and energy policy. The Italians are from the only Mediterranean country in the community and hence have special interests in the field of agriculture and horticulture and in their policy of importing oil from the Socialist bloc. However, one would not expect that degree of cohesion from the otherwise strongly polarised Italian party system. It should be borne in mind that the roll-call vote data is very selective in character and represents a somewhat limited basis for an analysis. Specifically, in the Italian case, there has been a tendency to overweight the government parties in the delegation to the European parliament and to exclude the opposition; however, that cannot explain away an undoubted cohesion. It is, however, strange that the Italian national delegation should come out more cohesive than the UDE.

Another point of interest is that the Liberals do not show any less cohesion than the Christian Democrats; indeed in the period 1958-63 they are more cohesive and in the second period only marginally less so. This would appear to contradict much of our earlier analysis. The conclusion is based on inadequate data, but it may mean that the Christian Democrats are not a great deal more cohesive than the Liberals, but merely are more successful at appearing to be so. The UDE seems to be less cohesive than the Socialist group. To the extent that this remarkable finding is not merely based on too limited data, it attests to the strength of cohesion of the Socialists and probably to the diversity of the UDE group on social and economic questions.

The figure for the German delegation at 35.9 (1958-63) and 26.5 (1963-66) gives an indication of intergroup polarisation, at least for the

Socialist and the Christian Democrat groups, because the German delegation is dominated by the CDU and SPD members, in their turn dominant in their groups. However, the roll-call vote is atypical and the near unanimous compromise resolution is the norm for the European parliament.

Notes

1   Henig and Pinder, *European Political Parties,* p. 487.
2   Paper to the Lyon Colloque (1960), 'Le rôle de Parlement européen dans la formation de décision des Communautés européenes.'
3   See: *Débats,* December Session, 12 December 1972.
4   See: Report in *The Times* of 13 December 1972, p. 4.
5   See: G. Zellentin, 'Form and Function of the Opposition in the European Communities' *Government and Opposition,* vol. 2, no. 3, April-July 1967.
6   Rules of Procedure, Rule 35.

PART III

Parliamentary Processes:
the Groups and the Parliament
as a Political System

12 The Intervention of National Parliaments

Up to now we have confined our analysis to the activities of the groups and their members in the European parliament itself. If we are to judge the effectiveness of the political groups and the possibility of the development of European parties with coherent policy positions and strategies, we must also examine the work of the groups within the total political environment which contributes to the making of European policy — which at present very definitely includes national politics. Furthermore, in some sense the European parliament and the groups within it are merely outposts of the 'europeanist' avant-garde. It is just as important, if not more important, to promote the European dimension of politics in the national political arena, indeed in what is a much less receptive and even potentially hostile atmosphere. For, at the moment, whatever may have been the initial intentions and whatever hopes may still be held, the fundamental truth of the Gaullist article of faith that the nation state is in reality the source of all international action, must be recognised. The power of the nation states cannot be ignored by all who wish to remain within the realm of practical politics. Thus the European cause must enter the arena of national politics and contend with other issues for attention and support.

This was not initially realised to any great degree; national parliaments had not expected to play any role in community affairs. The German parliament indeed had a doctrinal aversion to doing so to any strong degree lest the role of the European parliament be undermined. Gradually, however, the need for national intervention was felt instinctively in national parliaments and ruefully accepted at the European level. This process has been greatly accelerated by the accession to the community of Britain, Denmark and Ireland, all jealous of parliamentary control.

The 'prise de conscience' came about less through the realisation that a revision of strategy was needed in order to underpin the community at the national level, than from a reaction, albeit belated and fragmentary, to the loss of parliamentary control at the national level entailed by the legislative power of the council-commission tandem, from which the European parliament was, in terms of real power, excluded. National parliaments were involved, but always in a one way process: national parliaments had made possible the community treaties; all new progress towards integration requires their consent; many trade agreements require national ratification. Community directives may need implementation by legislation or delegation of rule-making power to ministers. Ministers depend on their parliament for the budgets of their ministries and for general political support in carrying out community policy. The national parliaments have seen in the development of the community, which they otherwise welcome, a threat to parliamentary control, both at the national and the European level, through the potential degradation of parliamentary institutions and the ever wider sphere of executive discretion. However hesitantly and ineffectively it may be, national parliaments are involved in the community decision-making process and they have reacted to that fact.

An examination of the extent of that involvement shows that it is indeed considerable: debates on European policy, on agriculture, ratification debates, parliamentary questions, ministerial statements. Since the publication of Michael Niblock's book[1] the notion of the national parliaments as part of the community decision-making process has become common currency. Our analysis will follow this and subsequent more detailed studies[2] and makes no claim to completeness, since it is only one aspect of our subject here. We shall outline the procedures which have been established in the various national parliaments and the use actually made of them; the impact of such activity and the 'echoing' of issues from the European parliament to the national parliaments.

Procedures fall into two broad categories: those involving the information of national parliaments and those involving control. In a number of member states the laws of ratification placed on the government an obligation to report on community developments to parliament. In Germany, Article 2 requires general reports to both houses of the German parliament, but also specific information on community legislation which would have direct effect in Germany or require national legislation. Article 6 of the Danish law contains very similar provisions. In Germany since 1959 there have been annual and, since 1966, six monthly reports of a long and factual nature. Similarly the Dutch government provides an annual report which is debated in the second chamber. A report has been tabled in Italy since 1967 (long — up to two hundred pages). In Belgium the practice lapsed in 1967 after two reports. Article 2 of the French law requires a report on the activity of the communities, but no such report has ever been presented, since the government considers that members are adequately informed by other means.[3] The British government refused to write a commitment into the European Communities Act, but have agreed to keep the Commons informed by ministerial statements and documents.

Formal and informal reports to parliament, committees or political groups from members of the European parliament are an alternative source of information. In France the delegation is required by the 'réglement des Assemblées' to give an annual report on their activity; a UDR member has usually been the rapporteur. The same occurs in Belgium, where the report is given to the European affairs committee of the chamber and the rapporteur is usually one of the more activist members (M. Dewulf (CVP) was rapporteur in 1971 and 1972). No plenary debate occurs on such reports.

In Germany and Belgium a more immediate reporting occurs after each session of the European parliament. In the Bundestag one member reports to the foreign affairs committee. In Belgium a 'résumé of debates and resolutions is drawn up by the section of the senate secretariat dealing with liaison with international assemblies, and distributed to all members of parliament.

Such reports are naturally factual and non-partisan in character. Only in the political groups can more incisive information be given, but the extent to which this is actually done varies greatly. In France occasional reports are made to the various political groups in the two houses. In Belgium the PSC/CVP has a party committee (including non-parliamentarians) linked to CEPES (a study centre for European problems) chaired by M. Dewulf, an active European parliamentarian, which follows the work of the European parliament very closely. The Dutch Labour party group in the second chamber receives the agenda of the European parliament sessions in advance,[4] but debate within the group has been cursory or non--existent and there is no formal reporting back. One of the 'Arbeitskreise' of the German SPD is concerned with external policy, and includes most of the SPD members of the EP. This 'Arbeitskreise' has a small specialised staff, of which one attends all sessions, in order to assist the SPD members in Strasbourg and to carry out an information function within the SPD Bundestag Fraktion as a whole. The Fraktion publishes regularly a bulletin for those members who have no contact with the European parliament, giving a summary of the work of the parliament and especially the SPD members, but also opening its columns to members who wish to present an analysis or opinion on certain problems of a community character.[5]

When we turn to procedures for control we find various mechanisms: committees, parliamentary questions, debates. The committee work has been the most effective form of control and breaks down into two main forms: special European affairs committees or the use of the normal committee system. In the German Bundestag a special committee, the Integrations-ältestenrat was set up in 1963 and functioned until 1967 but was abolished in 1969. It was based on an inter-party agreement and was composed of 15 members, chosen proportionately to the party strengths in the Bundestag. It was never an organ for controlling ministers in their activity in the council of ministers, but was solely concerned with the co-ordination of initiatives relating to the community in the Bundestag. Though no doubt a useful and necessary function, its overall impact was small and many considered that normal informal channels could achieve the same result.

Since 1957 (with a change of name in 1965) the German Bundesrat has had a committee for affairs relating to the European communities. This committee has a general mandate to draw up reports on matters referred to the Bundesrat under Article 2 of the law of ratification. This committee alone is competent on community matters, co-ordinating opinions received from other committees. The position of the Bundesrat is made more unusual in that is is permitted an observer in council meetings and the 'Länder' maintain a liaison office in Brussels. These special features, together with its small size and character as an 'inter-governmental conference' makes its procedure unique and not exportable to other assemblies.

With the exception of the Danish case, the Belgian chamber's European affairs committee (EAC) represents the most durable and in some ways the most effective example of such a specialised committee. The EAC was set up in 1962 and its terms of reference are found in Article 83 of the rules of procedure. It received a mandate to 'obtain all information on the consequences of the application of the treaties in respect of European co-operation, and supervise the execution of the latter and follow the development of the organisations they create'. In particular the EAC is to examine the reports from the government and the delegations to European assemblies; require the presence of ministers; present reports on the progress of integration; report to the chamber on any matter referred to it or otherwise worthy of attention or requiring the intervention of the chamber by virtue of its constitutional prerogatives. Under Article 83(2c) the committee has 23 members, who may not be members of the EP. This is to ensure that the EAC extends knowledge of the communities beyond a small group of experts and 'Europeans'. However, many of the members are past or potential members of the EP (MM. Fayat, Glinne, Dewulf have been members of the EAC and EP).

Since 1962, 40-50 meetings have been held, but these have been rather unevenly spaced: 11 in 1962, 9 in 1963 and only 3 in 1964. It was largely the existence of a state secretary in the foreign ministry charged with European affairs in the period up to 1967 which made for the activism and effectiveness of the EAC in its heyday around 1965-66. This minister developed close relations with the EAC. Other ministers also attended: the agriculture minister in 1964 and 1966; finance; science and technology and foreign affairs. For example, in April 1967 the finance minister spoke on international monetary problems. Joint meetings have also been held with other committees, which have not abdicated their interest in European matters which touch their competence.

In 1968 the Italian senate set up a 'Giunta Consultativa' or consultative subcommittee of the foreign affairs committee, to which, technically, the 'Giunta' reports. The 'Giunta' has met, on average, once a month and has discussed matters such as the government report previously mentioned, which led to a full debate on the floor in 1969 for the first time. It also discussed agriculture and the law delegating powers to the government to implement community legislation. As in Belgium and Germany, the 'Giunta' does not control or co-ordinate the work of other committees, which retain an interest in community matters.[6]

In Denmark, entry to the community was strongly opposed, not least by the Socialist People's party and by minorities in the Social Democratic Party and the Radical party (some 31 MPs). The 'social contract' under which entry was approved at the referendum was a limited one: integration was to be restricted to the present treaties. These special factors, together with a tradition of parliamentary involvement in foreign affairs, led inevitably to the installation of powerful control machinery. The instrument of the Folketing (single chamber parliament) is the market relations committee (MRC). This 17 member committee receives, fortnightly, a list of commission proposals from the government of which the important ones are sifted out for consideration with the minister concerned. The minister presents to the MRC the mandate that he proposes to take with him to the council of ministers, and if so required presents a written statement. The MRC may take the advice of other specialised committees, and in particular the Udenrigsnaevnet (foreign affairs committee). If at the end of the discussion there is no majority in the MRC against the proposed mandate, then the minister may negotiate on that basis. If the commission's proposal is changed in the course of the discussion in the council, then the minister must reconsult the committee, even if only by telephone from Brussels. The MRC does not report back to the floor of the Folketing — its members are usually their party's spokesmen on EEC affairs and so have the confidence of their party groups, to which they report.

In the United Kingdom the matter of parliamentary control over EEC acts loomed very large; the Labour opposition attempted to write into the European Communities Bill various safeguards, but these were not accepted by the government. In December 1972 both houses of parliament set up select committees to study the problem of scrutiny of community legislation. These committees reported in July (Lords) and October (Commons) 1973. The recommendations of both select committees were broadly similar, with the House of Commons' report placing more weight on the need to promote debate on the floor of the house and less enthusiastic about entrusting scrutiny to a specialist committee. The Lords' committee[7] proposed a select committee to consider community proposals. This committee, with a paid chairman and small expert staff would first sift proposals and only discuss the most important, whereupon appropriate evidence would be taken. A report would be made on the legal and other implications of the proposal, which any peer or the government could have debated by putting down a motion to that effect. The Commons[8] SC proposed a scrutiny committee of 9-15 members with an expert staff, which would report on major proposals. It would be necessary to provide for a full debate on the floor for such major reports. It also wished to strengthen ministerial responsibility in respect to EEC matters. However, the task of the committee would not be to debate the mertis of a proposal, but merely to give the house as a whole the fullest information as to its implications. The Commons SC proposed sixth-monthly general reports from the government on community matters.

The Irish Dail and Senate have set up a joint committee on European affairs, composed of 26 members, with a chairman from the opposition. The task of the committee, which includes all ten Irish members of the EP, is to report to both houses on draft regulations and directives, with particular reference to administrative or legislative changes which would be required and their effect on Irish interests. The committee hears ministers and senior civil servants. It is intended to set up a number of subcommittees. Some difficulties have arisen in that the committee members consider that the government has not provided them with adequate information.

In France the constitutional position makes the formation of new committees difficult, since Article 43 limits each house to six. This has not prevented the establishment, in 1967, of a less formal body, 'Le Groupe d'Action pour l'Europe'. This group is open to all deputies and some 80 have joined. It has no formal powers and no place in the rules of the assembly, but does act as a forum for the dissemination of information and discussion, albeit limited since ministers do not attend and no record is taken of discussions. The foreign affairs committee alone has a special competence for community matters, but only along with other foreign policy issues.

Special European affairs' committees have not been an unqualified success. They have had difficulty in attaining sufficient status and attracting a high enough calibre of membership. If they were to include say, the chairmen of all other committees, they would then hold a preeminence vis-à-vis the other committees which may not be desired since community policy is not a neatly demarcated area, but spills over into every domain of national policy. There is another danger that such committees will become the preserve of EP members and a small group of specialists, cut off from the main stream of parliamentary opinion. This is not to deny their usefulness: they have become centres of co-ordination, of dissemination of information and for discussion, pursuing an educative function. However, severe limitations must be recognised, except in the Danish committee and the German Bundesrat, where a clear and un-equivocal central role has been given to the committee.

The second form of committee scrutiny, found in the German Bundestag, in the Dutch second chamber and to a lesser extent in the Italian chamber, is leaving scrutiny to the normal committee structure, each in its own sphere of competence, without central co-ordination. The Dutch second chamber relies on the activism of certain members and the normal specialised committees to do the job. The foreign affairs budgetary committee does not act as, nor even seek to act as, a European affairs' committee. It has both wider and narrower functions: it deals only with the general aspect, providing in May/June of each year the forum for a set-piece debate on the annual report presented by the government; on the other hand it deals with more general foreign affairs' matters. It does not control or co-ordinate the discussion of community questions in the second chamber. The Dutch specialist committees (those on agriculture, commerce and finance and transport) have developed a strong interest in the community aspect of their work. Politically important proposals of the commission are considered by the responsible committee in the presence of the competent minister, who will inform the committee, in closed session, of the position of the government on the draft, its reservations and the urgency which will be accorded to the proposal. The committee will hold an exchange of views with the minister and may challenge him on some points and may seek certain undertakings. The committee will then expect a report on the deliberations of the council and, if the matter comes up at several council meetings, an interim report on progress, when the minister may be pressed hard to change his tack or to insist on certain basic principles. This procedure stops well short of the degree of control exercised by the Danish market committee. Even this ideal is seldom attained; however, the Dutch committees are less likely than others (except the Danish committee) to be content with *ex post facto* control and more likely to be able to insert itself into the decision-making process at a formative stage, at least on important matters.[9] All this control is carried out in committee; especially since

G

1967 there has been very little debate on the floor of the house.

The German Bundestag (in spite of an experiment with a special committee) employs a more formalised version of the Dutch system. Under Article 2 of the law of ratification, all commission proposals are sent to the Bundestag (and Bundesrat) by the federal government and then referred by the Bundestag to one committee as the leading committee 'federführrender Ausschuss' and such other committees as might be involved are asked to give an opinion. Ministers are summoned before, during and after council deliberations. The report will either merely take note of the proposal if it is unimportant and technical or may instruct the government in detail on the line it should follow and the amendments it should seek. In special cases (value added tax proposals and those on beer) the committee concerned may seek information from a wide range of outside interests and even travel to Brussels for discussions with commission officials. Few reports have led to full dress debates on the floor (only those dealing with major agricultural proposals or economic and monetary union), but others may lead to a brief exchange of views or the presentation of observations when the report comes up for formal adoption by the Bundestag. This procedure achieves the same results as the Dutch procedure, but has the same drawback in greater measure — that is the danger of clogging up the system with detail in a morass of technical matters and the problem of controlling a fluid and complex activity like the deliberations of the council, bearing in mind that each national parliament can only call its own minister to account and not those of other member states.

These forms of control are supplemented by other forms such as debates and parliamentary questions. The parliamentary question (PQ) is a major method of eliciting information and seeking action, either in form of written questions or more elaborate questions with debate. There are far fewer PQs asked in continental legislatures than at Westminster and of the total (5,527 in France in 1971, and 6,666 in 1973; 1,113 in 1971 in the Netherlands and 1,662 in 1973) only a small number have concerned the community, but there has been a tendency to growth. In France and Belgium the number in each house was less than 10 over the period 1962-67, but by 1972 the number had risen to 92 written PQs in the assembly alone and in Belgium there were 12 community questions in 1970, but 14 in the first half of 1971. Only Germany and the Dutch second chamber show a consistently high figure from 1962 onwards. In the Netherlands the number had risen to 75 PQs in 1972-73.[10]

The questions, especially in Germany and France, are likely to concern agriculture, but a large number of the Dutch questions are what might be called 'institutional questions', such as the competence of community institutions, the supremacy of community law, procedure in the council, the powers of the European parliament, fulfilment of treaty obligations. Dutch questions are more likely to have been put from a 'European point of view', that is asking the government to support community institutions, carry out obligations under community law, rather than the defence of national interests and here the Dutch members of the European parliament (and in the past particularly Vredeling, Oele and Westerterp) have been particularly important, asking over half the questions asked in any one year on European topics.

Another means by which national parliaments express themselves is in the numerous debates on community topics. These fall into three broad categories: formal debates — ratification debates, debates on laws implementing community legislation; regular debates — foreign affairs and agriculture budget debates and debates on annual reports; occasional debates — debates on some unique event or to draw attention to specific problems (summit Conference, economic and monetary union, powers of the EP); such debates may sometimes be introduced by a motion or oral question from a backbench member. Debates are normally set-piece affairs: statements from group spokesmen, from the minister and finally interventions from backbenchers. Except in France the debate may be concluded by the adoption of a motion. In Denmark, general debates are to be organised on a regular basis — two or three times per year. In Britain, too, such debates will tend to increase in number. Several general debates have already been initiated in the Lords (e.g. on EEC-USA relations). Otherwise it is clear that such debates engender little controversy and are relatively ineffective instruments of control.

As the table on page 190 shows, in the period from December 1969 to June 1971 there were several debates in each member state and each category mentioned was well represented. As well as the topic shown there were debates on EEC-USA relations (Germany and Italy); the gas centrifuge agreement (Netherlands); the Greek association (Belgium); problems of wine growers (France); the appointment of a new member of the commission (Luxemburg). There were 43 debates altogether.[11]

In all these debates European parliamentary members were active: in the agriculture debates in the Italian chamber and senate (15 and 22 January 1970; 30 April 1970; 27 November and 1 December 1970; and in the chamber, 10-11 and 14 November 1970) interventions were made by MM. Vetrone (DC), Ciferelli (Rep.), Boano (DC), Scardaccione (DC), Cantalupo (Soc), Bersani (DC), Sandri, Cipolla, Marras and Fabrinni (PCI). All these were, or were to become, members of the EP. Another example in the Belgian debate on foreign affairs (11-12 February 1970), M. Radoux was the rapporteur and there were interventions from MM.

Califice, Dewulf and Glinne. However, the role of European parliamentarians should not be exaggerated. In Holland, only Berkhouver is foreign affairs spokesman for his party and Vredeling was for many years not Labour's spokesman on agriculture (the post, was held by Hr Van der Ploeg, who was never in the EP). Dutch European parliamentarians have not generally spoken in the most important political debates, such as the debate on the speech from the throne, opening the parliamentary session, but have been prominent only in special debates on European issues. Here one sees the danger of European questions becoming isolated from politics in general and the preserve of specialists.[12]

Issues brought up in the European parliament are frequently referred to in these debates and the proceedings of the EP themselves mentioned, but one may doubt the political punch of such debates: attendance may be low (as low as 3 or 4 out of 212 in the 1972 foreign affairs' debate in Belgium) and confined to European 'cognoscenti'. Ministers are not in general required to commit themselves to a line, nor is the house able to exert control beyond the level of generalities. The only real exceptions are the pledges given by Foreign Minister Luns to the Dutch second chamber on the budgetary powers of the European parliament during the debate on the 1965 'triptych' proposals and the similar, but weaker pledge extracted in Germany.

It is difficult to trace in detail issues which have been 'echoed' in national and European parliaments. Analysis of every community act published in the official *Journal* in February 1972 showed no follow-up of a direct character to any such act in the following four months in national parliaments. In the Netherlands, from 1970-75 some 46 separate issues were the subject of parliamentary intervention both in one or other House of the States General and in the European parliament, but usually the intervention was limited to the tabling of a written question, given again in response to parliamentary pressure.

However, more important than these procedures is the dynamism and activism of the small number of members of the European parliament in the national parliaments. These members have an organic link between the European parliament and their national parliaments — the double mandate. The European parliament has only been able to have a repercussive effect in the national parliaments and issues have only been echoed from one level to another where this has been taken up by members of the European parliament, assisted sometimes by a small group of pro-Europeans who are involved only at the national level (e.g. former members of the European parliament, members of the Belgian chamber's committee for European affairs, or former European personalities, such as Walter Hallstein[13] — first president of the EEC commission and now

CDU deputy in the Bundestag).

The activism of members varies greatly. It is instructive to the take the members of a national delegation and examine what they did in their national parliaments that was of European interest. This analysis was undertaken for the French members of the national assembly for 1971. Of the 24 members, 15 appeared to have made no 'European' contribution and, of the others, 2 had done no more than to ask one written question on a European subject. On the other hand, Monsieur Cousté had been rapporteur for one (minor) matter, had intervened in two major debates, asked two oral questions and six (out of 40) written questions.

Certain members have sought to devote themselves almost entirely to the European scene and have thus been particularly active. In Germany one can mention Hr Kriedemann (this has not been universally popular: the December 1972 issue of *Europäische Gemeinschaft* contains an article which states that Hr Kriedemann was pressurised to stand down at the recent federal election for this reason). In Italy, as we have seen, the PCI members have been largely chosen for their professionalism, moderation and expertise and have been largely assured of being re-elected and been given the explicit task of working largely in the European arena and bringing European issues up in the Italian parliament. In Belgium one can mention Monsieur Dewulf as a good example. From France one can cite Monsieur Cousté. The Luxemburg Socialist, Mlle. Lulling, is also very active.

However, the main exponents of the European mandate are the Dutch and, in particular, the Dutch Socialists from the second chamber, such as Oele and Vredeling. The position of the Dutch is exceptionally favourable in that all 150 members of the second chamber are elected on a national list system; hence no member has to 'nurse' a constituency or local party organisation. He only has to retain a place near the top of his party's national list. The Dutch Labour party is prepared to allow some members to devote the major part of their time to European activity either in the European parliament or in the national parliament.

Hr Vredeling was a special case; he spent 80-90 per cent of his time on 'European' activity. His party accepted this priority and public opinion was for the most part indifferent, but certainly not hostile. Hr Vredeling has made the written question into his forte, both in the European parliament and in the second chamber. Of the written questions tabled in the European parliament, he tabled in some years as many as 60 per cent of the total. He was responsible for over half the total of 508 tabled in 1969-70 and of the almost 600 asked in 1970-71. He covered a wide area, but mostly probed the community institutions on matters of an institutional or procedural nature, such as the powers of the parliament, court and commission, why the council acted in a certain way or refused to act in another, or brought to the attention of the institutions certain measures which should have been taken or matters which might have represented a breach of treaty obligations — in short a watch-dog. He would ·test reaction to a question in his own parliament and compare the answer of his own government and that given by the commission, and may base a new question on any discrepancy noted. In general terms, he wished to use the written question to sensibilise public opinion and to show that the executive was being controlled.[14] Hr Vredeling was sensitive to the possibilities afforded by the 'double mandate' and was ready to undertake parallel action on both levels whenever it seemed useful. However, in addition to using the written question, he was active in the European parliament in the agriculture committee (of which he is vice-president) and the social affairs committee; he has written important reports for both committees. He was also active in the Socialist group, of which he is a member of the bureau.

In the second chamber he was active on European questions and often spoke in debates on European affairs and intervened in committee discussions. However, he considers that, if public opinion is to support the community and enable the necessary measures to be taken at a European level, more is needed. This view led and still leads him to be active in his own party and to take all opportunities to sensibilise public opinion on European questions. To this end he submits the agenda of the European parliament to his group in the second chamber and seeks to stimulate discussion. He was able to tap a vein of public interest; he finds a willingness to discuss European matters among the rank and file party members in small, local, party meetings. He was also active in agricultural circles: he was a prominent speaker at the agricultural congress of the PvdA held on 21 January 1971. It is worth mentioning in parenthesis here that many members of the European parliament are active in sectorial pressure groups and seek to give to these a more European outlook; here one can mention, for example, Vetrone (President of COPA) and Dupont (chairman of the Belgian milk producers' association).

However, in the long run such activity will not be enough; if the community is to gain the place it should have in political life, then in the opinion of Hr Vredeling the political tendencies and parties must be re-organised and re-orientated to reflect this new priority. This is a particularly Dutch concern, which has been echoed by Hr Westerterp (CD),[15] when he proposed the formation of 'European parties', that is federations of national parties, able to bind the national parties by majority vote, based on the classic political tendencies of the community: Conservatives, Christian Democrats, Liberals, Socialists and Communists.

Under the impulsion of Hr Vredeling and others the congress of the PvdA (6 February 1971) passed a resolution calling for a conference of the Socialist parties of the Six, which would take measures leading to a 'federative partnership' of the parties.

What measures has the European parliament itself, as an institution, taken to foster links with the national Parliaments? In general one is forced to say that the attitude has been negative. There are, though, good reasons for this negative approach; in the first place, unlike the Council of Europe and the Western European Union, which depend entirely on national action to enact their recommendations, the community has supranational powers of its own which by-pass the national parliaments. This situation has made the need for co-operation less obvious and less intense. By the same token, the 'integrative' nature of the community decisions is such as to arouse fierce political controversy along the same lines of force in both the European and national parliament; this means that national parliaments which have a majority of government supporters (in the nature of things) cannot be harnessed to the cause of the European parliament against their national government, or only rarely. Lastly, there is a doctrinal point; the European parliament sees itself as a pre-federal and ultimately a federal parliament, replacing the national parliaments in those areas where competences have been transferred to the community. This implies a slacking of links with the national parliaments rather than closer links. The European parliament appears to take the view, or at any rate foresee the danger, that increased links with the national parliaments could be institutionally regressive, even as a temporary, stop-gap measure to fill the void arising from the present weakness of the European parliament.

As a result, the measures which have been taken so far have been, to say the least, tentative, hesitant and ineffective. Two reports[16] have examined this question, but came out against a greater role for the national parliaments. In January 1963 a special meeting was held in Rome at the initiative of Signor Martino, president of the European parliament. This was a meeting between the presidents of the national parliaments and their secretary generals and those of the European parliament. This meeting considered how each parliament could better organise its sessions to enable the European parliament to function better; little was achieved. On the question of giving community affairs a wider echo in the national parliaments, the final declaration limited itself to vague statements of good intentions − more debates, and so on. The only practical consequence was the designation of 'liaison members' of each national delegation who would meet together to co-ordinate their work of information and co-ordination in the national parliaments. This procedure was not effective and soon fell into abeyance. On the initiative of Hr Behrendt, president of the European parliament, a colloque (colloque parlementaire européen) was held on 15-16 March 1972, at which there were representatives of the national parliaments and the European parliament. In the debate, statements were made by the national and European party groups on the theme 'The state of European Unification and the role of Parliaments'. It was intended that this colloque should become a permanent, annual fixture. Useful points of view were put and some suggestions made, but no firm conclusions were reached.[17]

When one turns to actual cases where the parliament has sought to involve national parliaments, the result is meagre. It has not been done often and it is difficult to be sure whether or not it is in reality a case of a 'private initiative' by an active member of the European parliament. One clear case is outlined in the *Glesener Report* on the Euratom budget adopted by the council on 21 December 1971 and the agreements on common research activities signed by certain European states and by the Commission.[18] Here the committee concerned (energy, research and atomic questions) was disturbed at the failure of the council to adopt a budget which would safeguard the future of Euratom. The resolution of the European parliament adopted on 16 December on the basis of the *Strobel Report* on the proposed bi-annual programme for 1972-74 was sent not only, as is usual, to the commission and to the council, but also to the governments of the member states, which produced a reply from the German government in the form of a letter from the federal chancellor to the president of the European parliament. During its deliberations, the committee then decided to have asked identical questions in each national parliament by a member of the committee (Messieurs Jarrot, Biaggi, Vandewiele, Glesener, Oele and Madame Orth).

The 1965 crisis, where the power of the parliament was one of the contentious issues, included considerable involvement by the national parliaments, not least because any action based on Article 201 of the Treaty of Rome would require ratification of the national parliaments, as would any amendment of the treaty to increase the powers of the European parliament. From the time of the 1963 foreign affairs' debate in the Dutch second chamber, the issue was followed closely in the Dutch parliament and at the public session of the Foreign Affairs' Budgetary Committee of 9 June 1965 a commitment, in the form of a statement by the foreign minister that the government would press for increased powers for the European parliament and (most important) that it would support the commission viewpoint as long as the commission upheld it, was obtained largely by the pressure of Dutch members of the European parliament, such as Vredeling, Westerterp, Berkhouver.[19]

In the German Bundestag similar pressure was brought to bear, from a written question by SPD members in November 1963 to the debate on the report of the Budgetary Affairs' Committee on the commission proposal held on 30 June 1965. Here a resolution, albeit in a weaker form than in the Dutch second chamber, was passed and accepted by the government; this resolution held the government to support actively increased budgetary powers for the parliament as the *sine qua non* of the remainder of the 'package'. It is interesting that in the council discussions of later the same day Dr Schröder (the German Foreign Minister) made much play with this resolution.

It was in 1969, after the Luxemburg Agreement of 1966 and the Hague Summit of 1969, that the issue of 'Own Resources' for the community and the associated question of the budgetary powers of the parliament was seriously re-opened. To the parliament, the initial decision of principle which resulted from the council meeting of 22 December 1969 seemed to permit a certain initial optimism, which was soon dispelled by subsequent elaboration and interpretation of that decision. It was no longer possible to demand that the parliament should have equal powers over the budget with the council. All five delegations were agreed to exclude the parliament from the final decision on those parts of the budget which resulted from prior decisions of the council (e.g. the FEOGA), and France sought to limit the discretion of the parliament even over the remaining 5 per cent of the budget. Thus it was that in the debates of the sessions from March to May 1970, the question of whether to advise the national parliaments to withhold ratification was the crucial issue. It was suggested in the resolution of 28 February 1970[20] that this course might be recommended if the council did not meet the parliament on certain vital points. After the final adoption of the Treaty of Luxemburg on 21 April 1970, the parliament took its stand on its own interpretation of that treaty — namely, that the parliament could reject the whole budget in order to provoke new proposals. The resolution adopted in the May session was a judgement of the treaty as a whole and therefore did not recommend that the national parliaments refuse to ratify the treaty; indeed, the reverse. The resolution insisted on the parliament's interpretation of the treaty and emphasised the solemn agreement of the council and commission that new proposals on the powers of the parliament should be presented within two years. What is interesting here is not the result obtained, but the fact that the European parliament had directly involved the national parliaments as part of its leverage against the council, and, indeed, the danger of this procedure for the national governments appeared not to be lost on the UDE group who, through their then president, Monsieur Habib-Deloncle, indicated that

European debates in the national parliaments

	Belgium	Germany	France	Italy	Luxemburg	Netherlands
Prices Agriculture Structures	Senate April 1970	9. 2.71 10. 3.71		CAP (Senate) 15. 1.70 Budget: Senate 30. 4.70 Chamber 17. 5.70 Senate 27.11.70	15.12.70 (Budget)	•
Foreign Policy Debate — General Matters	February 1970 Budget April 1971	Debate 6.11.70 27. 5.70 17. 6.70	Senate rejects budget Debate 5.11.70 29. 4.70 20. 4.71	Senate 17.12.69 (Budget)	11.11.70 (Budget)	12. 2.70
Direct Elections	4. 5.71 Bill		30. 6.71 Bill			26. 4.71 Westerterp Bill
Enlargement		Debate 24. 6.71	19. 2.70		23. 4.70	27. 8.70
Economic and Monetary Union		Debate 11. 5.71				28. 4.70 25. 4.71 Bill
The Association Yaoundé and Arugha Conventions	Chamber 3. 6.71 Senate 25. 6.71			Chamber 12.10.70 Senate 26.11.70		
The Hague Summit		3.12.69			4.12.69	23.12.69

Source: European Documentation

190

they had doubts about the legality of such action.

Our brief examination of the many facets of the relationship between the European parliament and the national parliaments and their involvement in the community decision-making processes, has shown that the results have been limited and patchy and that on both sides there have been reservations on closer involvement and interrelationships. No one method seems to lead to better results; there seems to be no general model. Indeed, it appears that it is the dynamism and involvement of a small number of individual activists which has produced the most intense and fruitful results, rather than institutional devices and organisational perfection.

Notes

1   *The EEC: National Parliaments in Community Decision making,* PEP/Chatham House, April 1971.

2   There are currently a number of studies being carried out in this area. Since late 1973 research led by Professor Coombes (in which the author has participated) has been studying the impact of community membership on national parliaments, partly as one section of a project for the Thysen Foundation, co-ordinated by the 'Institut de la Communauté européenne pour les Études universitaires', and partly under a grant made to the Department of European Studies at Loughborough University of Technology by the Social Sciences Research Council.

3   See 'question écrite' no. 14425 from M. Tremloet de Villiers in J.O., *Débats de l'Assemblée nationale* of 17 March 1962, p. 402.

4   Information supplied to the author by Hr Vredeling.

5   Information supplied to the author by Frl. Köhnen, official of the SPD Arbeitskreis I.

6   See A. Chiti-Batelli, 'La Giunta degli Affari Europei del Senato e i rapporti fra parlamenti nazionale e Parlamento europeo' in *Revista di Diretto Europeo,* July/September 1969.

7   See: *Second Report from Select Committee on Procedures for the Scrutiny of Proposals for European Instruments,* 25 July 1973. Recommendations pp. ix-liv.

8   See: House of Commons. *Second Report of the Select Committee on European Community Secondary Legislation.* 463, I & II, 25 October 1973. Recommendations in vol. I. Both these reports contain much useful information on other countries, which has been drawn on in this chapter.

9   Niblock, op. cit, pp. 36-8.

10 *For Germany and the Netherlands:*

Bundestag	1962-3	'63-4	'64-5	'65-6	'66-7	'69-70	'72-3
Oral Questions	13	33	46	20	32	59	–
Second Chamber							
Written Questions	9	26	11	20	10	67	75

For France:

	1971	1972	1973
Written Questions total	48	92	113
of which agriculture	25	72	85
Questions 'd'actualité' total	4	21	11
agriculture	1	15	6
Oral questions and debate total	1	2	3
agriculture	1	1	1
Oral Questions without debate	3	4	4
	–	–	1

11 Source: European Documentation.

12 Information from interviews with Dutch MPs who are not members of the European parliament. These members (from all parties) indicated that in the past there had been no great effort to influence the government but that interest was growing, mainly in committee. Participation in floor debates was limited to specialists and the parliament as a whole was not well informed.

13 Resigned at the 1972 Election.

14 Based on information supplied to the author by Hr Vredeling.

15 See: his speech to the Colloque of the Dutch Branch of EUCD on 20 June 1970.

16 The *Strobel Report,* Document 110/1966-67, and the *Illerhaus Report,* Document 118/1966-67.

17 Colloque parlementaire européen, Compte rendu in extenso des séances.

18 Report by Monsieur Glesener, Doc. 57/72, of 13 June 1972, paras. 100-14.

19 For the statement, see *European Documentation,* July 1965, p. 12.

20 See: *Journal Officiel,* 28 February 1970.

13 The Concept of Opposition in the European Parliament

It is useful to examine the extent to which an 'opposition' exists in the European parliament because such an analysis will give a clearer idea of the inter-group dynamics which take place there. Naturally, we should be wary of concluding that the British concept of 'loyal' opposition is general throughout Europe, but it does not strain reality too much to see this characteristic in all the parliaments of the six member states. The multiplicity of parties precludes the existence of a one-party opposition as in Britain, but the tendency in all the member states is for blocs of parties to form, which then take on the characteristic of a government majority and an opposition. In general this means that the smaller parties cluster around the two most polarised large parties to form the two blocs. Indeed, one can see some conscious imitation of the British system in certain countries. In Germany, the outparty is called in the press the 'opposition' and it elects a permanent 'chancellor candidate' who becomes the alternative chancellor, elected by the whole opposition in the case of the CDU and CSU. This man is sometimes referred to in the press as the 'leader of the opposition'. In France before the 1967 elections the federation of the left signed an electoral pact with the other parties of the opposition (PCF and PSU) and formed a 'Contre Gouvernement', a shadow cabinet, presided over by Monsieur Mitterand, who would have been the undisputed candidate for the post of prime minister if the left had won. In the Netherlands too, with 14 parties represented in the second chamber, efforts at simplification have been made. For the 1971 election, a shadow coalition, an alternative government, was formed before the election by the Labour party and several other small parties. In Belgium and Italy (and Luxemburg) the situation remains confused. Here the characteristics of one single opposition are less easily found. In Italy, for example, it is true that a government bloc has formed around the dominant Christian Democrats, either to the centre-left or to the centre-right. But there has been no opposition bloc: the other large party, the PCI, has not acted as a focus for the other opposition parties. Indeed, the Christian Democrat led coalitions since 1947 have always had opposition both on the left and on the right (here always the MSI and monarchists and sometimes the Liberals, up to a total of about 12 per cent of the votes). Belgium has tended to prefer grand-coalitions of the PSC and PSB, leaving the other small parties of varied hues in opposition, but naturally not a coherent opposition. Sometimes (as seems likely at the present) the Liberals have also been in the government; some governments have been led by one major party and the Liberals. What can be said is that since 1945 each of the three major parties has been in government for over half the time. There is no pattern of opposition.

This brief examination of the national scene has shown us that even in multiparty systems there is a tendency towards the formation of an opposition. Even where this has not been successfully achieved, there seems to be some belief that such a system would lend coherence to much that is confused at present. If such is the 'model' of parliamentary government, what is its effect on the institution of parliament? As Bagehot rightly pointed out, modern politics have become 'the action and reaction between the Ministry and the Parliament'. We can approve L. S. Amery's updating of this statement to read between 'Ministry and Opposition'.[1]

What this means is that the functions of control which formally belong to parliament as a whole have by and large been abdicated in favour of the opposition alone. Parliament is split into two warring camps, with little or no common purpose, little or no identity *qua* parliament. The majority bloc has, so to speak (with exceptions by certain individuals and on certain issues) 'suspended disbelief' for the period of the legislature. Its main task is to sustain the ministry and enact its programme and not to exercise functions of control, of which the opposition then becomes the sole custodian. The separation of powers is no more; parliament as an institution is a weak and imprecise notion. In the nature of parliamentary government, the whole parliament cannot act as an institution to control the government without thereby unmaking the government.[2]

From this point of view, in spite of the pretensions and aspirations of the European parliament, it must be stated that the European parliament does not in fact go far towards meeting this 'model'. Certain features of behaviour in the common assembly and the European parliament, such as debates on the future programme of the commission, parliamentary questions, the motion of censure, can be compared to the government-opposition model, as we have seen. However, many difficulties lie in the path of such a development. In our consideration of the concept of opposition we noted that the main feature of modern political life was the action and the reaction between the ministry and the opposition (part of the parliament), with the majority viewing its task to support the government and assist it to get on record by words and deeds a level of accomplishment that will enable it to be returned to power at the subsequent election. The opposition seeks to deny this credibility to the majority both through obstruction of its programme and through demolishing (verbally) its content. In general terms the model presupposes certain characteristics: an executive power dependent on the parliament and in which alternation can occur through periodic elections; that executive action is based on a coherent political programme; that coherent parties or blocs of parties exist in the legislature, organised to dispute before the electorate for control over the executive. Where any of these characteristics is lacking, the political system must conform to another type.

It is in these 'institutional' prerequisites that the European communities are deficient. There is no government of the communities; there are only the institutions, each endowed with its own attributions. The executive power is divided between the commission and the council. Both are to an extent dependent on the other: as has often been said, 'the Commission proposes and the Council disposes'. Neither institution, nor the two if taken collectively, meets our requirements. They are not politically or formally dependent on the parliament, or only to a very limited extent. The parliament cannot remove the council, nor can it impede or amend council legislation. It cannot refuse to approve the credits which must finance the operations of the communities. The council members derive their political support from the national legislatures. As for the commission, it can be formally removed by a motion of censure, but political reality, plus the fact that the parliament has no role in the appointment of new members, make this weapon at best a blunt instrument. Politically the commission has sought the support of the parliament, but legally is able to make whatever proposals it thinks fit, irrespective of the position of the parliament and where the commission has autonomous rules; making powers under the treaty, it may exercise them without conforming to the opinion of the parliament.

The commission and council are not politically coherent and offer no scope for 'alternation'. The council is politically an arbitrary coalition of the tendencies of the governments of the member states and has mostly included both Liberal, Christian Democrat and Socialist ministers at one and the same time. It functions by suppressing this incoherence and avoiding party political type controversy and makes no claims to political coherence. The commission likewise is a coalition, a forced coalition. The commissioners must obey the rules of 'political balance' and are in effect imposed on one another from outside; neither they themselves, the parliament, nor increasing the council itself has any role in their appointment, which tends in practice to be in the hands of the national governments alone. No programme could be defined by a community institution (say, the commission) in collaboration with a majority in the European parliament. The programme of the community is in the first place limited by the treaties and their deadlines and demands; in the second place by statements of principle by such meetings as the summit conferences (those of both The Hague and Paris gave a heavy programme of action) and by resolutions and declarations by the council which enjoin action. Even though within the limits of the treaty, the powers of initiative of the commission are unfettered; in reality it is limited to what the council is likely to be able to adopt. The parliament has itself no power of initiative (although it can make suggestions) and is thus a passive responder to the initiatives from elsewhere, which usually themselves depend on some other imperative.

Even if contending groups were organised in the parliament, it would be a sham battle, for there is no electoral contest, since the members are not directly elected and, in any case, to capture a majority in the European parliament could change little, as power does not lie there and, above all, in our context, it could not effect the alteration of the executive.

In spite of the formidable difficulties and the limitations of such an analysis, we shall examine whether after all opposition of a different or attenuated form does exist. If we follow the thesis of Professor Coombes[3] then the parliament remains itself an organ of opposition. The parliament is in an ambivalent state, as is indicated by its title of 'Assembly' with its nascent flavour. This fits with the position of a body in an early stage of development, fighting for powers and unsure of its position in the institutional structure, and compares with the behaviour of national parliaments at a similar formative period in their development. As Coombes says: 'It would seem in general that up to now most members of the Parliament have interpreted its role as that of an institution of opposition.' This does not mean that the parliament is opposed to the process of integration; on the contrary, it is rather opposed to the dilatoriness with which the community progresses. What is meant, to quote Coombes again, is that:

> ... the Parliament has not been seen as a body concerned with supporting a Government ... The Parliament has no programme of its own to put in place of that of the Commission ... Most members go there not to seat or unseat a Government, but to react to initiatives already taken ...

Such a position would have as its basis a low degree of politicisation as compared with national parliaments. The level of debates would be technical and repetitive and 'politically boring'. Unanimity would be the

196

general rule or broad majorities with only a few abstentions in favour of general and uncontroversial resolutions. Such resolutions would be balanced carefully to represent almost all points of view. The aim would be to present a united front to the other institutions of the community in the hope that they would be impressed and influenced by such a position.

Indeed, it is not hard to recognise these characteristics in the European parliament. The reports of the debates show little evidence of votes of principle on important areas of disagreement. Amendments of a controversial nature are more often than not withdrawn and not voted upon. Texts are long and bland and balanced to gain near unanimity; it is certainly rare that a whole group should take its opposition to a measure to a negative vote in the plenary session. Roll-call votes were ever rare and have become rarer. Experience of committee and group meeting discussions indicates that the parliament is over-concerned with consensus: debate (almost as in the council!) is continued in order to 'arrange and filter' the smallest of minority dissent. The aim is precisely to be able to present a united position to the council (and one which incidentally, will not be repudiated in national parliaments) and commission in the hope that a near unanimous opinion will carry more weight and be less easily dismissed by some, or all, of the commissioners or national governments for political, national or technical reasons.

This implied view of the role of the parliament, whilst it may in realistic terms represent the most that can be expected at the present time, does have within it certain difficulties, if not incoherence. In the first place, in the community system there is no identifiable government to oppose. The natural target for the views of the majority of the parliaments would be the council of ministers, and behind that the national governments, from which the ministers come and from which they derive their authority. To quote Coombes again: 'To play the role of institutional opposition effectively the Parliament would need means of subjecting the acts and decisions of these other bodies to its own approval.'

On the other side, if such an approach is to succeed, then the parliament will have to organise itself to that end and project an effective image of what it seeks to achieve. Hitherto any advance which has been made along this line — such as the limited increase in the budgetary powers of the parliament, deriving from the Luxemburg Treaty (1970) — have come about almost entirely through the activism of a small number of 'Europeanists', who have occupied the major posts of responsibility in the parliament from the beginning (president, bureau, committee chairmen, group chairmen). These are individuals from all political tendencies, often active as individuals only, without the support of organised groups and national parties to which they belonged, which have more often been

H

at best indifferent to the European endeavours of some of their colleagues. (Indeed, in the Belgian parliament some members feel that their colleagues are uncomprehending, uninterested and even hostile to the work of members of the European parliament.[4]) In short, this is an amalgam. It has no semblance of being a 'European Party' with a coherent programme, immediate goals, strategy and organisation. Without such impetus, it is difficult to see how progress can be achieved by this path.

An alternative analysis is to seek opposition or partial oppositions inside the parliament. As we have seen, in the early days of the common assembly and the first years of the European parliament, the Socialist group acted as a 'supranational opposition'. It took the lead in attacking the high authority on a whole range of issues, from its timidity in using its legal prerogatives to its lack of a socially-orientated, interventionist policy to meet the coal crisis. The Socialist group has tabled what amounted to a motion of censure against the high authority[5] and in the debates of the fourth and fifth *Annual Report* of the high authority was extremely critical of the general policy being pursued. The Socialists had a clear line: a more supranational and a more social, interventionist policy was required. This attitude provoked party conflict and forced the Liberals and Christian Democrats to defend the high authority in the name of the free-market system. At this time the Socialists called themselves a 'supranational opposition'[6] and the Christian Democrats were to 'appoint themselves' a government coalition.[7]

Although there have been similar attacks on the coal policy of the high authority since 1958 (as late as 1963), this community has taken a lesser role since the Rome treaties came into force. Under these treaties, and the more so since the merger treaty (1965) abolished the high authority (if not its functions), there has been no easily identifiable 'government' institution and policies have been more technical and complex and less emotionally charged for the Socialists than unemployment and run down in primary industries such as coal and steel. In any case, the problem of the institutional weakness of the parliament has loomed larger, since the powers delegated to the new communities were wider and potentially more destructive of parliamentary control. Consciousness of the government-opposition role has declined with the level of political controversy. As we have seen, general consensus has been the goal and has in general been attained, even if at the expense of incisiveness.

There have been fragmented, partial oppositions in the parliament. Some of the national delegations have shown a level of cohesion which might qualify them for the position of 'national oppositions'; however, even the Dutch and Italian delegations, the most cohesive, cannot really qualify due to lack of ideological cohesion, small size or lack of organisational homogeneity or constructive programme.[8] Such groups are issue-orientated and have no consciousness of their role; indeed, rather the contrary, since[9] the national delegations have been overtly downgraded in the European parliament. National 'oppositions' form over certain issues — the Dutch over cereal prices in 1962, the Italians over the *Lulling Report* on the application of the CAP to tobacco, the Italians (who held a national delegation meeting) over the reform of the social fund (June session 1971) — but just as rapidly dissolve into divided ideological groups. Interest groups, such as the free-trade interest and the agricultural interest, can be clearly identified in the parliament. In the votes on ratification of the Rome treaties in the national parliament, some Liberal parties opposed the community on the grounds that it would be 'protectionist'. This argument, prolonged into a general opposition to 'dirigisme', has been identified in the Liberal group and among certain members of the Christian Democrat group. This is not an opposition for the same reasons that the national delegations do not qualify — lack of cohesion and intensity. Although the agricultural interest is strong, especially in the Liberal group (some 21 members of the parliament have had a connection with agriculture: Christian Democrats 8, Socialists 5, Liberals 6, UDE 1, PCI 1), this group is too disparate and disorganised to qualify as an 'opposition': there is no other interest group of comparable size in the parliament.

Of the potential political oppositions, only the Socialists are seen by Zellentin as having the necessary characteristics for that role: 'No other Group links its economic and social aims with the desire to strengthen the supranational executive while at the same time bringing it under parliamentary control.' The Socialists have a long-range, dominant aim. As we have seen, they have established strong organisation both in the European parliament and between the constituent Socialist parties. They have a programme and were the first (and to date the only) group to seek to draw up a manifesto for European elections[10] and the whole movement in the European communities has its programme, the general resolution adopted at the eighth congress of the Socialist parties of the communities (June 1971). The Socialists are not opposed to the communities; on the contrary, they seek a more rapid development than has hitherto been possible. The group has been, in Haas's phrase,[11] a 'precursor opposition', which has opposed the entrenched and dominant national systems and structures which stand in the way of the development of the community. It does not oppose the executive as such, but only where it acts too timidly and allows its areas of competence to be curtailed by a self-denying ordinance in order, for example, to reach a compromise with the national systems as represented in the council — an ever more frequent occurrence since the Luxemburg Agreement (1966). Thus the general resolution of the eighth congress states: 'The parties therefore call upon the Commission to bring into the open all conflicts arising with the Council, the permanent Representatives, national governments . . .' Much of Hr Kriedemann's attack on the commission during the debate on the programme for 1972[12] was based on just this premise; the commission had avoided conflict, had managed the disagreements to its own detriment and had accepted a reduction in its own role in favour of the council. The threat of a censure motion which lay behind the failure of the new commission (in 1970) to withdraw its complaint against the council[13] came largely from the Socialist group, for the same reason. This position has made the Socialist group the most assiduous in the use of the (limited) means of control at the disposal of the parliament. As we have seen, the Socialists, aided by Hr Vredeling, have largely appropriated the device of the written question, accounting for at least half the number asked in each year since 1958, and approximately 60 per cent of the total since then. Zellentin argues that, of the total, about 50 per cent concern criticism of policy and 25 per cent concern the relationship between the supranational executive and the member states and 10 per cent directly concern institutional matters. Thus a large majority of all questions – and here particularly those asked by the Socialists – concern criticism from a supranational point of view; 'upgrading the common interest'.

It is noticeable that some of the most violent clashes which occur in the parliament are between Socialists and the UDE (Gaullist) members. This was especially so at the time of the 1965 crisis, when relations between the UDE members, the commission, and the Socialists in particular, were at an all-time low. This is understandable; the UDE represents an 'opposition' – not a 'precursor opposition', nor so much an opposition to the communities as they are, but to what they might become. Their opposition is to a certain concept of Europe, to a certain anti-national view of the development of the communities. This position is in direct contradiction to the Socialist ideal. Some analysis (Zellentin, for example) does not consider the UDE to be a genuine 'structural opposition'; the opposition of the group to the federalist idea is admitted, but its alternative schema is held to be too vague – the adherence to 'L'Europe des Patries' is not an alternative of sufficient precision, and, for the rest, the UDE acts in accordance with economic interests, those of France, but more generally as a non-Socialist party. However, one can say that the UDE first broke the quasi-unanimity of the European parliament and acted with the flavour of an opposition. It has become clear that the 'alternative schema' is adequate, is sufficiently precise to condition the effective, concrete, everyday political action of the group. Indeed, the precision of the notion has gained in definition since the advent of President Pompidou in 1969 and has effectively dominated the statements of the UDE group in the European parliament. Examination of the debates of the parliament, even from before 1958 and increasingly since then, especially after 1965, shows that the Gaullists have made a distinctive contribution to the discussions of the parliament, a consistent opposition to supranationalism as a practice or as an aim, to the attempted extension of the powers of the parliament, to the 'political' use of the powers that it has.

The UDE has accordingly made little use of the instruments of control: from 1958 to 1966, the UDE members asked only a total of 13 written questions, with a maximum of 6 in any one year (1963-64), with none in the years 1959 to 1963. When the problem of ratification of the Treaty of Luxemburg was debated and some members wanted the European parliament to come out against ratification, it was the UDE member, Monsieur Habib-Deloncle, who raised the legal objection that the parliament was not permitted to address such a demand to the national parliaments. In the discussion of the censure motion of Monsieur Spénale in the December 1972 session (later withdrawn), the UDE opposed the motion because they considered that the parliament had no right to adopt a 'political' censure motion.

The UDE is then a 'partial opposition'. It should be remembered that, to put matters in perspective, any oppositions, except anti-system oppositions, only oppose certain aspects of policy. The opposition in Britain may dispute the content of politics, but it does not oppose the political system itself, whereas in a sense the UDE could be said to oppose the system, that is the community system, or at least its potential development.

It would seem natural to place the PCI and their allies in the European parliament in the opposition. As we have seen, the communist members see themselves as the 'avant-garde' of a political tendency; they have supranational aspirations. One could expect theirs to be an attitude of ideological opposition. Indeed, such was the attitude of the Soviet Communist party and those of the Community member states, with the early exception of the Italians, who soon developed a position which held a somewhat more positive view of the community. The PCI, and now the PCF, have moved from almost denial of the existence of the community to demands for participation in the existing organs of the community (satisfied in the case of the economic and social committee and the Italian delegation to the European parliament). Even after four years in the European parliament the position of the Communists remains in some ways enigmatic and obscure, even ambiguous. The Communists have continued to press their objections to the policies pursued by the community — their 'cold war' character. One of the consistent themes of the group has been that only in complete independence from the United States can Europe develop its unity, a view which has come through in debates on foreign policy, the monetary crisis, economic and monetary union, energy policy and other areas. Another area of opposition is the capitalistic, or free-market, nature of the communities. It is not so much that the capitalist ownership structure as such is attacked, but that the consequences, as it appears to the communists, are criticised. This is particularly noticeable in the economic debates where the subject of the control of inflation has been to the fore. The Communists have taken a different view from the other groups; inflation is blamed on subservience to the American economy and upon the activities of monopoly capitalists. By the same token, the inadequacy of the social and regional policies (also a key Italian interest) is subject to a sharp and penetrating attack. As is to be expected, the Communists have an opposition social-economic schema (which by and large the UDE do not have and the Socialists only to a limited extent).

What is less clear is the attitude of the Communists to the system. It is true that they have moved from virtual 'non-recognition' of the communities to participation, but on what basis? It seems that the Communists now accept that the community is an objective fact and seek to work within it for its transformation and not to seek its destruction from without. It could be that in the end there is little difference between these two approaches — at least as far as goals are concerned — or it could represent a total shift of attitude. Statements by Communist members seem to vary between two extreme poles — ultra-caution, smacking more of their attitude in the 1950s, and on the other hand an almost positive evaluation of the Community. Compare:

> Thus they (the Communists) do not propose breaking the Rome Treaties, but rather their revision — a revision aimed at the democratic transformation of the Community, enabling it to promote a process of broader economic and cultural co-operation in Europe, within the context of collective security and respect for the independence and equality of all states, whatever their political or social régime,[14]

and:

> I find no difficulty in supporting wholeheartedly the transfer of certain powers from the national level to the European level, and

that in spite of all the consequences that this might have on the constitutional level. The process of economic integration, the need to harmonise social legislation, the dynamic and modern confrontation of different political positions are powerful elements which impose progress going beyond the traditional strict defence of national interests.[15]

The Communists may themselves be unclear as to the direction in which events should move: or one can say that even conversion to a cautious 'Europeanism' cannot be achieved overnight. It is reasonable to suppose that the Communists retain some reservations on the 'structural' plane. They are not an outright opposition in this sphere any more, but they are more sceptical and questioning than the other groups — in their distrust of the social and economic content of the community and in its lack of democratic control.

Notes

1   L. S. Amery, *Thoughts on the Constitution*, London 1947, pp. 10-11.
2   See C. Sartori, 'Opposition and Control: Problems and Prospects', *Government and Opposition*, vol. 1, no. 2, January 1966.
3   Coombes and Wiebcke, 'The Power of the Purse' *The Budgetary Powers of the European Parliament*, PEP/Chatham House, 1972.
4   Information supplied to the author by Monsieur Dewulf.
5   Statement of Hr Kreysig, June 1956.
6   See: *Débats*, May 1955, on investment policy in the ECSC.
7   See: Debates on fifth *Annual Report*, June 1957.
8   See: G. Zellentin, Forms and Function of the Opposition in the European Communities, in *Government and Opposition*, vol. 2, no. 3, April-July 1967.
9   See: Neunreither, op. cit.
10   The *Birkelbach Report*, 1962.
11   In *The Uniting of Europe*, London, 1958.
12   See: *Débats*, February 1972.
13   Case 22/70, Commission v Council.
14   Amendola, CESPE Colloque, *I Communisti italiani e l'Europa*.
15   Boiardi, *Colloque parlementaire européen*, Strasbourg 16-18 March 1972.

14 The Future of the European Parliament

In many ways the European parliament today has the character of the eighteenth-century House of Commons: it is an emergent entity. It is not, as the commons was then not, the unequivocal focus of political life; influence and power lay elsewhere; men making political careers did not need to choose that route any more than today a political career can be made exclusively in the European parliament. Both the eighteenth-century Commons and the modern European parliament had that 'irresponsible' character, which stems from the fact that neither derives from universal suffrage and neither faces the strong control of electoral pressure which weighs so heavily on a modern national parliament, forever in the glare of public opinion. In both cases public opinion was (or is), except for small, specialised segments, uninformed or indifferent. In both, the role of individuals can be observed; party not being the all pervasive factor that it is in modern national parliaments. In the eighteenth-century Commons, as in the modern European parliament, much depended on the individual activist parliamentarian, who created issues and followed them up. As is the case of the European parliament today, the Commons was struggling to define its place in the constitution, to enlarge its powers and bring the executive under control. Although history may have treated the parliamentary institutions of the other member states differently, the same basic struggle for parliamentary supremacy can be observed in one form or another in each member state. It must therefore be counted a necessary evolutionary phase toward parliamentary maturity.

Compared with the centuries-long evolution of national parliaments the development of the European parliament has been rapid. Within the short span of less than twenty years a parliamentary ethos has been evolved, synthesised out of first six then nine national parliamentary traditions; party groups, albeit weak have formed and the powers of the parliament have already been considerably extended beyond those laid down in the original treaties. However the parliament is not the repository of the main thrust of political activity in the community. Fundamental problems remain and stand in the way of development.

The parliament is a developing parliament, an embryonic parliament, in an emergent political unit. It faces all the difficulties inherent in that situation: what should be the role of a parliamentary institution in the evolution of the whole political unit; at what stage can the parliament meaningfully insert itself into the process. Some have argued that the power sought by the European parliament is there to be seized and indeed could already have been attained if the task had been undertaken with sufficient vigour and aggression.[1] However this may be true in the sense that the parliament has suffered from certain internal weaknesses and lack of incisive direction as to its role, this cannot be the whole explanation. Indeed the parliament is well on the way to achieving as much as can reasonably be expected in this direction: question time, more lively political debates on topical issues, a simplified consultation procedure for purely technical matters, more use of committee hearings. However all these reforms meet the inexorable external constraints.

These limits belong to the general context — to the political environment of the western world as a whole and to the specific context of the communities' institutional structure. The general near crisis of classic parliamentary institutions cannot but be magnified at the European level. Parliaments everywhere are grappling with the problem of adapting to the challenge of the complexities and contradictions of the modern world and enormously enlarged role of government. Parliaments are seeking a new role and effectiveness. This new role may lie less in the traditional task of legislation, of control, of 'resistance au pouvoir' than in legitimising government.

The *Vedel Report*[2] reached to the heart of the matter when it spoke of 'effectiveness and democracy'. In the specific community context it attempted to apply this prescription in a realistic manner through a limited shift of power among the institutions, leaving a central role to the council for some time to come.[3] The commission was to be given a pivotal role, legitimised by the European parliament. The present consultative powers of the European parliament would be replaced, over a transition period of say five years, by a power of co-decision with the council. This co-decision power would first apply to 'constitutive acts' — amendments to the treaties, use of Article 235, admission of new members; and then extended to the external competences of the community, harmonisation of legislation and common policies. In this way some new matters would become subject to parliamentary control (aviation and maritime transport) and others would remain as now subject only to consultation. The arbitrary distinction between 'expenses necessarily resulting from the treaty . . .' and other so called 'non-obligatory expenses' would be able to be abolished, as its logic would no longer exist, since the European parliament would have approved the acts provoking the expenditure. Hence a power of co-decision over the whole budget is

206

proposed. The report also proposed that the president of the commission should be subject to investiture by the parliament and that he should then choose the remaining members of the commission as a compact team.

The *Vedel Report* is clearly the best thought out examination of the future role of the parliament. Since the Paris summit the matter has had considerable attention from the institutions of the community. The summit conference communiqué declared:

> The Heads of State and Government, having set themselves the major objective of transforming, before the end of the present decade, and with the fullest respect for the Treaties already signed, the whole complex of the relations of the member states into a European Union, request the Community institutions to draw up a report on this subject before the end of 1975.

Clearly, such a commitment, if it was to mean anything, held considerable implications for the institutions themselves. The communiqué also asked the institutions to take measures to strengthen the powers of control of the European parliament.[4]

Already, at the time of signature of the Treaty of Luxemburg in April 1970, the council and the commission had committed themselves to a review of the budgetary powers of the European parliament within two years of the ratification of that treaty.[5] It was only on that understanding that the European parliament recommended to the national parliaments that they should ratify what was otherwise an unsatisfactory result. Thus, not without some delay, which provoked the first motion of censure against the commission[6] the new proposals on the budgetary powers were presented by the commission in June 1973.[7] The commission's proposals were intended to be realistic and hence were limited in scope. In response to the opinion of the parliament the commission modified its proposals in October 1973. It should be said that under the impulsion of the Conservative and Christian Democratic groups, the position adopted by the parliament was extremely moderate. The parliament did not demand the last word, nor even the right of veto (as proposed in the *Vedel Report*) over acts with financial consequences. The commission, in its revised procedure, has a conciliation procedure between the council and parliament, to be invoked in the case of disagreement over certain acts with financial consequences. The procedure would involve no formal modification of the treaties. There would be discussion between a delegation of the parliament and a council delegation, consisting of a minister from each member state. In event of continued disagreement after a given period (as yet undefined), the council would retain its right to reach a decision in accordance with the normal rules of the treaty: the parliament would have no increased legal powers, only the possibility of an extended dialogue with the council. In addition the parliament would have the right of outright rejection of the whole budget and the council would have to find a majority to reject any amendment on the 'obligatory' expenditure. The commission, too, proposed to enlarge gradually the category of 'non-obligatory' expenditure. An audit court would also be set up to assist the parliament in its task of control of the application of community funds. Clearly, the political climate for such proposals was not good. There has been no notable change in the French position since 1970; the Danes are opposed to treaty amendments and any institutional change. In the middle of council discussions came the uncertainty arising from the British general election and the death of President Pompidou. The Dutch government even seemed to accord less importance to this problem than in the past. Certainly, the commission's proposals must constitute a maximum at the present time. More radical progress on this issue and on legislative powers must be postponed for consideration in the framework of European union.

For any such proposals to be effective a redefinition of the role of the institutions would be required. Early theories had predicted that this would come about through the process of 'engrenage'; as the community developed a 'shift of loyalties' would occur away from national power centre towards the community institutions. In its unadulterated form such theories have proved over-optimistic. Indeed, interdependence has increased as between the member states, which has increased the political and economic cost of resisting common action, but has certainly not made independent national action impossible, nor undermined its legitimacy. The community has completed the customs' union phase when the programme was clearly defined in the treaty, to enter the phase when issues of high politics are increasingly involved and when precisely the promotive and creative role of the commission is most needed, but is most difficult to exercise. It is precisely at this point that some have reproached the commission with falling into a passive 'implementive' role, abandoning its earlier creative and promotive role.[8] In this view, the commission should concern itself more with long term strategic planning of goals, giving itself a central position in the community structure as the only body capable of imposing a coherent position. The argument is that the commission would thus (through its strategic thinking, perhaps expressed through firmer control over the use of the community budget) gain a pivotal role in the community process.

The problem here is not one of diagnosis but of cure. How is such a new relationship to be brought about? The role that the commission is here required to assume entails confrontation with the national governments and opposition to the existing structures which oppose community action. Such action would require from the commission a political authority which it has not got and clearly under present circumstances could scarcely obtain. Governments have legitimacy arising from their democratic base, from traditional loyalties, and compared with unknown international centres of power, from relative efficiency and above all they command the levers of power: financial, coercive and persuasive. The commission would require an equivalent and countervailing source of legitimacy if it is to assume a role in which it can mobilise opinion in support of European action, if need be against the national governments. This alternative legitimacy, which could not be traditional, would have to be based both on effectiveness — that is a manifest ability to perform tasks which have overgrown the dimension of the individual nation state, and would have to have a democratic legitimacy. This democratic basis is essential, because whatever bureaucratic elements may have intervened, the legitimacy of all public authority in the western world flows ultimately from election — parliamentary, presidential or referendum. Clearly, unless the commission (or its president) were to be directly elected, the only manner in which the legitimacy of election could be attained would be by linking the commission closely to a directly elected European parliament with real legislative and budgetary powers, at least as great as those proposed in the *Vedel Report*. The commission, or other governmental type institution at the European level, would occupy a pivotal position, but would be dependant on the European parliament — it would emanate from and execute the will of the majority of the European parliament. The council would remain a powerful element in the system, and behind it the states would retain a powerful and legitimate role, for the forseeable future. The powers of the council would become more powers of a negative character — blocking and delaying. The community structure, would accordingly be (if one dare use the term) more confederal than federal in character, but with a certain dynamic for development.

The present inhospitable political climate makes the implementation of such a structure within the reasonable future very doubtful, but an even more fundamental question must be raised. How would the political forces, which are at present essentially national in character, react to such a construction? If parliaments are essentially 'reflective, secondary' institutions, reacting to initiatives rather than the source of initiative; if it is inopportune to introduce strong parliamentary institutions at too early a stage in the development of emergent political entities, then the 'parliament first' strategy as a means of breaking out of the present institutional 'impasse' may have some highly contradictory (and in some minds undesirable) consequences.

National parties would sense that a new (and potentially rival) centre of power was in the making and react to that fact through their members in the European parliament, who are after all at present arms of their national parties, albeit at present relatively autonomous arms. Parties are about power and the exercise of power; they react to a new power centre by attempting to structure it according to their own point of view, by reacting to control it. In the first instance the parties would re-evaluate the European parliament, since there would at long last be a worthwhile power struggle in the European parliament — a majority in the European parliament would mean something in terms of real power. The state of affairs described by Spinelli[9] would stop: the parliament would cease to be the preserve of representatives of certain particular interest groups: agriculture and the 'europeanist' interest. More influential national parliamentarians would join the delegations. Members of the European parliament would be called to account by their national parties for their votes and actions in the European parliament and pressure groups affected by community measures would gravitate towards the parliament as a potential defence against the executive. Party discipline would be imposed, but it might well not be the discipline of the present European party groups but of national parties. Then two tendencies would emerge: those who accepted the transfer of power to the European level and those who opposed this transfer and reacted in a national orientated manner. The present fragile groups might have difficulty in surviving this schism and all the other centrifugal pressures. The more so in that they are structured on classic left-right lines which is a mirror of the national party structures and hence may have increasingly little relevance to the situation which would develop. The reaction of parties would be in danger of being fragmented and essentially national in character. Unless as a precondition more power was vested in the executive institution at the European level, then it would be realised that the power of the parliament was essentially negative only: a blocking power, to be used on a piecemeal, ad hoc basis, in response to national reactions to issues without any overall strategy being evolved. In this way it might emerge that democratisation did not equal integration. This is not to oppose democratisation of the community, but merely to indicate that the introduction of more democratic procedures might require certain parallel measures as a precondition, such as the development of stronger executive powers on the community level at which point the parliament could effectively enter on the scene.

Another such parallel development would be the development of a new party structure, adapted to the political battle at the European level. This restructuring of the party system would require the creation of communitywide parties, with communitywide programmes, appropriate to community issues and supported by communitywide organisations with subdivisions for every electoral district of the European parliament. Such parties would require a decision-making apparatus of a federal character, capable of imposing majority rule on the national sections of the party. Such parties would have to be geared to the struggle for power at all levels: local, national and community. Other parties of a purely local character would continue to exist without a European vocation, in that they would not represent any communitywide political tendency and would not articulate any 'European' issues. Here one can think of parties such as the Belgian linguistic parties (FDF-RW and the Flemish Volksunie). It is likely that such parties would be confined to national and local representation.

Certain efforts to promote change in this direction have already been made, but as yet there has been no definite progress, for as yet the European parliament does not have the powers, nor does the community have the dynamism which would justify, indeed make inevitable, such a development. It may be that such a restructuring will remain premature until a real centre of executive power has been created on the European level. Until then the political forces will resist any development in this direction, as the German SPD have done, precisely because political parties and parliaments react to new power centres; only when a new centre has been created will a shift of activity and hence of organisation occur.

Hr Vredeling and Mr Moser (Chef de Cabinet to Mr Mansholt) have been active in promoting action in this field. At its congress of 6 May 1971 the Dutch Labour party passed a resolution calling upon the party to request a special congress of the Socialist parties of the community and calling upon the executive of the party to present proposals to a subsequent Labour party congress – proposals which would form a position paper at the subsequent European congress, making suggestions for a European Socialist programme and for an agreement to set up an organisation of European socialist parties. This organisation would be based on majority rule, binding on all the parties represented, and would take the form of a federative partnership as the preliminary to the formation of a European Progressive party.

At the colloquium of the Dutch branch of the European Union of Christian Democrats (Schevenigen, 20 June 1970), Mr Westerterp, then a member of the European parliament and subsequently state secretary in the foreign ministry, made the proposal that a European party system should be formed on the basis of the predominant structure in the member states: Communists, Socialists, Christian Democrats, Liberals and Conservatives. He did not consider the Gaullists to be a permanent and distinct political tendency in their own right. Giving particular attention to the Christian Democrats and how they could work within such a structure, he argued that the existing 'interstate' structure of the EUCD was not satisfactory, as it does not lead to decisions binding on the national parties, which remain independent. He urged the formation of a European Christian Democratic People's party to which the national parties could affiliate, but only on the condition that they accepted a logical policy for progress and the necessary collective discipline.

These are examples of thinking in this field, which it must be said has not as yet achieved any great progress as a result of the resistance that such proposals have met in national political parties. There is however a more radical analysis, which holds that any party system on the European level, which does no more than to reproduce the pattern found at national level, would be totally inadequate. Essentially the left-right cleavage is the basis of the European states' party system and this pattern is found in the European parliament, allowing for the fact that a nine-nation parliament will have to accommodate some special factors unique to one country. The question must be asked as to whether this cleavage is the most relevant, or indeed whether it is at all relevant, at the European level. We have seen that, in fact, apart from the early period of the ECSC common assembly, the classic right-left confrontation has played relatively little part in the work of the European parliament. Political divisions have been more complex and of a different nature. The main cleavages have been along an 'integrationist-nationalist' axis; or along a centralist-devolutionist axis; or again along an 'autarchist-mondialist' axis. The tendency has been for these attitudes to become entrenched in a given committee. Much of the political conflict in the parliament can be seen in terms of divergences between the committees on agriculture, foreign trade, development co-operation. Members in this situation identify as much with a committee position as with a group position. Under these circumstances it must at least be raised whether a party system which was merely the national system writ large would be appropriate. Outmoded structures would be repeated and reinforced. Indeed such groups would be in this analysis: 'only parasitical elements which prevent the development, separation and articulation of deep trends within European Assemblies'.[10] If a political community is to have any meaning, then it must mean that new political issues faced in a new way will replace former issues, which in turn requires a re-definition of the party structure.

It is clear that little progress has been made in this direction. It is not clear how such restructuring should be achieved. All that has occurred is a

212

certain clearing of the ground. There is now a fairly clear consensus as to the problems involved and as to the complexity of the issues, though some reinforcement of the 'Internationals' of the various political tendencies at the European level can be expected. Indeed, the Socialist organisation at the community level is in the process of strengthening its structures; its decisions will now in the future be 'recommendations' with a correspondingly greater weight. However, it is now recognised, that very severe problems stand in the way of forming European political parties. Parties with the same label may in reality have little in common; for example the Liberal parties of the community are very varied, as we have seen.[11] The Socialist parties, the most united, would have difficulties in defining their relations with the Communist party at the European level, as well as that toward nationalisation. What is needed is a more flexible approach, based on the creation of common platforms among similar parties, the intensive work of 'Europeans' inside all parties, intensified co-operation among parties with a more or less common outlook and for some co-operation across political divides.[12]

Notes

1 See the Memorandum submitted to the parliament in January 1973 by Mr Kirk. Mr Grimond has argued that a Scottish assembly, for example, would once set up − whatever were its initial powers, assume rapidly the powers it considered necessary − and has contrasted the European parliament unfavourably.

2 Report of the working party on the problems of enlarging the powers of the European parliament (March 1972), chaired by M. Vedel.

3 *Vedel Report,* p. 111: 'The proposals in no way impair the position of the Council whose legislative and executive role continues to be of primary importance'.

4 Paragraph 15 of the *Final Communiqué.*

5 The following declaration was annexed to the Treaty: 'The Commission declared its intention to present, after the ratification of the Treaty of 22 April 1970 by all member states, and at the latest within two years, proposals in that respect.
'The Council declared that it would examine such proposals in conformity with the procedure laid down in article 236 of the Treaty . . .'

6 Presented by M. Spénale in December 1972 in protest against the delay and finally withdrawn.

7 Document Com(73) 1000 and Com(73) 1000 final.

8 For the development of such an analysis see Lindberg. 'The

dynamics of European Integration' and D. Coombes *Politics and Bureaucracy in the European Community,* London 1970.

9   A. Spinelli, *The Eurocrats: Crisis and Conflict in the European Communities,* John Hopkins Press, 1966, p. 171

'That strange negligence which prevails among parliamentarians as soon as they leave Strasbourg' arises because 'when they return to their Capitals they are caught up in the discipline of their parties . . . in other words by the logic of the internal power struggle. As European Parliamentarians they would only count in their own countries if there were an incipient power struggle in Strasbourg in which their party were involved for which it could ask for their support'.

10   Levy in *Elections européennes au suffrage universel directe,* Institut de Sociologie, Solvay, Paris 1960, pp. 132-3.

11   For example a survey has shown that Belgian Christian Democrats at Louvain University would vote SPD if in Germany, and Liberal if in Britain, by large majorities.

12   The recent 'XXVII Table Ronde des Problemes de l'Europe' (Brussels, 26-27 April 1974) was devoted to this theme of party re-alignments, and from the discussions the consensus indicated in the text could be seen.

Bibliography

The documents and works included in this bibliography are by no means a complete conspectus of the literature of the subject. Only those works of a more general interest are repeated here of those works quoted in the text. Otherwise the works are those of general relevance to the subject.

General

The Commission

W. Hallstein, 'The EEC Commission: a new factor in international decision making, *International and Comparative Law Quarterly*, 1965, p. 727.
D. Coombes, *Politics and Bureaucracy in the European Communities* PEP/Allen and Unwin, London 1970.
K. Van Miert, 'Les aspects politiques de la partique du droit d'initiative de la Commission des Communautés européennes' *Chronique de politique étrangère*, March 1969.

The Council

Buerstedde, *Der Ministerrat im konstitutionellen System der Europäischen Gemeinschaften*, Sijthoff, Leiden 1965.
E. Noel, 'The Committee of Permanent Representatives' *Journal of Common Market Studies* vol. 1, no. 1.

The Decision-making Process

A. H. Robertson, *European Institutions*, Library of World Affairs 1973.
Everling, Wohlfahrt, Gläsner, 'Kommentar zum EWG-Vertag' in M. Waelbroeck (ed.) *Droit des Communautés Européennes*, Brussels 1969.
Weisermüller, 'Zur Machtsverteilung in den Gremium der EWG' *Schweizer Zeitschrift für Volkswirtschaft und Statistik*, June 1971.
Hogan, *Representative Government and European Integration*, University of Nebraska Press, 1967.
Gerbet & Pépy, *Le Décision dans la CEE,* Presse universitaire de Bruxelles, 1969.

G. Zellentin, 'The Economic and Social Committee' *Journal of Common Market Studies*, vol. 1, no. 1.

J. Lambert, 'Decision making in the European Communities' *Government and Opposition*, April-July 1967.

D. Didjanski, 'L'Originalité des Communautés européennes et leurs pouvoirs' *Revue générale du Droit public international'* 1961, p. 40.

H. Wallace, 'The Machinery of national Government and the EEC' *Government and Opposition* Autumn 1971.

D. Sidjanski, 'The European Pressure Groups' *Government and Opposition* April-July 1967.

R. Dahl, *Political Oppositions in Western Democracies,* Yale University Press, 1966. Communiqué of the Conference of Heads of State and Government, Paris 1972.

W. Feld, *The Court of Justice of the European Communities*, The Hague 1964.

F. Willis, *Italy Chooses Europe.* OUP, New York 1971.

A. Spinelli, *The Eurocrats: Conflict and Crisis in the European Communities,* Baltimore 1966.

The European Parliament

The Official Journal, Annexe Debates of the European Parliament.

European Parliament, Annuaire-Manuel (Annual publication).

European Parliament, Pour l'élection du Parlement européen au Suffrage universel directe (1970).

European Parliament, Les ressources propres aux Communautés européennes et les pouvoirs budgétaires du Parlement européen (1970).

Conservative Group, Memorandum of 18 January 1973.

B. Cocks, *The European Parliament: Structure, Procedure and Practice*, HMSO, 1973.

W. Birke, *European Elections by Universal Suffrage*, Sijthoff, Leiden 1961.

M. Forsyth, *The Parliament of the European Communities*, PEP/Chatham House, 1964.

E. Ginestet, *Le Parlement européen*, Paris 1960.

A. M. Houdebine & J. R. Verges, *Le Parlement européen dans la construction de l'Europe des Six,* Paris 1966.

H. A. H. Andretsch, 'Les questions écrites au Parlement européen, quelques statistiques' *Revue du March Commun* no. 105, September 1965.

E. Bubba, 'A propos de designation des membres du Parlement européen par les parlements nationaux' *Revue du Marche commun* no. 89.

A. Schaub, Die Anhörungsrecht des Europäischen Parlements.

Schutzer, 'Legal Aspects of the work of the European Parliament' *Common Market Law Review*, 1967.

K-H. Neunreither, 'Le role du Parlement européen dans la formation de la decision dans les Communautés européennes' *Europa Archiv,* 1966.

Reifferscheid, *Die Ausschüsse des Europäischen Parlaments*, Pontes Verlag 1966.

G. Zellentin, 'Form and Function of the Opposition in the European Parliament' *Government and Opposition*, April-July 1967.

D. Coombes & I. Wiebeke, *The Power of the Purse: The budgetary powers of the European Parliament*, PEP/Chatham House, 1972.

P. C. J. F. Van Erve, 'Eigen middelen der Europeese Gemeenschappen en budgetaire bevoegdheden van het Europeese Parlement' *TMC Assenaar Institut,* Willink/Sijthoff 1973.

Vedel Committee, *Report on the enlargement of the powers of the European Parliament.*

National Parliaments

M. Niblock, *The EEC: National Parliaments in Community decision making,* PEP/Chatham House, April 1971.

K.-H. Neunreither. 'Les rapports entre le Parlement européen et les parlements nationaux' *Annuaire européen* 1967.

European Parliament, Papers on national parliaments by various authors prepared for the Symposium of May 1974.

HMSO, *Report of the Select Committee of the House of Lords on procedures for the scrutiny of proposals for European instruments,* July 1973.

HMSO, *Report of the Select Committee of the House of Commons on European Community secondary legislation,* October 1973.

E. Damgaard, 'Stability and Change in the Danish Party system in half a century' *Scandinavian Political Studies* vol. 9, 1974.

The Groups

M.-F. Reinbold, 'Le PCF et le Marche commun', Thesis, Strasbourg 1967.

Beckel, Reiring, Roegele, *Christliche parteien in Europa,* Verlag From, Osnabrück 1964.

G. Marchal Van Belle, *Les Socialistes belges et l'integration européenne*, Brussels 1965.

Colloque, (Bruges 1968) *Les partis politiques et l'integration européenne* Geneva 1969.

G. Van Oudenhouve, *The Political Parties in the European Parliament,* Leiden 1965.

G. Zellentin, *Die Kommunisten und die Einigung Europas,* Frankfurt 1964.

CESPE, *I Communisti italiani e l'Europa,* Report of the Colloque held in Rome 23-25 November 1971.

Timmerman, 'Autonomie der Italienischen und Franzözischen Kommunisten' *Gegenwartskunde* 20(1), 1971, pp. 13-25.

J. Leich, 'The Italian Communists and the European Parliament' *Journal of Common Market Studies* vol. X, pp. 271-81.

A. Fontaine, 'What is French Foreign Policy' *Foreign Affairs* 1966.

Thesis, *Le Groupe socialiste au Parlement européen,* Strasbourg 1963.

Socialist Group, Rules of Procedure.

Socialist Group, VIIIth Congress of the Social Democratic Parties in the European Communities: Resolutions.

D C Europe, Various numbers.

Courrier socialiste européen: various numbers.

European Documentation; until 1971 quarterly.

T. Westerterp, 'Europeese Fractievormning' *Internationale Spectator* 1958.

H. Vredeling, 'European Political Parties' *Government and Opposition* Autumn 1971.

Index

economic and social issues 79–80; and inflation 80–1; and energy problems 81–2; and agriculture 82–5; and sociology 85; important role of 85; cohesion of 166–7, 170

Christian Democrats (CD) in ECSC 19, 20, 23–36 *passim*

Christian Socialism 111

CHU (Christelijk Historische Unie, (Dutch) 69, 70, 72

Cipolla, Signor 130, 141, 168, 183; and Conte: *Report* 140, 141

CISL (Italian Christian trade union) 71

Clerical and anti-clerical 'divide' 111,116

Coal: crisis (1952) 32–3; policy 33; supplies 104; *see also* Energy

Cohesion of the Groups, comparative 163–71; index of 169–70

Colombo, Signor 75

Commission, The 3–8, 10, 14–17 *passim*, 39, 40, 42, 43, 78, 111, 200; role of 3–4, 14; and EP 15–16, 48–55, 59–60, 61–3 *passim*, 148; represented in committee meetings 59–60; too powerful 135; not powerful enough 137; supported by Conservative group 147–9 *passim*; censure motion against (1972) 166; status and power of 195, 196; future role of 206–13 *passim*

Committee of Permanent Representatives (COREPER) 7–8 *passim*

Committees of EP 10, 42–3, 53–64, *see also under their names;* ad hoc 42–3; specialised 6; microcosms of EP 53; appointments to 53–4; composition of 54, 55; 'replacement' members 55; 'self-selection' of members 55; rapporteurs of 55–8 *passim;* Commission represented on 59–60; reports of 60–1; role of secretariats in 61; presidents of 61, 119

Committees, standing (of EP) 58, 90–1, 101; *named* 42

Common Agricultural Policy (CAP) 17, 82, 83, 102–3, 117, 122, 125, 140, 149–51; British objections to 149

Common Assembly (of ECSC) 13–37, 40–1, 45, 194; members, number and distribution of 23, 25; volume of work 40; groups in 43; polarisation in 126

Common Market for Europe, a: proposed and discussed 31–6, 39; requirements of, CDs 31–2, Liberals 32, Socialists 31, 96, 102

'Common Programme of the Left' (1972) 109, 134

Communist and Allies group in EP 58–9, 129–44; and rapporteurships 59; membership and organisation of 129–33; composition of 130; policy of 132–44; on democratisation of EEC 132–7; and economic policy 137–8; and multi-national companies 138–9; on inflation and public expenditure 139; and regional policy 139–40; and social policy 140; and agriculture 140–1; and price policy 140–1; and energy 142; cohesion of 168; as an opposition party 201–3

Communist parties of Western Europe: conferences of (1971 & 1974) 131, 134; and the EEC 131, 132

Communists in EEC 44, 45; how excluded from EP 44; Italian (1969) 45

Confédération européenne des Syndicats libres dans la Communauté 60

Conference (congress) of SD parties in the European communities 94, 95, 110

Conference on Co-operation and Security in Europe 133

Consensus sought 7–9, 89, 126, 197, 198

Conservatism, British, and *laissez-faire* 145

Conservative Group in EP 145–53; British membership (by parties) 145; membership and organisation of 145–7; composition of 146; policy of 147–52; and Commission and Council 147–9; and EP 147–8; and institutional matters 147–8; and British national interests 149; and CAP 149–50; and external relations 150–1; and harmonisation 151; and economic matters and inflation 151; and energy 152; cohesion of 168–9

Consultative Assembly of EEC (CA, 1958) 39–66; members, number and distribution of 39, election and powers of 39–40; volume of work 40; *see also* European Parliament

Coombes, David 18, 44–5, 196, 197

Co-operatives, agricultural, advocated 141

COPA (Confédération d'Organisations Professionales Agricoles) 5, 10, 55, 71, 83, 186

Council of Ministers of EEC 4–10 *passim*, 14–17 *passim*, 39, 42, 43, 58, 111, 123, 197, 200; powers of 4, 9, 14; decisions, directives, regulations and resolutions

Institutional reforms proposed 74–9, 147–8; *see also* Summit Conference, Paris

Integration of Europe 30–6 *passim*, 81–5 *passim*, 88, 93, 96–8 *passim*, 105, 121, 122, 142, 164, 165, 196, 210; and democratic control of EP 96, 137; requires consent of national parliaments 176

International Federation of Free Trade Unions (IFFTU) 94

Intervention of National Parliaments 175–92; by EAC, *q.v.* 178–82; by parliamentary questions 182–3; by debates in parliament 183–4, 190; national activism and dynamism of members 184–6, 191; attempt to co-ordinate EP and national parliaments 187–8; and budgetary powers of EP 189

Investment policy 35–6

Iotti, Signora 130, 132, 135–6

IRI (Italian state holdings) 80

Irish Dail and Senate joint committee on European Affairs 180

Irish parties, *see* Fine Fáil *and* Fine Gail

Italian: delegation to EP 43–5; farmers 83, 140

Italian parties: Christian Democrats (DC) 64, 69, 71, 72, 82–3; Christian Trade Unions (CISL) 71; Communist party (PCI) 18, 45, 58, 126, 128, 130–4 *passim*, 136, 142, 157, 167, 168, 185, 193, 199, 201, on committees of EP 54, 55, 59, in Communist and Allies group 130, cohesion of 167–9; Liberal party (PLI) 107–8 *passim*; Monarchists (PDIUM) 44, 108; Republican party (PRI) 87, 88; Social-Democratic party (PSDI) 87; Socialist Movement – National Right (MSL–DN) 44, 108; Socialist party (PSI) 87, 97; 'Statists' 79, 80, 97

Italy: centre-left government in (after 1968) 45; agriculture in 82, 83, 140; and CAP 83

Jahn, Hr 71

Journées d'études (study days) 73, 75, 110, 117, 131, 146

Jozeau-Marigné, Monsieur 56–7, 63

Judicial power, *see* Court of Justice

Kirk, Peter 148–50, 152

Klinker, Hr (of Schleswig-Holstein) 71

Korthals, Monsieur 20, 21

KPD (German party) 18, 45

Kreyssig, Monsieur 21, 28

'Kreyssig Declaration' (1956) 34

Kreyssig Report 34

Kriedemann, Hr 89, 90, 166, 185, 200

KVP (Katholieke Volkspartij), *see* Dutch Catholic Peoples party

Labour, mobility of 137

Laffargue, Monsieur 27

'Laissez-faire' in economic matters 108, 110, 116, 145

Lapie, Monsieur 34

Laudrin, Monsieur 125; Declaration of 124

Legal Committee of EP 53, 54, 60

Legislative power 3; *see also* Council of Ministers

Leonardi, Signor 59, 130, 137–9, 142, 168

Liberal and Allies group in EP 43, 44, 95, 107–16; definition of 110; on committees of EP 54, 55; rapporteurs 56; and agriculture 83; membership and organisation 107–10; policy 110–16; ideological diversity in 108; individualism of 111, 112; two tendencies in 111–12; and inflation 112–13; social and regional policy 113–14; and agriculture 114; and energy 115; positive characteristics of 116; UNR in 118; cohesion of 166, 167, 170

Liberal International 110, 124

Liberals in ECSC 19, 20, 23–36 *passim*

Liogier, Monsieur 62, 124

Löhr, Hr 79–80

Longo, Signor 132

Lücker, Hr 75–7, 79, 82

Lulling, Mademoiselle 57, 62, 100–1, 185

Lulling Report 83, 124, 140, 199

Luns, Hr 184

Luxemburg: and EEC 45; rapporteurs 56, 57; Agreement (1966) 8, 78, 111, 189, 200; Treaty of, *see* Treaty

Luxemburg parties: Christian Socialist party (PCS) 69; Democratic party (PD) 107; Social Democratic party (PSD) 87; Workers' Socialist party (POSL) 87

Maigaard, Jens 129, 131

Majority principle 8

Malfatti, Signor 90

reforms under consideration 91–3; internationalist 90, 93, 96; liaison bureau (international) 94, 95; Congress of SD parties 94; and IFFTU 94; political position of 94; its agrarian programme (1961) 95; and the market economy 95–6; and the common market 96, 102; internationalism and democracy of 97–8; social and economic policy of 99–102; energy policy of 103–4; transport policy of 105; cohesion of 164; discipline and a free vote 165–6; as an opposition group 198–200; and UDE 200